Marx Machiavelli Chesterton Cooper Emerson Joyce
Abbott Hardy Montaigne Haggard Austen
Defoe Melville Hugo
Christie Eliot Grimm
Stoker Carroll Molière
Wilde Maupassant Byron
Engels Schiller
Garnett Einstein Fitzgerald Smith
Goethe Hawthorne Kafka
Cotton Dostoyevsky Hall
Baum Kipling Doyle Willis
Leslie Dumas Henry Nietzsche
Flaubert Turgenev Balzac
Stockton Vatsyayana Crane
Burroughs Whitman Verne
Curtis Tocqueville Gogol Vinci
Homer Widger Tolstoy Busch
Darwin Thoreau
Potter Freud Zola Twain Plato Scott
Lawrence
Kant Jowett Stevenson Dickens
Andersen Cervantes Burton Hesse Harte
London Descartes
Poe Aristotle Wells Voltaire
Hale James Hastings Cooke
Bunner Shakespeare
Richter Chambers Irving
Doré Swift Dante Chekhov da Shaw Wodehouse Benedict Alcott
Pushkin
Newton

tredition®

tredition was established in 2006 by Sandra Latusseck and Soenke Schulz. Based in Hamburg, Germany, tredition offers publishing solutions to authors and publishing houses, combined with worldwide distribution of printed and digital book content. tredition is uniquely positioned to enable authors and publishing houses to create books on their own terms and without conventional manufacturing risks.

For more information please visit: www.tredition.com

TREDITION CLASSICS

This book is part of the TREDITION CLASSICS series. The creators of this series are united by passion for literature and driven by the intention of making all public domain books available in printed format again - worldwide. Most TREDITION CLASSICS titles have been out of print and off the bookstore shelves for decades. At tredition we believe that a great book never goes out of style and that its value is eternal. Several mostly non-profit literature projects provide content to tredition. To support their good work, tredition donates a portion of the proceeds from each sold copy. As a reader of a TREDITION CLASSICS book, you support our mission to save many of the amazing works of world literature from oblivion. See all available books at www.tredition.com.

Project Gutenberg

The content for this book has been graciously provided by Project Gutenberg. Project Gutenberg is a non-profit organization founded by Michael Hart in 1971 at the University of Illinois. The mission of Project Gutenberg is simple: To encourage the creation and distribution of eBooks. Project Gutenberg is the first and largest collection of public domain eBooks.

Ferdinand De Soto, The Discoverer of the Mississippi American Pioneers and Patriots

John S. C. (John Stevens Cabot) Abbott

Imprint

This book is part of TREDITION CLASSICS

Author: John S. C. (John Stevens Cabot) Abbott
Cover design: Buchgut, Berlin – Germany

Publisher: tredition GmbH, Hamburg - Germany
ISBN: 978-3-8472-2108-1

www.tredition.com
www.tredition.de

Ferdinand de Soto,

THE

DISCOVERER OF THE MISSISSIPPI

BY

JOHN S. C. ABBOTT.

NEW YORK:
DODD & MEAD, No. 762 BROADWAY.
1873.

Wm. McCrea & Co., Stereotypers,
Newburgh, N. Y.

Lange, Little & Hillman,
PRINTERS,
108 to 114 Wooster Street, N. Y.

AMERICAN PIONEERS AND PATRIOTS.

FERDINAND DE SOTO.

THE

DISCOVERER OF THE MISSISSIPPI.

By JOHN S. C. ABBOTT.

ILLUSTRATED.

NEW YORK:
DODD & MEAD, No. 762 BROADWAY.
1873.

PREFACE.

Mr. Theodore Irving, in his valuable history of the "Conquest of Florida," speaking of the astonishing achievements of the Spanish Cavaliers, in the dawn of the sixteenth century says:

"Of all the enterprises undertaken in this spirit of daring adventure, none has surpassed, for hardihood and variety of incident, that of the renowned Hernando de Soto, and his band of cavaliers. It was poetry put in action. It was the knight-errantry of the old world carried into the depths of the American wilderness. Indeed the personal adventures, the feats of individual prowess, the picturesque description of steel-clad cavaliers, with lance and helm and prancing steed, glittering through the wildernesses of Florida, Georgia, Alabama, and the prairies of the Far West, would seem to us mere fictions of romance, did they not come to us recorded in matter of fact narratives of contemporaries, and corroborated by minute and daily memoranda of eye-witnesses."

These are the wild and wondrous adventures which I wish here to record. I have spared no pains in obtaining the most accurate information which the records of those days have transmitted to us. It is as wrong to traduce the dead as the living. If one should be careful not to write a line which dying he would wish to blot, he should also endeavor to write of the departed in so candid and paternal a spirit, while severely just to the truth of history, as to be safe from reproach. One who is aiding to form public opinion respecting another, who has left the world, should remember that he may yet meet the departed in the spirit land. And he may perhaps be greeted with the words, "Your condemnation was too severe. You did not make due allowance for the times in which I lived. You have held up my name to unmerited reproach."

Careful investigation has revealed De Soto to me as by no means so bad a man as I had supposed him to have been. And I think that the candid reader will admit that there was much, in his heroic but melancholy career, which calls for charitable construction and sympathy.

The authorities upon which I have mainly relied for my statements, are given in the body of the work. There is no country on the globe, whose early history is so full of interest and instruction as our own. The writer feels grateful to the press, in general, for the kindly spirit in which it has spoken of the attempt, in this series, to interest the popular reader in those remarkable incidents which have led to the establishment of this majestic republic.

CHAPTER I.

Childhood and Youth.

Birthplace of Ferdinand De Soto.—Spanish Colony at Darien.—Don Pedro de Avila, Governor of Darien.—Vasco Nuñez.—Famine.—Love in the Spanish Castle.—Character of Isabella.—Embarrassment of De Soto.—Isabella's Parting Counsel.

In the interior of Spain, about one hundred and thirty miles southwest of Madrid, there is the small walled town of Xeres. It is remote from all great routes of travel, and contains about nine thousand inhabitants, living very frugally, and in a state of primitive simplicity. There are several rude castles of the ancient nobility here, and numerous gloomy, monastic institutions. In one of these dilapidated castles, there was born, in the year 1500, a boy, who received the name of Ferdinand de Soto. His parents were Spanish nobles, perhaps the most haughty class of nobility which has ever existed. It was, however, a decayed family, so impoverished as to find it difficult to maintain the position of gentility. The parents were not able to give their son a liberal education. Their rank did not allow them to introduce [Pg 10] him to any of the pursuits of industry; and so far as can now be learned, the years of his early youth were spent in idleness.

Ferdinand was an unusually handsome boy. He grew up tall, well formed, and with remarkable muscular strength and agility. He greatly excelled in fencing, horseback riding, and all those manly exercises which were then deemed far more essential for a Spanish gentleman than literary culture. He was fearless, energetic, self-reliant; and it was manifest that he was endowed with mental powers of much native strength.

When quite a lad he attracted the attention of a wealthy Spanish nobleman, Don Pedro de Avila, who sent him to one of the Spanish universities, probably that of Saragossa, and maintained him there for six years. Literary culture was not then in high repute; but it was deemed a matter of very great moment that a nobleman of Spain should excel in horsemanship, in fencing, and in wielding every weapon of attack or defence.

Ferdinand became quite renowned for his lofty bearing, and for all chivalric accomplishments. At the tournaments, and similar displays of martial prowess then in vogue, he was prominent, exciting the envy of competitive cavaliers, and winning the admiration of the ladies.

[Pg 11]

Don Pedro became very proud of his foster son, received him to his family, and treated him as though he were his own child. The Spanish court had at that time established a very important colony at the province of Darien, on the Isthmus of Panama. This isthmus, connecting North and South America, is about three hundred miles long and from forty to sixty broad. A stupendous range of mountains runs along its centre, apparently reared as an eternal barrier between the Atlantic and Pacific oceans. From several of the summits of this ridge the waters of the two oceans can at the same time be distinctly seen. Here the Spanish court, in pursuit of its energetic but cruel conquest of America, had established one of its most merciless colonies. There was gold among the mountains. The natives had many golden ornaments. They had no conception of the value of the precious ore in civilized lands. Readily they would exchange quite large masses of gold for a few glass beads. The great object of the Spaniards in the conquest of Darien was to obtain gold. They inferred that if the ignorant natives, without any acquaintance with the arts, had obtained so much, there must be immense quantities which careful searching and skilful mining would reveal.

The wanton cruelties practised by the Spaniards [Pg 12] upon the unoffending natives of these climes seem to have been as senseless as they were fiendlike. It is often difficult to find any motive for their atrocities. These crimes are thoroughly authenticated, and yet they often seem like the outbursts of demoniac malignity. Anything like a faithful recital of them would torture the sensibilities of our readers almost beyond endurance. Mothers and maidens were hunted and torn down by bloodhounds; infant children were cut in pieces, and their quivering limbs thrown to the famished dogs.

The large wealth and the rank of Don Pedro de Avila gave him much influence at the Spanish court. He succeeded in obtaining the much-coveted appointment of Governor of Darien. His authority was virtually absolute over the property, the liberty, and the lives of a realm, whose extended limits were not distinctly defined.

Don Pedro occupied quite an imposing castle, his ancestral mansion, in the vicinity of Badajoz. Here the poor boy Ferdinand, though descended from families of the highest rank, was an entire dependent upon his benefactor. The haughty Don Pedro treated him kindly. Still he regarded him, in consequence of his poverty, almost as a favored menial. He fed him, clothed him, patronized him.

It was in the year 1514 that Don Pedro entered [Pg 13] upon his office of Governor of Darien. The insatiate thirst for gold caused crowds to flock to his banners. A large fleet was soon equipped, and more than two thousand persons embarked at St. Lucar for the golden land. The most of these were soldiers; men of sensuality, ferocity, and thirst for plunder. Not a few noblemen joined the enterprise; some to add to their already vast possessions, and others hoping to retrieve their impoverished fortunes.

A considerable number of priests accompanied the expedition, and it is very certain that some of these at least were actuated by a sincere desire to do good to the natives, and to win them to the religion of Jesus:—that religion which demands that we should do to others as we would that others should do to us, and whose principles, the governor, the nobles, and the soldiers, were ruthlessly trampling beneath their feet. Don Pedro, when measured by the standard of Christianity, was proud, perfidious and tyrannical. The course he pursued upon his arrival in the country was impolitic and almost insane.

His predecessor in the governorship was Vasco Nuñez. He had been on the whole a prudent, able and comparatively merciful governor. He had entered into trade with the natives, and had so far secured their good will as to induce them to bring in an ample supply of provisions for his colony. He [Pg 14] had sent out Indian explorers, with careful instructions to search the gold regions among the mountains. Don Pedro, upon assuming the reins of government, became very jealous of the popularity of Nuñez, whom he supplanted. His enmity soon became so implacable that, without any cause, he accused him of treason and ordered him to be decapitated. The sentence was executed in the public square of Acla. Don Pedro himself gazed on the cruel spectacle concealed in a neighboring house. He seemed ashamed to meet the reproachful eye of his victim, as with an axe his head was cut off upon a block.

All friendly relations with the Indians were speedily terminated. They were robbed of their gold, of their provisions, and their persons were outraged in the most cruel manner. The natives, terror-stricken, fled from the vicinity of the colony, and suddenly the Spaniards found all their supplies of provisions cut off. More than two thousand were crowded into a narrow space on the shores of the gulf, with no possibility of obtaining food. They were entirely unprepared for any farming operations, having neither agricultural tools nor seed. Neither if they had them could they wait for the slow advent of the harvest. Famine commenced its reign, and with famine, its invariable attendant, pestilence. In [Pg 15] less than six months, of all the glittering hosts, which with music and banners had landed upon the isthmus, expecting soon to return to Europe with their ships freighted with gold, but a few hundred were found alive, and they were haggard and in rags.

The Spaniards had robbed the Indians of their golden trinkets, but these trinkets could not be eaten and they would purchase no food. They were as worthless as pebbles picked from the beach. Often lumps of gold, or jewels of inestimable value, were offered by one starving wretch to another for a piece of mouldy bread. The colony would have become entirely extinct, but for the opportune arrival of vessels from Spain with provisions. Don Pedro had sent out one or two expeditions of half-famished men to seize the rice, Indian corn, and other food, wherever such food could be found.

The natives had sufficient intelligence to perceive that the colonists were fast wasting away. The Indians were gentle and amiable in character, and naturally timid; with no taste for the ferocities of war. But emboldened by the miseries of the colonies, and beginning to despise their weakness, they fell upon the foraging parties with great courage and drove them back ignominiously to the coast. The arrival of the ships to which we have referred with provisions [Pg 16] and reinforcements, alone saved the colony from utter extinction.

Don Pedro, after having been in the colony five years, returned to Spain to obtain new acquisitions of strength in men and means for the prosecution of ever-enlarging plans of wealth and ambition. North and south of the narrow peninsula were the two majestic continents of North and South America. They both invited incursions, where nations could be overthrown, empires established, fame won, and where mountains of gold might yet be found.

It seems that De Soto had made the castle of Don Pedro, near Badajoz, his home during the absence of the governor. There all his wants had been provided for through the charitable munificence of his patron. He probably had spent his term time at the university. He was now nineteen years of age, and seemed to have attained the full maturity of his physical system, and had developed into a remarkably elegant young man.

The family of Don Pedro had apparently remained at the castle. His second daughter, Isabella, was a very beautiful girl in her sixteenth year. She had already been presented at the resplendent court of Spain, where she had attracted great admiration. Rich, beautiful and of illustrious birth, many noblemen had sought her hand, and among the rest, one [Pg 17] of the princes of the blood royal. But Isabella and De Soto, much thrown together in the paternal castle, had very naturally fallen in love with each other.

The haughty governor was one day exceedingly astounded and enraged, that De Soto had the audacity to solicit the hand of his daughter in marriage. In the most contemptuous and resentful manner, he repelled the proposition as an insult. De Soto was keenly wounded. He was himself a man of noble birth. He had no superior among all the young noblemen around him, in any chivalric accomplishment. The only thing wanting was money. Don Pedro loved his daughter, was proud of her beauty and celebrity, and was fully aware that she had a very decided will of her own.

After the lapse of a few days, the governor was not a little alarmed by a statement, which the governess of the young lady ventured to make to him. She assured him that Isabella had given her whole heart to De Soto, and that she had declared it to be her unalterable resolve to retire to a convent, rather than to become the wife of any other person. Don Pedro was almost frantic with rage.

As totally devoid of moral principle as he was of human feelings, he took measures to have De Soto assassinated. Such is the uncontradicted testimony of contemporary historians. But every day revealed to him more [Pg 18] clearly the strength of Isabella's attachment for De Soto, and the inflexibility of her will. He became seriously alarmed, not only from the apprehension that if her wishes were thwarted, no earthly power could prevent her from burying herself in a convent, but he even feared that if De Soto were to be assassinated, she would, by self-sacrifice, follow him to the world of spirits. This caused him to feign partial reconciliation, and to revolve in his mind more cautious plans for his removal.

He decided to take De Soto back with him to Darien. The historians of those days represent that it was his intention to expose his young protégé to such perils in wild adventures in the New World, as would almost certainly secure his death. De Soto himself, proud though poor, was tortured by the contemptuous treatment which he received, even from the menials in the castle, who were aware of his rejection by their proud lord. He therefore eagerly availed himself of the invitation of Don Pedro to join in a new expedition which he was fitting out for Darien.

He resolved, at whatever sacrifice, to be rich. The acquisition of gold, and the accumulation of fame, became the great objects of his idolatry. With these he could not only again claim the hand of Isabella, but the haughty Don Pedro would eagerly seek [Pg 19] the alliance of a man of wealth and renown. Thousands of adventurers were then crowding to the shores of the New World, lured by the accounts of the boundless wealth which it was said could there be found, and inspired by the passion which then pervaded Christendom, of obtaining celebrity by the performance of chivalric deeds.

Many had returned greatly enriched by the plunder of provinces. The names of Pizarro and Cortez had been borne on the wings of renown through all the countries of Europe, exciting in all honorable minds disgust, in view of their perfidy and cruelty, and inspiring others with emotions of admiration, in contemplation of their heroic adventures.

De Soto was greatly embarrassed by his poverty. Both his parents were dead. He was friendless; and it was quite impossible for him to provide himself with an outfit suitable to the condition of a Spanish grandee. The insulting treatment he had received from Don Pedro rendered it impossible for him to approach that haughty man as a suppliant for aid. But Don Pedro did not dare to leave De Soto behind him. The family were to remain in the ancestral home. And it was very certain that, Don Pedro being absent, ere long he would hear of the elopement of Ferdinand and Isabella. Thus influenced, he offered De Soto a free passage to Darien, a captain's [Pg 20] commission with a suitable outfit, and pledged himself that he should have ample opportunity of acquiring wealth and distinction, in an expedition he was even then organizing for the conquest of Peru. As Don Pedro made these overtures to the young man, with apparently the greatest cordiality, assuming that De Soto, by embarking in the all-important enterprise, would confer a favor rather than receive one, the offer was eagerly accepted.

Don Pedro did everything in his power to prevent the two lovers from having any private interview before the expedition sailed. But the ingenuity of love as usual triumphed over that of avarice. Isabella and De Soto met, and solemnly pledged constancy to each other. It seems that Isabella thoroughly understood the character of her father, and knew that he would shrink from no crime in the accomplishment of his purposes. As she took her final leave of her lover, she said to him, very solemnly and impressively,

"Ferdinand, remember that one treacherous friend is more dangerous than a thousand avowed enemies."

[Pg 21]

CHAPTER II.

The Spanish Colony.

Character of De Soto.—Cruel Command of Don Pedro.—Incident.—The Duel.—Uracca.—Consternation at Darien.—Expedition Organized.—Uracca's Reception of Espinosa and his Troops.—The Spaniards Retreat.—De Soto Indignant.—Espinosa's Cruelty, and Deposition from Command.

It was in the year 1519, when the expedition sailed from St. Lucar for Darien. We have no account of the incidents which occurred during the voyage. The fleet reached Darien in safety, and the Spanish adventurers, encased in coats of mail, which the arrows and javelins of the natives could not pierce, mounted on powerful war horses, armed with muskets and cannon, and with packs of ferocious bloodhounds at their command, were all prepared to scatter the helpless natives before them, as the whirlwind scatters autumnal leaves.

De Soto was then but nineteen years of age. In stature and character he was a mature man. There are many indications that he was a young man of humane and honorable instincts, shrinking from the deeds of cruelty and injustice which he saw everywhere [Pg 22] perpetrated around him. It is however probable, that under the rigor of military law, he at times felt constrained to obey commands from which his kindly nature recoiled.

Don Pedro was a monster of cruelty. He gave De Soto command of a troop of horse. He sent him on many expeditions which required not only great courage, but military sagacity scarcely to be expected in one so young and inexperienced. It is however much to the credit of De Soto, that the annalists of those days never mentioned his name in connection with those atrocities which disgraced the administration of Don Pedro. He even ventured at times to refuse obedience to the orders of the governor, when commanded to engage in some service which he deemed dishonorable.

One remarkable instance of this moral and physical intrepidity is on record. Don Pedro had determined upon the entire destruction of a little village occupied by the natives. The torch was to be applied, and men, women and children, were to be put to the sword. Don Pedro had issued such a command as this, with as much indifference as he would have placed his foot upon an anthill. It is not improbable that one of the objects he had in view was to impose a revolting task upon De Soto, that he might be, as it were, whipped into implicit obedience. [Pg 23] He therefore sent one of the most infamous of his captains to De Soto with the command that he should immediately take a troop of horse, proceed to the doomed village, gallop into its peaceful and defenceless street, set fire to every dwelling, and with their keen sabres, cut down every man, woman and child. It was a deed fit only for demons to execute.

De Soto deemed himself insulted in being ordered on such a mission. This was not war,—it was butchery. The defenceless natives could make no resistance. Indignantly and heroically he replied:

"Tell Don Pedro, the governor, that my life and services are always at his disposal, when the duty to be performed is such as may become a Christian and a gentleman. But in the present case, I think the governor would have shown more discretion by entrusting you, Captain Perez, with this commission, instead of sending you with the order to myself."

This reply Captain Perez might certainly regard as reflecting very severely upon his own character, and as authorizing him to demand that satisfaction which, under such circumstances, one cavalier expects of another. He however carried the message to the governor. Don Pedro was highly gratified. He saw that a duel was the necessary result. Captain Perez was a veteran soldier, and was the most expert swordsman in the army. He was famed for his quarrelsome [Pg 24] disposition; had already fought many duels, in which he had invariably killed his man. In a rencontre between the youthful De Soto and the veteran Captain Perez, there could be no doubt in the mind of the governor as to the result. He therefore smiled very blandly upon Captain Perez, and said in language which the captain fully understood:

"Well, my friend, if you, who are a veteran soldier, can endure the insolence of this young man, De Soto, I see no reason why an infirm old man like myself should not show equal forbearance."

Captain Perez was not at all reluctant to take the hint. It was only giving him an opportunity to add another to the list of those who had fallen before his sword. The challenge was immediately given. De Soto's doom was deemed sealed. Duels in the Spanish army were fashionable, and there was no moral sentiment which recoiled in the slightest degree from the barbaric practice.

The two combatants met with drawn swords in the presence of nearly all the officers of the colonial army, and of a vast concourse of spectators. The stripling De Soto displayed skill with his weapon which not only baffled his opponent, but which excited the surprise and admiration of all the on-lookers. For two hours the deadly conflict continued, without any decisive results. De Soto had received [Pg 25] several trifling wounds, while his antagonist was unharmed. At length, by a fortunate blow, he inflicted such a gash upon the right wrist of Perez, that his sword dropped from his hand. As he attempted to catch it with his left hand, he stumbled and fell to the ground. De Soto instantly stood over him with his sword at his breast, demanding that he should ask for his life. The proud duellist, thus for the first time in his life discomfited, was chagrined beyond endurance. In sullen silence, he refused to cry for mercy. De Soto magnanimously returned his sword to its scabbard, saying: "The life that is not worth asking for, is not worth taking."

He then gracefully bowed to the numerous spectators and retired from the field, greeted with the enthusiastic acclaim of all who were present. This achievement gave the youthful victor prominence above any other man in the army. Perez was so humiliated by his defeat, that he threw up his commission and returned to Spain. Thus the New World was rid of one of the vilest of the adventurers who had cursed it.

The region of the peninsula, and the adjoining territory of South America, were at that time quite densely populated. The inhabitants seem to have been a happy people, not fond of war, and yet by no means deficient in bravery. The Spanish colonists [Pg 26] were but a handful among them. But the war horse, bloodhounds, steel coats of mail and gunpowder, gave them an immense, almost resistless superiority.

There was at this time, about the year 1521, an Indian chief by the name of Uracca, who reigned over quite a populous nation, occupying one of the northern provinces of the isthmus. He was a man of unusual intelligence and ability. The outrages which the Spaniards were perpetrating roused all his energies of resentment, and he resolved to adopt desperate measures for their extermination. He gathered an army of twenty thousand men. In that warm climate, in accordance with immemorial usage, they went but half clothed. Their weapons were mainly bows, with poisoned arrows; though they had also javelins and clumsy swords made of a hard kind of wood.

The tidings of the approach of this army excited the greatest consternation at Darien. A shower of poisoned arrows from the strong arms of twenty thousand native warriors, driven forward by the energies of despair, even these steel-clad adventurers could not contemplate without dread. The Spaniards had taught the natives cruelty. They had hunted them down with bloodhounds; they had cut off their hands with the sword; they had fed their dogs with their infants; had tortured them at slow fires and cast [Pg 27] their children into the flames. They could not expect that the natives could be more merciful than the Spaniards had been.

Don Pedro, instead of waiting the arrival of his foes, decided to assail the army on its march, hoping to take it by surprise and to throw consternation into the advancing ranks. He divided his army of attack into two parties. One division of about one hundred men, he sent in two small vessels along the western coast of the isthmus, to invade the villages of Uracca, hoping thus to compel the Indian chief to draw back his army for the defence of his own territories. This expedition was under the command of General Espinosa.

The main body of the Spanish troops, consisting of about two hundred men, marched along the eastern shore of the isthmus, intending eventually to effect a junction with the naval force in the realms of the foe. The energetic, but infamous Francisco Pizarro, led these troops. A very important part of his command consisted of a band of dragoons, thirty or forty in number, under the leadership of De Soto. His steel-clad warriors were well mounted, with housings which greatly protected their steeds from the arrows of the natives.

The wary Indian chieftain, who developed during the campaign military abilities of a high order, had [Pg 28] his scouts out in all directions. They discerned in the distant horizon the approach of the two vessels, and swift runners speedily reported the fact to Uracca. He immediately marched with a force in his judgment sufficiently strong to crush the invaders, notwithstanding their vast superiority in arms.

The Spaniards entered a sheltered bay skirted by a plain, which could be swept by their guns, and where the Indian warriors would have no opportunity to hide in ambush. Uracca allowed the Spaniards to disembark unopposed. He stationed his troops, several thousand in number, in a hilly country, several leagues distant from the place of landing, which was broken with chasms and vast boulders, and covered with tropical forest. Here every Indian could fight behind a rampart, and the Spaniards could only approach in the scattered line of skirmishers. The proud Spaniards advanced in their invading march with as much of war's pageantry as could be assumed. They hoped that nodding plumes and waving banners, and trumpet peals, would strike with consternation the heart of the Indians.

Uracca calmly awaited their approach. His men were so concealed that Espinosa could form no judgment of their numbers or position. Indeed he was scarcely conscious that there was any foe there who would venture to oppose his march. Accustomed as [Pg 29] he was to ride rough shod over the naked Indians, he was emboldened by a fatal contempt for the prowess of his foe. Uracca allowed the Spaniards to become entangled in the intricacies of rocks and gullies and gigantic forest trees, when suddenly he opened upon them such a shower of poisoned arrows as the Spaniards had never encountered before. The touch of one of these arrows, breaking the skin, caused immediate and intense agony, and almost certain death. The sinewy arms of the Indians could throw these sharp-pointed weapons with almost the precision and force of a bullet, and with far greater rapidity than the Spaniards could load and fire their muskets.

Espinosa found himself assailed by a foe outnumbering him ten or twenty to one. The air was almost darkened with arrows, and every one was thrown with unerring aim. The rout of the Spaniards was almost instantaneous. Several were killed, many wounded. In a panic, they turned and fled precipitately from the trap in which they had been caught. The natives impetuously pursued, showing no quarter, evidently determined to exterminate the whole band.

It so happened that De Soto, with his dragoons, had left Pizarro's band, and in a military incursion into the country, was approaching the bay [Pg 30] where Espinosa had landed his troops. Suddenly the clamor of the conflict burst upon his ear—the shouts of the Indian warriors and the cry of the fugitive Spaniards. His little band put spurs to their horses and hastened to the scene of action. Very great difficulties impeded their progress. The rugged ground, encumbered by rocks and broken by ravines, was almost impassable for horsemen. But the energy of De Soto triumphed over these obstacles, even when the bravest of his companions remonstrated and hesitated to follow him. At length he reached the open country over which the Spaniards were rushing to gain their ships, pursued by the Indians in numbers and strength which seemed to render the destruction of the Spaniards certain.

The natives stood in great dread of the horses. When they saw the dragoons, glittering in their steel armor, come clattering down upon the plain, their pursuit was instantly checked. Espinosa, thus unexpectedly reinforced, rallied his panic-stricken troops, and in good order continued the retreat to the ships. De Soto with his cavalry occupied the post of danger as rear-guard. The Indians cautiously followed, watching for every opportunity which the inequalities of the ground might offer, to assail the invaders with showers of arrows. Occasionally De Soto would halt and turn his horses' heads towards the Indians. [Pg 31] Apprehensive of a charge, they would then fall back. The retreat was thus conducted safely, but slowly.

The Spaniards had advanced many leagues from the shores of the Pacific. They were now almost perishing from hunger and fatigue. Indian bands were coming from all directions to reinforce the native troops. The sun was going down and night was approaching. All hearts were oppressed with the greatest anxiety. Just then Pizarro, with his two hundred men, made his appearance. He had not been far away, and a courier having informed him of the peril of the Spaniards, he hastened to their relief. Night with its gloom settled down over the plain, and war's hideous clamor was for a few hours hushed. The morning would usher in a renewal of the battle, under circumstances which caused the boldest hearts in the Spanish camp to tremble.

In the night Generals Espinosa and Pizarro held a council of war, and came to the inglorious resolve to steal away under the protection of darkness, leaving Uracca in undisputed possession of the field. This decision excited the indignation of De Soto. He considered it a disgrace to the Spanish arms, and declared that it would only embolden the natives in all their future military operations. His bitter remonstrances were only answered by a sneer from General [Pg 32] Espinosa, who assured him that the veteran captains of Spain would not look to his youth and inexperience for guidance and wisdom.

At midnight the Spaniards commenced their retreat as secretly and silently as possible. But they had a foe to deal with who was not easily to be deceived. His scouts were on the alert, and immediate notice was communicated to Uracca of the movements of the Spaniards. The pursuit was conducted with as much vigor as the flight. For eight and forty hours the fugitives were followed so closely, and with such fierce assailment, that large numbers of the rank and file perished. The officers and the dragoons of De Soto, wearing defensive armor, generally escaped unharmed. The remnant at length, weary and famine-stricken, reached their ships and immediately put to sea. With the exception of De Soto's dragoons, they numbered but fifty men. Deeply despondent in view of their disastrous campaign, they sailed several leagues along the western coast of the isthmus towards the south, till they reached a flourishing Indian village called Borrica. Conscious that here they were beyond the immediate reach of Uracca's avenging forces, they ventured to land. They found all the men absent. They were probably in the ranks of the native army.

General Espinosa, who was now chief in command, [Pg 33] meanly sacked the defenceless village and captured all the women and children, to be sent to the West Indies and sold as slaves. The generous heart of De Soto was roused by this outrage. He was an imperious man, and was never disposed to be very complaisant to his superiors. Sternly the young captain rebuked Espinosa as a kidnapper, stealing the defenceless; and he demanded that the prisoners should be set at liberty. An angry controversy ensued. De Soto accused Espinosa of cowardice and imbecility, in ordering the troops of Spain to retreat before naked savages. Espinosa, whose domineering spirit could brook no opposition, accused De Soto of mutinous conduct, and threatened to report him to the governor. De Soto angrily turned his heel upon his superior officer and called upon his troops to mount their horses. Riding proudly at their head, he approached the tent of Espinosa and thus addressed him:

"Señor Espinosa, the governor did not place me under your command, and you have no claim to my obedience. I now give you notice, that if you retain these prisoners so cruelly and unjustly captured, you must do so at your own risk. If these Indian warriors choose to make any attempt to recover their wives and their children, I declare to you upon my solemn oath, and by all that I hold most sacred, [Pg 34] that they shall meet with no opposition from me. Consider, therefore, whether you have the power to defend yourself and secure your prey, when I and my companions have withdrawn from this spot."

Pizarro does not seem to have taken any active part in this dispute, though he advised the headstrong Espinosa to give up his captives. While these scenes were transpiring, about one hundred of the men of the village returned. Most earnestly they entreated the release of their wives and children. If not peacefully released, it was pretty evident that they would fight desperately for their rescue. It was quite apparent that the Indian runners had gone in all directions to summon others to their aid. The withdrawal of De Soto left Espinosa so weakened that he could hardly hope successfully to repel such forces. Indeed he was so situated that, destitute of provisions and ammunition, he did not dare to undertake a march back through the wilderness to Darien. He therefore very ungraciously consented to surrender his captives.

Governor Don Pedro had established his headquarters at Panama. De Soto, accompanied by a single dragoon, who like himself was an admirable horseman, rode with the utmost possible dispatch to Panama, where he informed the governor of the disasters [Pg 35] which had befallen the expedition, and of the precarious condition in which he had left the remnant of the troops. He also made such representation of the military conduct of General Espinosa as to induce the governor to remove him from the command and send General Herman Ponce to take his place. The garrison at Panama was then so weak that only forty men could be spared to go to the relief of the troops at Borrica.

In the mean time the Indian chief Uracca had received full information of the position and condition of the Spanish troops. Very sagaciously he formed his plan to cut off their retreat. Detachments of warriors were placed at every point through which they could escape; they could not venture a league from their ramparts on any foraging expedition, and no food could reach them. They obtained a miserable subsistence from roots and herbs.

At length De Soto returned with a fresh supply of ammunition and the small reinforcement. By the aid of his cavalry he so far broke up the blockade as to obtain food for the famishing troops. Still it was very hazardous to attempt a retreat to Panama. With the reinforcements led by General Ponce, their whole army, infantry and cavalry, amounted to less than one hundred and fifty men. They would be [Pg 36] compelled on their retreat to climb mountains, plunge into ragged ravines, thread tropical forests and narrow defiles, where armies of uncounted thousands of natives were ready to dispute their passage.

[Pg 37]

CHAPTER III.

Life at Darien.

Reinforcements from Spain.—Aid sent to Borrica.—Line of Defense Chosen by the Natives.—Religion of the Buccaneers.—The Battle and the Rout.—Strategy of Uracca.—Cruelty of Don Pedro.—The Retreat.—Character of Uracca.—Embarrassment of Don Pedro.—Warning of M. Codro.—Expedition of Pizarro.—Mission of M. Codro.—Letter of De Soto to Isabella.

While governor Don Pedro was awaiting with intense anxiety the receipt of intelligence from Borrica, a ship arrived from Spain bringing three or four hundred adventurers, all of whom were eager for any military expedition which would open to them an opportunity for plunder. One hundred and fifty of these were regular soldiers, well taught in the dreadful trade of war. Don Pedro took these fresh troops and one hundred and fifty volunteers; and set out with the utmost expedition for Borrica. His impetuous nature was inspired with zeal to retrieve the disgrace which had befallen the Spanish arms. He took with him several pieces of ordnance,—guns with which the Indians thus far had no acquaintance.

Upon arriving at Borrica he very earnestly harangued his troops, reminding them of the ancient renown [Pg 38] of the Spanish soldiers, and stimulating their cupidity by the assurance that the kingdom of Veragua, over which Uracca reigned, was full of gold; and that all that was now requisite for the conquest of the country and the accumulation of princely wealth, was a display of the bravery ever characteristic of Spanish troops.

There was a deep and rapid river, the Arva, rushing down from the mountains, which it was necessary for the Spaniards to cross in their renewed invasion of Veragua. On the northern banks of this stream Uracca stationed his troops, selecting this spot with much skill as his main line of defence. He however posted an advanced guard some miles south of the stream in ground broken by hills, rocks and ravines, through which the Spaniards would be compelled to pass, and where their cavalry could be of very little avail.

By great effort Don Pedro had collected an army of about five hundred men. Rapidly marching, he soon reached the spot of broken ground where the native troops were stationed awaiting their approach.

It seems almost incomprehensible that this band of thieves and murderers, who, without the slightest excuse or provocation, were invading the territory of the peaceful natives, carrying to their homes death [Pg 39] and woe, that they might acquire fame for military exploits and return laden with plunder, could have looked to God for his blessing upon their infamous expedition. But so it was. And still more strange to say, they did not apparently engage in these religious services with any consciousness of hypocrisy. The thoughtful mind is bewildered in contemplating such developments of the human heart. Previous to the attack the whole army was drawn up for prayers, which were solemnly offered by the ecclesiastics who always accompanied these expeditions. Then every soldier attended the confessional and received absolution. Thus he felt assured that, should he fall in the battle, he would be immediately translated to the realms of the blest.

Thus inspired by military zeal and religious fanaticism, the Spaniards rushed upon the natives in a very impetuous assault. We are happy to record that the natives stood nobly on the defence. They met their assailants with such a shower of arrows and javelins that the Spaniards were first arrested in their march, then driven back, then utterly routed and put to flight. In that broken ground where the cavalry could not be brought into action, where every native warrior stood behind a tree or a rock, and where the natives did not commence the action till the Spaniards were within half bow shot of them, arrows [Pg 40] and javelins were even more potent weapons of war than the clumsy muskets then in use.

Upon the open field the arrows of the natives were quite impotent. A bullet could strike the heart at twice or three times the distance at which an arrow could be thrown. The Spaniards, hotly pursued, retreated from this broken ground several miles back into the open plain. Many were slain. Here the rout was arrested by the cavalry and the discharges from the field-pieces, which broke the Indian ranks.

The natives, however, boldly held their ground, and the Spaniards, disheartened and mortified by their discomfiture, encamped upon the plain. It was very evident that God had not listened to their prayers.

For several days they remained in a state of uncertainty. For five hundred Spaniards to retreat before eight hundred natives, would inflict a stigma upon their army which could never be effaced. They dared not again attack the natives who were flushed with victory in their stronghold. They were well aware that the band of warriors before them was but the advanced guard of the great army of Uracca. These eight hundred natives were led by one of Uracca's brothers. Even should these Indians be attacked and repulsed, they had only to retreat a few miles, cross the river Arva in their canoes, and on the northern banks join the formidable army of twenty [Pg 41] thousand men under their redoubtable chief, who had already displayed military abilities which compelled the Spaniards to regard him with dread.

Affairs were in this position when Uracca adopted a stratagem which completely deceived the Spaniards and inflicted upon them very serious loss. He caused several of his warriors to be taken captive. When closely questioned by Don Pedro where gold was to be found, and threatened with torture if they refused the information, they with great apparent reluctance directed their captors to a spot, at the distance of but a few leagues, where the precious metal could be obtained in great abundance. These unlettered savages executed their artifice with skill which would have done honor even to European diplomatists.

Don Pedro immediately selected a company of forty of his most reliable men and sent them to the designated spot. Here they were surrounded by Indian warriors in ambush, and the whole party, with the exception of three, put to death. The three who escaped succeeded in reaching the Spanish camp with tidings of the disaster. Don Pedro in his rage ordered his captives to be torn to pieces, by the bloodhounds. They were thrown naked to the dogs. The Spaniards looked on complacently, as the merciless beasts, with bloody fangs, tore them limb from limb, devouring their quivering flesh. The natives bore [Pg 42] this awful punishment with fortitude and heroism, which elicited the admiration of their foes. With their last breath they exulted that they were permitted to die in defence of their country.

The expedition of Don Pedro had thus far proved an utter failure. He had already lost one-fourth of his army through the prowess of the natives. The prospect before him was dark in the extreme. His troops were thoroughly discouraged, and the difficulties still to be encountered seemed absolutely insurmountable. Humiliated as never before, the proud Don Pedro was compelled to order a retreat. He returned to Panama, where, as we have mentioned, he had removed his seat of government from Darien. Panama was north of Darien, or rather west, as the isthmus there runs east and west. Its seaport was on the Pacific, not the Atlantic coast.

Uracca, having thus rescued his country from the invaders, did not pursue the retreating Spaniards. He probably in this course acted wisely. Could Don Pedro have drawn his enemies into the open field, he could undoubtedly have cut down nearly their whole army with grape shot, musketry, and charges by his strongly mounted steel-clad cavaliers. A panic had however pervaded the

Spanish camp. They were in constant apprehension of pursuit. Even when they had reached Panama, they were day after day in intense [Pg 43] apprehension of the approach of their outnumbering foes, by whose valor they had already been discomfited, and so greatly disgraced.

"When the Spaniards looked out towards the mountains and the plains," writes the Spanish historian Herrera, "the boughs of trees and the very grass, which grew high in the savannas, appeared to their excited imagination to be armed with Indians. And when they turned their eyes towards the sea, they fancied that it was covered with canoes of their exasperated foemen."

Uracca must have been in all respects an extraordinary man. We have the record of his deeds only from the pen of his enemies. And yet according to their testimony, he, a pagan, manifested far more of the spirit of Christ than did his Christian opponents. In the war which he was then waging, there can be no question whatever that the wrong was inexcusably and outrageously on the side of Don Pedro. We cannot learn that Uracca engaged in any aggressive movements against the Spaniards whatever. He remained content with expelling the merciless intruders from his country. Even the fiendlike barbarism of the Spaniards could not provoke him to retaliatory cruelty. The brutal soldiery of Spain paid no respect whatever to the wives and daughters of the natives, even to those of the highest chieftains.

[Pg 44]

On one occasion a Spanish lady, Donna Clara Albitez, fell into the hands of Uracca. He treated her with as much delicacy and tenderness as if she had been his own daughter or mother, and availed himself of the first opportunity of restoring her to her friends.

Though De Soto was one of the bravest of his cavaliers, and was so skilful as an officer that his services were almost indispensable to Don Pedro, yet the governor was anxious to get rid of him. It is probable that he felt somewhat condemned by the undeniable virtues of De Soto; for the most of men can feel the power of high moral principle as witnessed in others. De Soto, intensely proud, was not at all disposed to play the sycophant before his patron. He had already exasperated him by his refusal to execute orders which he deemed dishonorable. And worst of all, by winning the love of Isabella, he had thwarted one of the most ambitious of Don Pedro's plans; he having contemplated her alliance with one of the most illustrious families of the Spanish nobility.

Don Pedro did not dare to send De Soto to the scaffold or to order him to be shot. He had already braved public opinion by the outrageous execution of Vasco Nuñez, without a shadow of law or justice, and had drawn down upon himself an avalanche of condemnation from the highest dignitaries of both [Pg 45] church and state. He was trembling through fear that the Spanish government might call him to account for this tyrannic act. Thus situated, it was highly impolitic to send De Soto, who was greatly revered and admired by the army, to the block. He therefore still sought, though with somewhat waning zeal, to secure the death of De Soto on the field of battle. De Soto could not fail to perceive that Don Pedro was not his friend. Still, being a magnanimous man himself, he could not suspect the governor of being guilty of such treachery as to be plotting his death.

When the little army of Spaniards was beleaguered at Borrica, and De Soto with his cavalry was scouring the adjacent country on foraging expeditions, he chanced to rescue from captivity M. Codro, an Italian philosopher, who had accompanied the Spaniards to Darien. In the pursuit of science, he had joined the forty men who, under the command of Herman Ponce, had been sent as a reinforcement to Borrica. While at some distance from the camp on a botanical excursion, he was taken captive by the natives, and would have been put to death but for the timely rescue by De Soto.

M. Codro was an astrologer. In that superstitious age he was supposed by others, and probably himself supposed, that by certain occult arts he was [Pg 46] able to predict future events. Six months after the return of the Spaniards from their disastrous expedition against Uracca, this singular man sought an interview with De Soto, and said to him:

"A good action deserves better reward than verbal acknowledgment. While it was not in my power to make any suitable recompense to you for saving my life, I did not attempt to offer you any. But the time has now come when I can give you some substantial evidence of my gratitude. I can now inform you that your life is now in no less danger than mine was when you rescued me from the Indians."

De Soto replied: "My good friend, though I do not profess to be a thorough believer in your prophetic art, I am no less thankful for your kind intentions. And in this case, I am free to confess that your information, from whatever source derived, is confirmed in a measure by my own observations."

"Ferdinand De Soto," said the astrologer with great deliberation and solemnity of manner, "I think I can read the page of *your* destiny, even without such light as the stars can shed upon it. Be assured that the warning I give you does not come from an unearthly source. But if any supernatural confirmation of my words were needed, even on that score you might be satisfied. While comparing your horoscope with that of my departed friend Vasco Nuñez, [Pg 47] I have observed some resemblances in your lives and fortunes, which you, with all your incredulity, must allow to be remarkable. Nuñez and you were both born in the same town; were both members of noble but impoverished families; both sought to ally yourselves with the family of Don Pedro, and both thus incurred his deadly resentment."

"These coincidences are certainly remarkable," replied De Soto; "but what other similarities do you find in the destinies of Nuñez and myself?"

"You are a brave man," replied M. Codro, "and you are too skeptical to be much disturbed by the prognostications of evil. I may therefore venture to tell you that according to my calculations, you will be in one important event of your life more happy than Vasco Nuñez. It seems to be indicated by the superior intelligences, that your death will not be in the ordinary course of nature; but I find likewise that the term of your life will be equal to that which Nuñez attained. When I consider your present circumstances, this appears to me to be the most improbable part of the prediction."

Nuñez was forty-two years old at the time of his death. This gave De Soto the promise of nearly twenty years more of life. Reverently he replied, "I am in the hands of God. I rely with humble confidence on his protection."

[Pg 48]

"In that you do well," rejoined M. Codro. "Still it is your duty to use such human means as may be required to defend yourself against open violence or fraudful malice."

De Soto thanked the astrologer for the caution he had given him, and as he reflected upon it, saw that it was indeed necessary to be constantly on his guard. As time passed on Don Pedro became more undisguised in his hostility to De Soto. Ferdinand and Isabella exerted all their ingenuity to correspond with each other. Don Pedro had been equally vigilant in his endeavors to intercept their letters; and so effectual were the plans which he adopted, that for five years, while the lovers remained perfectly faithful to each other, not a token of remembrance passed between them.

These were weary years to De Soto. He was bitterly disappointed in all his expectations. There was no glory to be obtained even in victory, in riding rough-shod over the poor natives. And thus far, instead of victory attending the Spanish arms, defeat and disgrace had been their doom. Moreover, he was astonished and heartily ashamed when he saw the measures which his countrymen had adopted to enrich themselves. They were highway robbers of the most malignant type. They not only slaughtered the victims whom they robbed, but fired their dwellings, [Pg 49] trampled down their harvests and massacred their wives and children.

The most extravagant tales had been circulated through Europe respecting the wealth of the New World. It was said that masses of pure gold could be gathered like pebble stones from the banks of the rivers, and that gems of priceless value were to be found in the ravines. De Soto had been now five years on the isthmus of Darien, and had acquired neither fame nor fortune, and there was nothing in the prospect of the future to excite enthusiasm or even hope.

There was quite a remarkable man, made so by subsequent events, under the command of Don Pedro. His name was Francisco Pizarro. He was a man of obscure birth and of very limited education, save only in the material art of war. He could neither read nor write, and was thus intellectually hardly the equal of some of the most intelligent of the natives. We have briefly alluded to him as entrusted with the command of one portion of the army in the inglorious expedition against Uracca. De Soto had very little respect for the man, and was not at all disposed as a subordinate officer to look to him for counsel. Don Pedro, however, seems to have formed a high opinion of the military abilities of Pizarro. For notwithstanding his ignominious defeat and retreat from [Pg 50] Veragua, he now appointed him as the leader of an expedition, consisting of one hundred and thirty men, to explore the western coast of the isthmus by cruising along the Pacific Ocean.

Pizarro set sail from Panama on the fourteenth of November, 1524, in one small vessel. It was intended that another vessel should soon follow to render such assistance as might be necessary. De Soto was urged to become one of this party; but probably from dislike of Pizarro, refused to place himself under his command.

The vessel, which was soon joined by its consort under Almagro, coasted slowly along in a northerly direction, running in at every bay, and landing whenever they approached a flourishing Indian village, plundering the natives and maltreating them in every shameful way. At length they aroused such a spirit of desperation on the part of the natives, that they fell upon the buccaneers with resistless ferocity. Two-thirds of the miscreants were slain. Pizarro barely escaped with his life, having received severe wounds and being borne to his ship in a state of insensibility.

While Pizarro was absent on this ill-fated expedition, a new trouble befell Don Pedro. Las Casas, a devoted Christian missionary, whose indignation was roused to the highest pitch by the atrocities perpetrated [Pg 51] upon the Indians, reported the inhuman conduct of Don Pedro to the Spanish government. The King appointed Peter de Los Rios to succeed him. The new governor was to proceed immediately to Panama and bring the degraded official to trial, and, if found guilty, to punishment. The governor of a Spanish colony in those days was absolute. Don Pedro had cut off the head of his predecessor, though that predecessor was one of the best of men. He now trembled in apprehension of the loss of his own head. Conscious of his deserts, he was terror-stricken.

About four or five hundred miles north of Panama there was the magnificent province of Nicaragua. The isthmus is here about one hundred and fifty miles in breadth, and the province being about two hundred miles in a line from north to south, extended from the Atlantic to the Pacific shores. Don Pedro was popular with his brutal soldiery, since he allowed them unlimited license and plunder. He resolved, surrounded by them, to take refuge in Nicaragua. Nevertheless, to render himself as secure as possible, he decided to send an agent to plead his cause at the Spanish court.

Among those rude, unprincipled adventurers, men of violence and blood, it was very difficult to find a suitable person. At length he fixed with much hesitation [Pg 52] upon M. Codro, the astrologer. He was a simple-minded, good man; learned, though very artless. M. Codro was strongly attached to De Soto, the preserver of his life. As we have seen, he was well aware of the peril to which his benefactor was hourly exposed from the malignity of the governor. Gladly therefore he accepted the mission, as he hoped it would afford him an opportunity of conferring some favor upon his imperilled friend.

Don Pedro had adopted the most rigorous measures to prevent any communication between the colony and Spain, which was not subjected to his inspection. He was mainly influenced to this course that he might prevent the interchange of any messages whatever between De Soto and Isabella. The most severe penalties were denounced against all persons who should convey any writing across the seas, excepting through the regular mails. But the grateful M. Codro declared himself ready to run all risks in carrying a letter from De Soto to Isabella. Though De Soto at first hesitated to expose his friend to such hazard, his intense desire to open some communication with Isabella, at length induced him to accept the generous offer.

As we have mentioned, for five years not one word had passed between the lovers. It is said that the following is a literal translation of the letter which [Pg 53] De Soto wrote. We cannot be certain of its authenticity, but it bears internal evidence of genuineness, and a manuscript copy is in the library of a Spanish gentleman who has spent his life in collecting documents in reference to the past history of his country:

"Most Dearly Beloved Isabella:

"For the first time within five years, I write to you with some assurance that you will receive my letter. Many times have I written before; but how could I write freely when I had reason to fear that other eyes might peruse those fond expressions which your goodness and condescension alone could pardon? But what reason have I to hope that you can still look with favorable regard on my unworthiness? My mature judgment teaches me that this dream of my youth, which I have so long cherished, is not presumption merely, but madness.

"When I consider your many perfections, and compare them with my own little deserving, I feel that I ought to despair, even if I could empty into your lap the treasure of a thousand kingdoms. How then can I lift my eyes to you when I have nothing to offer but the tribute of an affection which time cannot change, and which must still live when my last hope has departed.

"O Isabella! the expectation which brought me [Pg 54] to this land has not been fulfilled. I can gather no gold, except by such means as my honor, my conscience and yourself must condemn. Though your nobleness may pity one on whom fortune has disdained to smile, I feel that your relations are justified in claiming for you an alliance with exalted rank and affluence; and I love you far too well to regard my own happiness more than your welfare. If, therefore, in your extreme youth you have made a promise which you now regret, as far as it is in my power to absolve you from that engagement, you are released. On my side, the obligation is sacred and eternal. It is not likely that I shall ever return to my country. While I am banished from your presence, all countries are alike to me.

"The person who brings you this exposes himself to great danger in his desire to serve me. I entreat you to use such precautions as his safety may require. If your goodness should vouchsafe any message to me, he will deliver it, and you may have perfect confidence in his fidelity. Pardon my boldness in supposing it possible that I still have a place in your remembrance. Though you may now think of me with indifference or dislike, do not censure me too severely for calling myself unchangeably and devotedly, Yours, De Soto."

[Pg 55]

CHAPTER IV.

Demoniac Reign.

Giles Gonzales.—Unsuccessful Contest of De Soto with Gonzales.—Bold Reply of De Soto to the Governor.—Cruelty of Don Pedro to M. Codro.—Assassination of Cordova.—New Expedition of Discovery.—Revenge upon Valenzuela.—Reign of Don Pedro at Nicaragua.—Unwise Decision of De Soto.

It was supposed at that time that there must be a strait somewhere north of Panama across the narrow isthmus, which would connect the waters of the Atlantic and Pacific oceans. Several expeditions had been fitted out in search of this all-important passage. Almost invariably a company of priests joined these expeditions, who exerted all their energies to convert the Indians to nominal Christianity. A fanatic adventurer by the name of Giles Gonzales, acquired much celebrity for his success in inducing the natives to accept the Christian faith and to acknowledge fealty to the king of Spain. He was at the head of one hundred steel-clad warriors. His mode of persuasion, though unique, was very potent. When he approached the seat of the chief of Nicaragua, he sent a courier to him with the following message:

[Pg 56]

"I am coming as a friend to teach you the only true religion, and to persuade you to recognize the most powerful monarch on the globe. If you refuse to yield to my teachings, you must prepare for battle, and I challenge you to meet me in the field."

The gentle and peace-loving natives contemplated with consternation these fierce Spaniards mounted on powerful war horses, animals which they had never before seen, and glittering in coats of mail. They had no religious creed to which they adhered with any tenacity. The Nicaraguan chief unhesitatingly expressed his readiness to accept the new faith, and in token of friendship, sent Gonzales a quantity of gold, equal it is said in value to seventy-five thousand dollars of our money. The Spanish historian Herrera, whose record is generally deemed in the main accurate, says that the chief, his family, and nine thousand of his subjects, were baptized and became Christians. Influenced by this example, and by the glowing representations of the rewards which were sure to follow the acceptance of the Christian faith, more than thirty-six thousand of the natives were baptized within the space of half a year. The baptismal fees charged by Gonzales amounted to over four hundred thousand dollars.

While Gonzales was engaged on his own responsibility in this career of spiritual conquest, with its [Pg 57] rich pecuniary accompaniment, Don Pedro sent two of his generals, Ferdinand de Cordova and Ferdinand De Soto, to explore Nicaragua and take possession of it in his name. He assumed that Gonzales, acting without authority, was engaged in a treasonable movement. The two parties soon came into collision.

De Soto, with a party of fifty men, twenty of them being well mounted cavaliers, encamped at a small village called Torebo. Gonzales was in the near vicinity with a little army of three hundred men, two hundred of whom were Indians. In the darkness of the night, Gonzales fell upon De Soto, and outnumbering him six to one, either killed or took captive all the thirty footmen; while the cavaliers, on their horses, cut their way through and escaped. Gonzales lost fifty of his best men in the conflict, and was so impressed with the military vigor of De Soto, that he was not at all disposed again to meet him on the field of battle. He therefore retired to a distant part of the province, where he vigorously engaged in the work of converting the natives, never forgetting his baptismal fee.

De Soto and Cordova established themselves in a new town which they called Grenada. Here they erected a church, several dwelling houses, and barracks for the soldiers. They also surrounded the village [Pg 58] with a trench and earthworks, as protection from any sudden assault. Gonzales was a fugitive from justice, having assassinated an officer sent by Hernando Cortes to arrest him.

Cordova was a mild and humane man. Under his sway the Indians were prosperous and happy. Two flourishing towns grew up rapidly quite near each other, Leon and Grenada. The climate was delightful, the soil fertile, the means of living abundant. Many of the inhabitants of Panama emigrated to this more favored region.

De Soto, leaving Cordova in command of Nicaragua, returned to Panama to report proceedings to Don Pedro. It was not till then that he learned, to his extreme regret, that the Governor had selected Nicaragua as a place for his future abode. He knew that the presence of the tyrannical governor could only prove disastrous to the flourishing colony, and ruinous to the happiness of the natives. The gloom with which the contemplation oppressed his mind spread over his speaking countenance. The eagle eye of the suspicious governor immediately detected these indications of discontent. With an air of deference, but in a tone of mockery, he said:

"I judge from your appearance, captain, that my Nicaraguan enterprise does not meet with your cordial approbation."

[Pg 59]

De Soto boldly, and with great deliberation of words, replied:

"Governor Don Pedro, I confess that I feel but little interested in any of your movements or intentions, except when they encroach upon the rights of others. Nicaragua is at this time well governed by Ferdinand de Cordova. The change you propose to make, is to be deprecated as one of the greatest misfortunes that could befall not only the Indian inhabitants of that district, but our own countrymen likewise, who have flocked thither to escape from your jurisdiction."

The countenance of Don Pedro became pallid with rage. Struggling, however, to suppress the unavailing outburst of his passion, he said, with a malignant smile:

"I thank you, Captain De Soto, for giving me this opportunity which I have so long desired. Were I to permit such insolence to go unpunished, my authority in this colony would soon be at an end."

"It is at an end," replied De Soto. "You must be aware that your successor, De Los Rios, is now on his way to Panama."

"I do not choose," replied Don Pedro, "to debate this matter with you. I still claim the right to command you as your superior military officer. I now command you to hold yourself and your company in [Pg 60] readiness to march. When we arrive at Leon, I promise you that full justice shall be done to your friend De Cordova, and to yourself."

De Soto fully comprehended the significance of these threats. He wrote immediately to Cordova, urging him to be on his guard. The inhabitants of Leon and Grenada, learning of the intention of Don Pedro,—to take the government into his own hands,—entreated De Cordova to resist the tyrant, promising him their unanimous and energetic support. But De Cordova declined these overtures, saying, that all the authority to which he was legitimately entitled was derived from Don Pedro, and that it was his duty to obey him as his superior officer, until he should be deposed by the Spanish crown.

Just before Don Pedro, with his suite, left Panama for Nicaragua, M. Codro returned from Spain. He brought dispatches to the governor, and also secretly a letter from Isabella to De Soto. The spies of the governor, in his castle in Spain, watched every movement of M. Codro. The simple minded man had very little skill in the arts of duplicity. These spies reported to Don Pedro that M. Codro had held a secret interview with Isabella, and had frankly stated that he was entrusted with a private message to her. Don Pedro knew that such a message could have gone only from De Soto; and that [Pg 61] unquestionably M. Codro had brought back from his daughter a response. We may remark in passing, that the letter from Isabella to De Soto informed him of the inflexible fidelity of Isabella, and filled the heart of De Soto with joy.

The malignant nature of Don Pedro was roused by these suspicions to intensity of action, and he resolved upon direful revenge. As the new governor was hourly expected, he could not venture upon any open act of assassination or violence, for he knew that in that case summary punishment would be his doom. Calling M. Codro before him, he assumed his blandest smile, thanked the artless philosopher for the services he had rendered him in Spain, and said that he wished to entrust him with the management of a mineralogical survey of a region near the gulf of San Miguel.

The good man was delighted. This was just the employment which his nature craved. He was directed to embark in a vessel commanded by one of the governor's tools, an infamous wretch by the name of De Valenzuela. This man had been for many years a private, and was then engaged in kidnapping Indians for the slave trade. He was ordered as soon as the vessel was at sea, to chain M.

Codro to the foremast, to expose him to all the tortures of the blaze of a tropical sun by day and chilling [Pg 62] dews by night. The crew were enjoined to assail him with insulting mockery. Thus exposed to hunger, burning heat, and incessant abuse, he was to be kept through these lingering agonies until he died.

For ten days the good man bore this cruel martyrdom, when he breathed his last, and was buried on a small island about a hundred miles southwest of Panama. This brutal assassination was so conducted, that De Soto at the time had no knowledge of the tragedy which was being enacted.

Early in the year 1526, Don Pedro, surrounded by a large retinue of his obedient soldiery, left Panama to assume the government of Nicaragua, to which he had no legitimate title. De Soto accompanied the governor. Much as he detested his character, he could not forget that he was the father of Isabella. When Don Pedro approached the little town of Leon, he sent a courier before him, to order De Cordova to meet him in the public square, with his municipal officers and his clergy, prepared to give an account of his administration.

De Soto with his horsemen was ordered to form in line on one side of the square. The foot soldiers of Don Pedro surrounded the governor on the other side. All the vacant space was filled with citizens and natives. By the side of the governor stood his [Pg 63] executioner; a man of gigantic stature and of herculean strength, whose massive sword few arms but his could wield. De Cordova advanced to meet Don Pedro, and bowing respectfully before him, commenced giving an account of the state of affairs in the province. Suddenly he was interrupted in his narrative by Don Pedro, who with forced anger exclaimed:

"Silence, you hypocrite! Your treasonable projects cannot be hidden under these absurd pretensions of loyalty and patriotism: I will now let your accomplices see how a traitor should be punished."

He made a sign to his executioner. His gleaming sword flashed through the air, and in an instant the dissevered head of Cordova rolled in the dust. The headsman grasped the gory trophy by the hair, and raising it high above his head exclaimed,

"Behold the doom of a traitor."

All this took place in an instant. The spectators were horror stricken. De Soto instinctively seized his sword, and would doubtless have put spurs to his horse, rushed upon the governor, and plunged the weapon to the hilt in his breast, but for the restraining memories of the past. Hesitatingly he returned his sword to its scabbard.

But Don Pedro had not yet finished the contemplated [Pg 64] work of the day. Another victim he had doomed to fall. A file of soldiers, very resolute men, led by a determined officer, crossing the square, approached De Soto, at the head of his troops. Don Pedro then exclaimed in a loud voice,

"Ferdinand De Soto, you are ordered to dismount and submit yourself to the punishment which you have just seen inflicted on your traitorous comrade. Soldiers! drag him from his horse if he refuse to obey."

The officer reached forth his hand to seize De Soto. Like lightning's flash, the sword of the cavalier fell upon the officer, and his head was cleft from crown to chin. The spurs were applied to the fiery steed. He plunged through the soldiers, knocking several of them down, and in an instant De Soto had his sword's point at the breast of the governor. Shouts of "kill the tyrant," rose from all parts of the square, which were echoed even from the ranks of Don Pedro's soldiers. Again De Soto held back his avenging hand; but in words which made Don Pedro quake in his shoes, he said,

"You hear the expression of public sentiment. You hear the wishes of those who are subject to your authority. It is the voice of justice speaking through these people. In refusing to obey the call, I am scarcely less guilty than yourself. But remember, [Pg 65] Don Pedro, that in sparing your life at this moment, I discharge all the obligations I have owed you. Miserable old man! Be thankful that the recollection of one that is absent, can make me forget what I owe to my murdered friend.

"I will now sheathe my sword, but I solemnly declare by the sacred emblem of the cross which it bears, that I will never draw it again in your service."

The assassination, for it could hardly be called execution, of De Cordova, excited the general indignation of the Spanish settlers. They all knew that Don Pedro had no authority from the king of Spain to assume the government of Nicaragua, and that he was therefore an usurper. The noble character which De Soto had exhibited, and his undeniable ability and bravery, had won for him universal regard. The Spaniards generally rallied around him, and entreated him to assume the command, promising him their enthusiastic support. They could not comprehend why De Soto so persistently refused their solicitations. They knew nothing of the secret reasons which rendered it almost impossible for De Soto to draw his sword against the father of Isabella.

As we have mentioned, it was generally supposed that there must be some strait between the Isthmus of Darien and the southern frontiers of Mexico, which [Pg 66] connected the waters of the Atlantic and Pacific Oceans. The king of Spain had offered a large reward for the discovery of this passage. Several of the wealthy citizens of Leon organized an expedition in pursuit of this object. De Soto was placed at its head. He selected, from his cavalry troop, five of his most intelligent and energetic young men. They started from Leon, and followed along the coast of the Pacific, in northwesterly course, penetrating every bay and inlet. They travelled on horseback and encountered innumerable difficulties from the rugged and pathless wilderness, through which they pressed their way. They also had much to fear from the unfriendly character of the natives, whose hostility had been aroused by the outrages which companies of vagabond Spaniards had inflicted upon them.

De Soto, however, and his companions, by their just and kindly spirit, soon won the regards of the Indians. They found that the natives possessed large quantities of gold, which they seemed to esteem of little value. Eagerly they exchanged the precious metal for such trinkets as the explorers took with them. Upon this arduous expedition, which De Soto managed with consummate skill, he was absent eleven months. Seven hundred miles of sea-coast were carefully explored, and he became fully convinced that the looked-for strait did not exist. [Pg 67] Though in this respect the expedition had proved a failure, he returned to Leon quite enriched by the gold which he had gathered. With honesty, rarely witnessed in those days, he impartially divided the treasure among the projectors of the enterprise.

As De Soto was returning, he discovered a small Spanish vessel anchored near the present site of San Salvador. As his men and horses were worn down by their fatiguing journey, he engaged a passage in the vessel to Leon. Upon embarking he found the captain and crew consisted of some of the most depraved and brutal men who had ever visited the New World. They were cruising along the coast, watching for opportunity to kidnap the natives, to convey them to the West Indies as slaves. The captain was the infamous Valenzuela, who, as agent of Don Pedro, had tortured M. Codro to death.

De Soto had no knowledge, as we have mentioned, of the dreadful doom which had befallen his friend. One day the fiendlike captain was amusing his crew with a recital of his past deeds of villany. He told the story of the murder of Codro.

"He was," he said, "an old wizard whom Don Pedro, the governor of Panama, commissioned me to torture and to put to death, in consequence of some treachery of which he had been guilty while on a mission to Spain."

[Pg 68]

The words caught the ear of De Soto. He joined the group, and listened with breathless attention and a throbbing heart, to the statement of Valenzuela.

"I chained the old fellow," said the captain, "to the mainmast, and the sailors amused themselves by drenching him with buckets of cold water, till he was almost drowned. After several days, he became so sick and exhausted, that we saw that our sport would soon be at an end. For two days he was speechless. He then suddenly recovered the use of his voice, and endeavored to frighten me by saying:

"'Captain, your treatment has caused my death. I now call upon you to hear the words of a dying man. Within a year from this time, I summon you to meet me before the judgment seat of God.'"

Here the captain burst into a derisive and scornful laugh. He then added:

"Come comrades, we'll have a hamper of wine, and drink to the repose of M. Codro's soul."

De Soto stepped forward, and repressing all external exhibition of the rage which consumed his soul, said calmly to the captain,

"You say that the astrologer prophesied that you should die within the year. When will that year expire?"

"In about two weeks," the captain replied. "But [Pg 69] I have no fear but that the prophet will prove to be a liar."

"He shall not," De Soto added. And drawing from his scabbard his keen, glittering sword, with one blow from his sinewy arm, severed the captain's head from his body. The ghastly trophy rolled gushing with blood upon the deck. These wild and savage men were accustomed to such scenes. They admired the courage of De Soto, and the marvellous skill with which, at one blow, he had struck off the head of the captain. De Soto then turned to the crowd and said:

"Gentlemen, if any of you are disposed to hold me accountable for what I have just done, I am ready to answer you according to your desires. But I consider myself bound, in reason and in courtesy, to inform you, that M. Codro, the man whom this villain murdered, was my friend; and I doubt not that he was condemned to death for doing me an important service."

All seemed satisfied with this explanation. These sanguinary scenes in those days produced but a momentary impression.

De Soto and Don Pedro no longer held any intercourse with each other. The reign of the usurping governor was atrocious beyond the power of language to express. With horses and bloodhounds he [Pg 70] ran down the natives, seizing and selling them as slaves. Droves of men, women and children, chained together, were often driven into the streets of Leon.

The assumption then was that a nominal Christian might pardonably inflict any outrages upon those who had not accepted the Christian faith. Several of the Indian chiefs had embraced Christianity. Don Pedro compelled them all to pay him a tribute of fifty slaves a month. All orphans were to be surrendered as slaves. And then the wretch demanded that all parents who had several children, should surrender one or more, as slaves to the Spaniards. The natives were robbed of their harvests, so that they had no encouragement to cultivate the soil. This led to famine, and more than twenty thousand perished of starvation. Famine introduced pestilence. The good Las Casas declares that in consequence of the oppressions of the Spaniards, in ten years, more than sixty thousand of the natives of Nicaragua perished.

About this time Francisco Pizarro had embarked in a hair-brained enterprise for the conquest of Peru, on the western coast of South America. Very slowly he had forced his way along, towards that vast empire, encountering innumerable difficulties, and enduring frightful sufferings, until he had reached a point where his progress seemed to be arrested. His army was greatly weakened, and he had not sufficient force to [Pg 71] push his conquests any farther. Threatened with the utter extermination of his band, he remembered De Soto, whom he had never loved. He knew that he was anxious for fame and fortune, and thought that his bravery and great military ability might extricate him from his embarrassments.

He therefore wrote to Don Pedro, praying that De Soto, with reinforcements, might be sent to his aid. For three years there had been no communication whatever between the governor and the lover of his daughter. But Don Pedro regarded the adventure of Pizarro as hazardous in the extreme, and felt sure that all engaged in the enterprise would miserably perish. Eagerly he caught at the idea of sending De Soto to join them; for his presence was to Don Pedro a constant source of annoyance and dread. He therefore caused the communication from Pizarro to be conveyed to De Soto, saying to the messenger who bore it:

"Urge De Soto to depart immediately for Peru. And I pray Heaven that we may never hear of him again."

De Soto, not knowing what to do with himself, imprudently consented, and thus allied his fortunes with those of one of the greatest villains of any age or country.

[Pg 72]

CHAPTER V.

The Invasion of Peru.

The Kingdom of Peru.—Its Metropolis.—The Desperate Condition of Pizarro.—Arrival of De Soto.—Character of the Spaniards.—Exploring tour of De Soto.—The Colony at San Miguel.—The General Advance.—Second Exploration of De Soto.—Infamous Conduct of the Pizarros.

The kingdom of Peru, skirting the western coast of South America, between the majestic peaks of the Andes and the mirrored waters of the Pacific Ocean, was one of the most beautiful countries in the world. This kingdom, diversified with every variety of scenery, both of the sublime and the beautiful, and enjoying a delicious climate, was about eighteen hundred miles in length and one hundred and fifty in breadth. The natives had attained a high degree of civilization. Though gunpowder, steel armor, war horses, and bloodhounds gave the barbarian Spaniards the supremacy on fields of blood, the leading men, among the Peruvians, seem to have been in intelligence, humanity and every virtue, far superior to the savage leaders of the Spaniards, who so ruthlessly invaded their peaceful realms.

[Pg 73]

The metropolis of the empire was the city of Cuzo, which was situated in a soft and luxuriant valley traversing some table-lands which were about twelve thousand feet above the level of the sea. The government of the country was an absolute monarchy. But its sovereign, called the Inca, seems to have been truly a good man, the father of his people; wisely and successfully seeking their welfare. The Peruvians had attained a degree of excellence in many of the arts unsurpassed by the Spaniards. Their houses were generally built of stone; their massive temples, though devoid of architectural beauty, were constructed of hewn blocks of granite, so admirably joined together that the seams could be with difficulty discerned.

Humbolt found, among the ruins of these temples, blocks of hewn stone thirty-six feet long, nine feet wide, and six feet in thickness. Their great highways, spanning the gulfs, clinging to the precipitous cliffs and climbing the mountains, were wonderful works of mechanical skill.

De Soto was thoroughly acquainted with the cruel, faithless, and treacherous character of Pizarro. A stigma must ever rest upon his name, for consenting to enter into any expedition under the leadership of such a man. It may however be said, in reply, that he had no intention of obeying Pizarro in any [Pg 74] thing that was wrong; that his love of adventure was roused by the desire to explore one of the most magnificent empires in the New World, which rumor had invested with wealth and splendor surpassing the dreams of romance. And perhaps, most important of all, he hoped *honestly* to be able to gather from the fabled mines of gold, with which Peru was said to be filled, that wealth with which he would be enabled to return to Spain and claim the hand, as he had already won the heart, of the fair and faithful Isabella.

Pizarro had entered upon his enterprise with an army of one hundred and eighty men, twenty-seven of whom were mounted. It seems to be the uncontradicted testimony of contemporary historians, that this army was composed of as worthless a set of vagabonds as ever disgraced humanity. There was no crime or cruelty from which these fiends in human form would recoil.

Pizarro, following down the western coast of South America five or six hundred miles, had reached the island of Puna, in the extreme northern part of Peru. It was separated from the mainland by a narrow strait. The inhabitants received him cordially, but the murders, rapine and other nameless atrocities, perpetrated by the Spaniards upon the friendly natives, soon so aroused their resentment [Pg 75] that a conspiracy was formed for the entire extermination of the invaders. The expedition had become so weakened and demoralized that even Pizarro saw that it would be the height of imprudence for him to venture, with his vile crew, upon the mainland, before reinforcements under some degree of military discipline should arrive. He was in this precarious condition, and on the eve of extermination, when De Soto and his select and well-ordered troops reached the island.

They came in two vessels, bringing with them an abundant supply of arms and ammunition. The party consisted of fifty men, thoroughly equipped. Thirty of them were steel-clad cavaliers, well mounted. De Soto had been offered the rank of second in command. But when he arrived at Puna, he found that Pizarro's brother—Hernando—occupied this post, and that he had no intention of relinquishing it. De Soto reproached Pizarro in very plain terms for this wrong and insult. He however did not allow it long to trouble him. Surrounded by his own brave and devoted followers, he felt quite independent of the authority of Pizarro, and had no intention of obeying him any farther than might be in accordance with his own wishes.

On the other hand, Pizarro had but little confidence in his brother, and was fully conscious that the [Pg 76] success of his enterprise would be mainly dependent upon the energy and skill of De Soto.

Pizarro, now finding himself at the head of really a formidable force, prepared to pass over to the mainland. There was quite a large town there called Tumbez, surrounded by a rich and densely populated country. The Peruvians had gold in abundance, and weapons and utensils of copper. With iron and steel, they were entirely unacquainted. As when fighting at a distance, the bullet of the Spaniard was immeasurably superior to the arrow of the native, so in a hand to hand fight, the keen and glittering sabre of steel, especially in the hands of steel-clad cavaliers left the poorly armed Peruvians almost entirely at their mercy.

Arrangements were made to cross the strait and make a descent upon Tumbez. Pizarro had already visited the place, where he had been kindly received by the inhabitants, and where he had seen with his own eyes that the houses and temples were decorated with golden ornaments, often massive in weight, and of almost priceless value. He floated his little band across the narrow strait on rafts.

The inhabitants of Tumbez and its vicinity had been disposed to receive their Spanish visitors as guests, and to treat them with the utmost courtesy and kindness. But the tidings had reached them of [Pg 77] the terrible outrages which they had inflicted upon the inhabitants of Puna. They therefore attacked the Spaniards as they approached the shore on their rafts and endeavored to prevent their landing. But the invaders, with musketry and a cannon which they had with them, speedily drove off their assailants, and with horses and hounds planted their banners upon the shore. They then marched directly upon Tumbez, confident of gathering, from the decorations of her palaces and her temples, abounding wealth. Bitter was their disappointment. The Peruvians, conscious of their probable inability to resist the invaders, had generally abandoned the city, carrying with them, far away into the mountains, all their treasures.

The Spaniards, who had entered the city with hideous yells of triumph, being thus frustrated in the main object of their expedition, found, by inquiry, that at the distance of several leagues easterly from the sea-coast, among the pleasant valleys of the mountains, there were populous cities, where abundance of booty might be found.

The whole number of Spaniards, then invading Peru, did not exceed two hundred and fifty. The Peruvians were daily becoming more deeply exasperated. With such a number of men, and no fortified base to fall back upon, Pizarro did not deem it safe to enter upon a plundering tour into the interior. [Pg 78] Keeping therefore about one hundred and thirty men with him, and strongly fortifying himself at Tumbez, he sent De Soto, at the head of eighty men, sixty of whom were mounted, back into the mountains, to search for gold, and to report respecting the condition of the country, in preparation for future expeditions.

The bad fame of Pizarro was spreading far and wide. And though De Soto enjoined it strictly upon his men, not to be guilty of any act of injustice, still he was an invading Spaniard, and the Peruvians regarded them all as the shepherd regards the wolf. De Soto had passed but a few leagues from the seashore, ere he entered upon the hilly country. As he was ascending one of the gentle eminences, a band of two thousand Indians, who had met there to arrest his progress, rushed down upon him. His sixty horsemen instantly formed in column and impetuously charged into their crowded ranks. These Peruvians had never seen a horse before. Their arrows glanced harmless from the impenetrable armor, and they were mercilessly cut down and trampled beneath iron hoofs. The Spaniards galloped through and through their ranks, strewing the ground with the dead. The carnage was of short duration. The panic-stricken Peruvians fled wherever there was a possibility of escape. The trumpets [Pg 79] of the conquerors pealed forth their triumphant strains. The silken banners waved proudly in the breeze, and the victors exultingly continued their march through one of the defiles of the mountains.

Whatever excuses De Soto may make for himself, humanity will never forgive him for the carnage of that day. Having thus fairly embarked upon this enterprise, where he was surely gaining military renown, infamous as it was, and where there was the prospect before him of plunder of incalculable worth, De Soto seems to have assumed to act upon his own responsibility, and to have paid very little regard to the authority of Pizarro, whom he had left behind. He had already penetrated the country much farther than he had been authorized to do by the orders of his superior. One of the men, whom Pizarro had sent with him, very probably as a spy upon his movements, deserted, and returned to Tumbez with the report that De Soto was already practically in revolt, and had renounced all dependence on Pizarro. For this alleged insubordination, Pizarro did not venture to call his energetic lieutenant to account.

In the mean time, Pizarro was exploring the country in the vicinity of Tumbez, for the site of the colony he wished to establish. He selected a position about ninety miles south of that city, in a rich and well-watered valley which opened upon the placid [Pg 80] surface of the Pacific. His troops were transported to the spot by the two vessels. Here he laid the foundations of a town, which he called San Miguel. With timber from the mountains, and stone from the quarries, and the labor of a large number of natives, who were driven to daily toil, not as servants, by the stimulus of well-paid labor, but as slaves, goaded by the sabres of their task masters, quite a large and strongly-fortified town rapidly arose.

De Soto continued his explorations in the interior for some time, and discovered a very magnificent highway, leading to the capital of the empire. It was smoothly paved with flat blocks of stone, or with cement harder than stone. He returned to San Miguel with the report of his discoveries, and quite richly laden with the gold which he had received as a present from the natives, or which he had seized as what he considered the lawful spoils of war. The sight of the gold inspired all the Spaniards at San Miguel with the intense desire to press forward into a field which promised so rich a harvest.

It was ascertained that the Inca had command of an army of over fifty thousand men. Pizarro, leaving sixty men in garrison at San Miguel, set out with one hundred and ninety men to visit the Inca in his capital. De Soto accompanied him. It was not ostensibly a military expedition, seeking the conquest of the [Pg 81] country, or moving with any hostile intent whatever. De Soto had a conscience; Pizarro had none. Whatever reproaches might arise in the mind of De Soto in reference to the course he was pursuing, he silenced them by the very plausible assumption that he was an ambassador from the king of Spain, commissioned to make a friendly visit to the monarch of another newly-discovered empire; that he was the messenger of peace seeking to unite the two kingdoms in friendly relations with each other for their mutual benefit. This was probably the real feeling of De Soto. The expedition was commissioned by the king of Spain. The armed retinue was only such as became the ambassadors of a great monarch. Such an expedition was in every respect desirable. The fault—perhaps we ought in candor to say the calamity—of De Soto was in allowing himself to be attached to an expedition under a man so thoroughly reckless and unprincipled as he knew Pizarro to have been. Perhaps he hoped to control the actions of his ignorant and fanatic superior officer. It is quite manifest that De Soto did exert a very powerful influence in giving shape to the expedition.

An Indian courier was sent forward to Cuzco, one of the capitals of the Peruvian monarch, with a friendly and almost an obsequious message to the Inca, whose name was Attahuallapa. The courier [Pg 82] bore the communication that Pizarro was an ambassador commissioned by the king of Spain to visit the king of Peru, and to kiss his hand in token of peace and fraternity. He therefore solicited that protection in passing through the country which every monarch is bound to render to the representatives of a foreign and friendly power.

Pizarro, as it will be remembered, was a rough and illiterate soldier, unable either to read or write. In this sagacious diplomatic arrangement, we undoubtedly see the movement of De Soto's reflective and cultivated mind. The expedition moved slowly along, awaiting the return of the courier. He soon came back with a very indefinite response, and with a present of two curiously carved stone cups, and some perfumery. The guarded reply and the meagre present excited some alarm in the Spanish camp. It was very evident that the expedition was not to anticipate a very cordial reception at the Peruvian court. Pizarro was much alarmed. He was quite confident that the Inca was trying to lure them on to their ruin. Having called a council of war, he urged that they should proceed no farther until he had sent some faithful Indian spies to ascertain the intentions of Attahuallapa.

But De Soto, whose youthful energies were inspired [Pg 83] by love and ambition, was eager to press forward.

"It is not necessary," said he, "for the Inca to use treachery with us. He could easily overpower us with numbers were he so disposed. We have also heard that he is a just and merciful prince; and the courtesy he has already shown us, is some token at least of his good will. But why should we hesitate? We have no longer any choice but to go forward. If we now retreat, it will prove our professions to be false; and when the suspicions of the Inca are once aroused, we shall find it impossible to escape from his country."

Pizarro's brother—Hernando—was a man of ignoble birth, of ruffianly manners, of low and brutal character. Tauntingly he inquired of De Soto, if he were ready to give proof of his confidence in the faith of the Peruvian monarch, by going forward to his court, as an envoy from the embassy.

De Soto turned his keen and flashing eye upon the man, whom he despised, and said in slow and measured words:

"Don Hernando, I may yet convince you that it is neither civil nor safe to call my sincerity in question. I have as much confidence in the honor of the Inca as I have in the integrity of any man in this company, not excepting the commander or yourself. [Pg 84] I perceive that you are disposed to go backward. You may all return, when and how you please, or remain where you are. But I have made up my mind to present myself to Attahuallapa. And I shall certainly do so, without asking the assistance or permission of any of your party."

This was certainly a very defiant speech. It asserted his entire rejection of the authority of Pizarro. De Soto could not have dared thus to have spoken, unless he had felt strong in the support of his own dragoons.

Hernando Pizarro was silent, indulging only in a malignant smile. It was not safe for him to provoke De Soto to a personal rencontre. Francisco Pizarro smothered his chagrin and very adroitly availed himself of this statement, to commission De Soto to take twenty-four horsemen, such as he might select, and accompanied by an Indian guide called Filipillo, go forward to the Peruvian court.

Both of the Pizarros seemed quite relieved when the sound of the departing squadron of brave cavaliers died away in the distance. De Soto, during the whole of his adventurous life, seems to have been entirely unconscious of the emotion of fear. During his residence in the camp of the Pizarros, he had exerted a powerful restraint upon their ferocious natures. He had very earnestly endeavored to impress [Pg 85] their minds with the conviction that they could not pass through the populous empire of Peru, or even remain in it, if their followers were allowed to trample upon the rights of the natives. So earnestly and persistently did he urge these views, that Pizarro at length acknowledged their truth, and in the presence of De Soto, commanded his men to abstain from every act of aggression.

But now that De Soto was gone, the Pizarros and their rabble rout of vagabonds breathed more freely. Scarcely had the plumed helmets of the cavaliers disappeared in the distance, when Hernando Pizarro set out on a plundering expedition into the villages of the Peruvians. The natives fled in terror before the Spaniards. Pizarro caught one of the leading men and questioned him very closely respecting the designs of Attahuallapa. The captive honestly and earnestly declared, that he knew nothing about the plans of his sovereign.

This demoniac Hernando endeavored to extort a confession from him by torture. He tied his victim to a tree, enveloped his feet in cotton thoroughly saturated with oil and applied the torch. The wretched sufferer in unendurable agony, said "yes" to anything and everything. Two days after, it was proved that he could not have known anything respecting the intended operations of the Inca. It is [Pg 86] a satisfaction to one's sense of justice to remember that there is a God who will not allow such crimes to go unpunished.

De Soto, with his bold cavaliers, pressed rapidly on towards the Peruvian camp. Very carefully he guarded against every act of hostility or injustice. Everywhere the natives were treated with the utmost courtesy. In the rapid advance of the Spaniards through the country, crowds flocked to the highway attracted by the novel spectacle. And a wonderful spectacle it must have been! These cavaliers, with their nodding plumes, their burnished armor, their gleaming sabres, their silken banners, mounted on magnificent war horses and rushing along over the hills and through the valleys in meteoric splendor, must have presented an aspect more imposing to their minds than we can well imagine.

De Soto, who had not his superior as a horseman in the Spanish army, was mounted on a milk white steed of extraordinary size and grace of figure, and wore a complete suit of the most costly and showy armor. It is said that on one occasion his path was crossed by a brook twenty feet wide. The noble animal disdained to wade through, but cleared it at a single bound.

The crowds who lined the highways seemed to understand and appreciate the friendly feelings De [Pg 87] Soto manifested in gracefully bowing to them and smiling as he passed along. He soon ascertained, though his guide Filipillo, that the headquarters of the Peruvian camp was at a place now called Caxamarca, among the mountains, about eighty miles northeast of the present seaport of Truxillo.

After a rapid ride of about six hours, the expedition approached quite a flourishing little town called Caxas. Several hundred Peruvian soldiers were drawn up in battle array in the outskirts, to arrest the progress of the Spaniards. De Soto halted his dragoons, and sent forward Filipillo to assure the commandant that he was traversing the country not with any hostile intent, and that he bore a friendly message from his own sovereign to the king of Peru.

The kindly disposed Peruvians immediately laid aside their arms, welcomed the strangers, and entertained them with a sumptuous feast. Thus refreshed, they pressed on several leagues farther, until they reached a much larger city called Guancabama. From all the accounts given it would seem that the inhabitants of this region had reached a degree of civilization, so far as the comforts of life are concerned, fully equal to that then to be found in Spain. This city was on the magnificent highway which traversed fifteen hundred miles through the very heart of the empire. The houses, which were built [Pg 88] of hewn stone, admirably jointed, consisted of several rooms, and were distinguished for cleanliness, order, and domestic comfort.

The men seemed intelligent, the women modest, and various arts of industry occupied their time. De Soto testified that the great highway which passed through this place far surpassed in grandeur and utility any public work which had ever been attempted in Spain. Happy and prosperous as were the Peruvians, compared with the inhabitants of most other countries, it is quite evident that the ravages of the Fall were not unknown there.

Just before entering the town, De Soto passed a high gibbet upon which three malefactors were hung in chains, swaying in the breeze. That revolting spectacle revealed the sad truth that in Peru, as well as elsewhere, man's fallen nature developed itself in crime and woe. The Emperor had also a large standing army, and the country had just been ravaged by the horrors of civil war.

De Soto was kindly received at Guancabama. Just as he was about to leave for Caxamarca, an envoy from the Inca reached the city on its way to the Spanish camp. The ambassador was a man of high rank. Several servants accompanied him, laden with presents for Pizarro. He entreated De Soto to return with him to the headquarters of the Spaniards. [Pg 89] As these presents and this embassy would probably convince Pizarro of the friendly feeling of the Peruvian monarch, De Soto judged it wise to comply with his request. Thus he turned back, and the united party soon reached Pizarro's encampment.

[Pg 90]

CHAPTER VI.

The Atrocities of Pizarro.

Fears of Pizarro.—Honorable Conduct of the Inca.—The March to Caxamarca.—Hospitable Reception.—Perfidious Attack upon the Inca.—His Capture and Imprisonment.—The Honor of De Soto.—The Offered Ransom.—Treachery and Extortion of Pizarro.

The report which De Soto brought back was in many respects quite alarming to the Pizarros. Though they were delighted to hear of the wealth which had been discovered, and the golden ornaments decorating houses, temples and shrines, they were not a little alarmed in the contemplation of the large population over which the Inca reigned, and of the power of his government. The spectacle of the gallows also at Guancabama, caused very uncomfortable sensations.

Both of these men were aware that they and their troops had committed crimes which would doom them to the scaffold, should the Inca be able to punish them according to their deserts. Indeed it subsequently appeared, that the Inca had heard of their outrages. But with humanity and a sense of justice which reflects lustre upon his name, he had resolved not to [Pg 91] punish them unheard in their own defence. He knew not but that false representations had been made of the facts. He knew not but that the Spaniards had been goaded to acts of retaliation by outrages on the part of the Peruvians.

He therefore invited the Spanish adventurers to meet him at Caxamarca, assuring them of a safe passage to that place. With fear and trembling Pizarro consented, with his little band of two hundred and fifty men, to visit the Peruvian camp, where fifty thousand soldiers might be arrayed against him. The path they were to traverse led through defiles of the mountains, where a few hundred men could arrest the march of an army. The Spaniards afterwards could not but admit, that had the Inca cherished any perfidious design, he might with the utmost ease have utterly exterminated them. Not a man could have escaped.

The march of these trembling men was not with the triumphant tramp of conquerors. They did not enter the Peruvian camp with flourish of trumpets and bugle blasts, but as peaceful ambassadors, with a showy retinue, who had been permitted to traverse the country unharmed. The sun was just sinking behind the rugged peaks of the mountains on the fifteenth of November, 1532, when Pizarro's band rode into the streets of Caxamarca. In the centre of the [Pg 92] town there was a large public square. On one side of that square was a spacious stone edifice, which the Inca had caused to be prepared for the accommodation of his guests. This building was a part of a strong fortress, within whose massive walls, a small party of well armed men might easily defend themselves against a host.

The fact that Attahuallapa assigned to them such quarters, proves conclusively that he had no intention to treat them otherwise than in the most friendly manner. The Inca, with the troops immediately under his command, was encamped at a distance of about three miles from the town. The treacherous Pizarro was ever apprehensive of treachery on the part of others. He was an entire stranger to that calm and peaceful courage which seemed always to reign in the bosom of De Soto.

Immediately after he reached Caxamarca he dispatched De Soto to inform the Inca of his arrival. The Peruvian camp covered several acres of ground, with substantial and commodious tents. In the centre there was truly a magnificent pavilion, gorgeous in its decorations, which was appropriated to the Inca. Attahuallapa was informed of the approach of the Spanish cavaliers. He came from his tent and took his seat upon a splendid throne prepared for the occasion. The Peruvian soldiers gazed with amazement [Pg 93] upon the spectacle of these horsemen as they were led into the presence of their sovereign.

De Soto, with the native grace which attended all his actions, alighted from his horse, bowed respectfully to the monarch, and said in words which were interpreted by Filipillo.

"I am sent by my commander, Don Francisco Pizarro, who desires to be admitted to your presence, to give you an account of the causes which have brought him to this country, and other matters which it may behoove your majesty to know. He humbly entreats you to allow him an interview this night or to-morrow, as he wishes to make you an offer of his services, and to deliver the message which has been committed to him by his sovereign, the king of Spain."

Attahuallapa replied with much dignity and some apparent reserve, that he cordially accepted the friendly offers of Pizarro, and would grant him the desired interview the following morning. The Inca was a young man about thirty years of age. He was tall, admirably formed, and with a very handsome countenance. But there was an expression of sadness overspreading his features, and a pensive tone in his address, indicating that he was a man who had seen affliction.

The splendid steed from which De Soto had alighted was restlessly pawing the ground at a short [Pg 94] distance from the tent of the Inca, attracting the particular attention and admiration of the sovereign. De Soto, perceiving the admiration which his steed elicited, remounted, and touching the spirited animal with the spur, went bounding with almost the speed of the wind over the level plain, causing his horse now to rear, and now to plunge, wheeling him around, and thus exhibiting his excellent qualities. He then came down at full speed to the spot where the Inca stood, until within a few feet of the monarch, when he checked his horse so suddenly as to throw him back upon his haunches. Some of the attendants of the Inca were evidently alarmed; but the Inca himself stood proudly immovable. He reproved his attendants for their timidity; and Mr. Prescott, who represents Attahuallapa as a very cruel man, intimates that he put some of them to death that evening for betraying such weakness before the strangers. Refreshments were offered to De Soto and his party, and a sort of wine was presented to them in golden cups, of extraordinary size.

As De Soto, having fulfilled his mission, was about to leave the royal presence and return to Caxamarca, Attahuallapa said:

"Tell your companions, that as I am keeping a fast, I cannot to-day accept their invitation. I will come to them to-morrow. I may be attended by a [Pg 95] large and armed retinue. But let not that give you any uneasiness. I wish to cultivate your friendship and that of your king. I have already given ample proof that no harm is intended you, though your captain, I am told, mistrusts me. If you think it will please him better, I will come with few attendants and those unarmed."

De Soto warmly assured the Inca that no man could doubt his sincerity, and begged him to consult his own taste entirely in reference to the manner in which he would approach the Spaniards.

Upon the return of the cavalier to Pizarro, with an account of the interview, that perfidious chieftain proposed to his men, that they should seize the Inca and hold him in captivity as a hostage. Mr. Prescott, in his account of this infamous procedure, speaks of it in the following apologetic terms:

"Pizarro then summoned a council of his officers, to consider the plan of operations, or rather to propose to them the extraordinary plan on which he had himself decided. This was to lay an ambuscade for the Inca, and take him prisoner in the face of his whole army. It was a project full of peril, bordering as it might well seem on desperation. But the circumstances of the Spaniards were desperate. Whichever way they turned they were menaced by the most appalling dangers. And better was it to confront the [Pg 96] danger, than weakly to shrink from it when there was no avenue for escape. To fly was now too late. Whither could they fly? At the first signal of retreat the whole army of the Inca would be upon them. Their movements would be anticipated by a foe far better acquainted with the intricacies of the Sierra than themselves; the passes would be occupied, and they would be hemmed in on all sides; while the mere fact of this retrograde movement would diminish the confidence and with it the effective strength of his own men, while it doubled that of the enemy."

The next morning was Saturday, the 16th of November, 1532. The sun rose in a cloudless sky, and great preparations were made by the Inca to display his grandeur and his power to his not very welcome guests. A large retinue preceded and followed the monarch, while a courier was sent forward to inform Pizarro of his approach. The Inca, habited in a dress which was glittering with gems and gold, was seated in a gorgeous open palanquin, borne upon the shoulders of many of his nobles.

It was five o'clock in the afternoon, when the Inca, accompanied by a small but unarmed retinue, entered the public square of the city. The tents of his troops left outside, spread far and wide over the meadows, indicating the presence of an immense host. The Inca was clothed in a flowing robe of [Pg 97] scarlet, woven of the finest wool, and almost entirely covered with golden stars and the most precious gems. His head was covered with a turban of variegated colors, to which there was suspended a scarlet fringe, the badge of royalty. The palanquin, or throne, on which he was seated, was apparently of pure gold; and the cushion upon which he sat was covered with the most costly gems. His nobles were also dressed in the highest possible style of Peruvian wealth and art. It was estimated that the number of the nobles and officers of the court who accompanied the king into the square, was about two thousand. A large company of priests was also in attendance, who chanted the Peruvian National Hymn.

It is very difficult for an honest mind to form any just conception of such a religious fanatic, and such an irreligious wretch as this Francisco Pizarro. Just before the Peruvians arrived he had attended a solemn mass, in which the aid of the God of the Christians was fervently implored in behalf of their enterprise. The mass was closed with chanting one of the psalms of David, in which God is called upon to arise and come to judgment. Friar Vincent, who was Pizarro's spiritual adviser, and grand chaplain of the so-called Christian army, was then sent forward with the Bible in one hand and a crucifix in the other, to expound to the Inca the doctrines of the Christian [Pg 98] faith, stating that it was for that purpose, and for that only, that the Spaniards had come into the country.

So far as we can judge from the uncertain records which have reached us, the views he presented were what are called evangelical, though highly imbued with the claims of the Papal Church. He described the creation of man, his fall, the atonement by the crucifixion of the Son of God, his ascension, leaving Peter and his successors, as his vicegerents upon earth. Invested with this divine power, one of his successors, the present Pope, had commissioned Pizarro to visit Peru, to conquer and convert the natives to the true faith.

The Inca listened attentively to the arguments of the priest, but was apparently unmoved by them. He calmly replied:

"I acknowledge that there is but one God, the maker of all things. As for the Pope, I know him not. He must be insane to give away that which does not belong to him. The king of Spain is doubtless a great monarch, and I wish to make him my friend, but I cannot become his vassal."

A few more words were interchanged, when the priest returned into the stone fortress, where Pizarro stood surrounded by his soldiers. The priest reported the conversation which had taken place; declared that the Inca, in the pride of his heart, had rejected [Pg 99] Christianity. He therefore announced to Pizarro that he was authorized by the divine law, to make war upon the Inca and his people.

"Go set on them at once," said he; "spare them not; kill these dogs which so stubbornly despise the law of God. I absolve you."

The extraordinary scene which then ensued cannot perhaps be better described than in the language of Mr. Prescott:

"Pizarro saw that the hour had come. He waved a white scarf in the air, the appointed signal. The fatal gun was fired from the fortress. Then springing into the square, the Spanish captain and his followers shouted the old war cry of 'St. Jago, and at them!' It was answered by the battle cry of every Spaniard in the city, as rushing from the avenues of the great halls in which they were concealed, they poured into the Plaza, horse and foot, and threw themselves into the midst of the Indian crowd.

"The latter, taken by surprise, stunned by the reports of artillery and musketry, the echoes of which reverberated like thunder from the surrounding buildings, and blinded by the smoke which rolled in sulphurous volumes along the square, were seized with a panic. They knew not whither to fly for refuge from the coming ruin. Nobles and commoners all were trampled down under the fierce charge of the [Pg 100] cavalry, who dealt their blows right and left, without sparing; while their swords, flashing through the thick gloom, carried dismay into the hearts of the wretched natives, who now, for the first time, saw the horse and his rider in all their terrors. They made no resistance, as indeed they had no weapons with which to resist.

"Every avenue to escape was closed, for the entrance to the square was choked up with the dead bodies of men who had perished in vain efforts to fly. And such was the agony of the survivors, under the terrible pressure of their assailants, that a large body of Indians, by their convulsive struggles, burst through the wall of stone and dried clay, which formed the boundary of the Plaza. It fell, leaving an opening of more than a hundred paces, through which multitudes now found their way into the country, still hotly pursued by the cavalry, who, leaping the piles of rubbish, hung on the rear of the fugitives, striking them down in all directions.

"There were two great objects in view in this massacre. One was to strike terror into the heart of the Peruvians; the other was to obtain possession of the person of the Inca. It seems that the nobles regarded their sovereign with almost idolatrous homage. They rallied thickly around him, placed their own bodies between him and the sabres of their [Pg 101] assailants, and made frantic endeavors to tear the cavaliers from their saddles. Unfortunately they were unarmed, and had neither arrows, javelins nor war clubs. The Inca sat helpless in his palanquin, quite bewildered by the awful storm of war which had thus suddenly burst around him. In the swaying of the mighty mass, the litter heaved to and fro, like a ship in a storm."

At length several of the nobles who supported it being slain, the palanquin was overthrown, and the Inca, as he was falling to the ground, was caught by the Spaniards. In the confusion of the affray, Pizarro was slightly wounded in the hand by one of his own men. This was the only hurt received by any Spaniard during the bloody affray.

The Inca being captured, the conflict in the square ceased. But there was another object in view, as has been stated, and that was to strike terror into the hearts of the Peruvians. Consequently the steel-clad cavaliers pursued the fugitives in all directions, cutting them down without mercy. Night, which followed the short twilight of the tropics, put an end to the carnage, and the trumpets of Pizarro recalled the soldiers, wiping their dripping sabres, to their fortress. The number slain is variously estimated. The secretary of Pizarro says that two thousand [Pg 102] fell. A Peruvian annalist swells the number of victims to ten thousand.

Attahuallapa, the monarch of the great kingdom of Peru, thus suddenly found himself a prisoner in one of his own fortresses; surrounded by a band of stern warriors, who had penetrated the heart of his empire from a distance of more than two thousand leagues. Pizarro treated the unhappy king with respect, and testifies to the dignity with which he met his awful reverses. What part De Soto took in the outrages just described, cannot now be known. He had unquestionably in good faith, and as an honorable man, invited the Inca to visit Caxamarca, by which invitation he had been enticed into the power of the Spaniards.

There is evidence that De Soto had no idea of the treachery which was intended, for it was not until after he had left on his visit to the Peruvian camp that the plot was formed for the seizure of the Inca. Pizarro had two bodies of horsemen. One was commanded by his brother Hernando, and the other by De Soto. There were thirty dragoons in each band. Unquestionably, Hernando was a very eager participant in the horrors of this day. It may be that De Soto, from the roof of the fortress, was an inactive spectator of the scene. It does not seem possible that with the character he had heretofore [Pg 103] developed, he could have lent his own strong arm and those of his horsemen to the perpetration of a crime so atrocious. Still military discipline is a terrible power. It sears the conscience and hardens the heart. The fact that De Soto was present and that there are no evidences of remonstrances on his part, has left a stigma upon his character which time cannot efface.

The next morning these Spaniards, so zealous for the propagation of the Christian faith, unmindful of their professed Christian mission, betook themselves, with all alacrity, to the work of pillage. The golden throne, and the royal wardrobe, were of very great value. The nobles were clad in their richest garments of state, and the ground was strewn with bodies of the dead, glittering in robes of gold and gems. Having stripped the dead, they then entered the houses and temples of Caxamarca and loaded themselves down with golden vases, and other booty of great value. As one suggestive item, which reveals the conduct of these brutal men, the good Las Casas states, that a Spanish soldier seized a young Peruvian girl. When the mother rushed to rescue her child, he cut off her arm with his sword, and then in his rage hewed the maiden to pieces.

Pizarro now assumed the proud title of "The Conqueror of Peru." With the sovereign as his prisoner, [Pg 104] and elated by his great victory, he felt that there was no resistance that he had to fear. It seems that Attahuallapa had penetration enough to discern that De Soto was a very different man in character from the Pizarros. He soon became quite cordial and unreserved in his intercourse with him. And there is no evidence that De Soto ever, in the slightest degree, betrayed his confidence. One day the Inca inquired of De Soto for what amount of ransom Pizarro would be willing to release him. De Soto was well aware of the timidity and avarice of the captain. The love of the Peruvians for their sovereign was such, that Pizarro was confident that so long as Attahuallapa was in his power, they would not make war upon him. De Soto felt therefore that there was no prospect that Pizarro would release his captive for any ransom whatever, and sadly advised him to resign all such hope. The Inca was greatly distressed. After a few moments of silence, he said:

"My friend, do not deprive me of the only hope that can make life supportable. I must be free, or I must die. Your commander loves gold above all things. Surely I can purchase my liberty from him at some price, and however unreasonable it may be, I am willing to satisfy his demand. Tell me, I entreat of you, what sum you think will be sufficient?"

For a moment De Soto made no reply. They [Pg 105] were sitting in a room, according to the statement of Pizarro's secretary, twenty-two feet long and seventeen feet broad. Then turning to the Inca, and wishing to impress his mind with the conviction that there was not any ransom which could effect his release, he said:

"If you could fill this room with gold as high as I can reach with my sword, Pizarro might perhaps accept it as your ransom."

"It shall be done," the Inca eagerly replied. "And I beg you to let Pizarro know, that within a month from this day, my part of the contract shall be fulfilled."

De Soto was troubled, for he had not intended that as an offer, but rather as a statement of an impossibility. He however felt bound to report the proposition to Pizarro. Much to his surprise the avaricious captain readily accepted it. The contract was drawn up, and

Pizarro gave his solemn pledge that upon the delivery of the gold the prison doors of the captive should be thrown open. But after the terms had all been settled, the perfidious Spaniard craved a still higher ransom, and declared that he would not release his victim unless another room of equal size was equally filled with silver.

Attahuallapa could fully appreciate such dishonorable conduct; for in all moral qualities he seems [Pg 106] to have been decidedly superior to his Spanish antagonist. But without any undignified murmurs, he submitted to this extortion also. Matters being thus arranged, De Soto, with his characteristic plain dealing, said to Pizarro:

"I hope you will remember, Don Francisco, that my honor is pledged for the strict fulfilment of the contract on the part of the Spaniards. Observe, therefore, that as soon as the gold and the silver are produced, Attahuallapa must have his liberty."

[Pg 107]

CHAPTER VII.

The Execution of the Inca, and Embarrassments of De Soto.

Pledges of Pizarro.—His Perfidy.—False Mission of De Soto.—Execution of the Inca.—His Fortitude.—Indignation of De Soto.—Great Embarrassments.—Extenuating Considerations.—Arrival of Almagro.—March Towards the Capital.

Pizarro gave his most solemn pledges, on his Christian faith, that so soon as the money was paid the Inca should be released. The idea does not seem to have entered the mind of Attahuallapa that Pizarro could be guilty of the perfidy of violating those pledges. The unhappy condition of the Inca excited the strong sympathies of De Soto. He visited him often, and having a natural facility for the acquisition of language, was soon able to converse with the captive in his own tongue. Quite a friendship, founded on mutual esteem, sprang up between them. By his strong intercession, Pizarro was constrained to consent that the gold should not be melted into ingots, thus to fill the designated space with its solid bulk, but that it should be received and packed away in the form of vases, and ornaments, and other manufactured articles, as brought in by the Peruvians.

[Pg 108]

Several of the principal officers of Attahuallapa's court were sent to Cuzco, the capital of the empire, where the main treasures of the kingdom were deposited. Three Spaniards accompanied these officers. The Inca issued his orders that they should be treated with respect. The people obeyed; for they knew that any injury or insult befalling the Spaniards would bring down terrible retribution upon their beloved sovereign. Peruvian agents were also dispatched to all the temples to strip them of their ornaments, and to the homes of the nobility to receive the plate and golden decorations which were eagerly contributed as ransom for the king. The cornices and entablatures of the temples were often of solid gold, and massive plates of gold encrusted the walls. For several weeks there seemed to be a constant procession of Peruvians entering the fortress, laden with golden vases and innumerable other utensils, often of exquisite workmanship.

Within the allotted time the ransom, enormous as it was, was all brought in. It is estimated that its value was equal to about twenty million dollars of our money. The Inca now demanded his release. The infamous Pizarro had perhaps originally intended to set him at liberty. But he had now come to the conclusion that the Inca might immediately rally around him, not only his whole army, but the whole population [Pg 109] of the kingdom, cut off the retreat of the Spaniards, exterminate them, and win back all the plunder so unrighteously extorted. Pizarro was consequently plotting for some plausible excuse for putting the monarch to death. The Peruvians thus deprived of their sovereign, and in a state of bewilderment, would be thrown into anarchy, and the Spaniards would have a much better chance of obtaining entire possession of the kingdom.

Pizarro did not dare to reveal to De Soto his treasonable designs. He feared not only his reproaches, but his determined and very formidable resistance. He therefore gave it as an excuse for postponing the liberation of the Inca, that he must wait until he had made a division of the spoils. The distribution was performed with imposing religious ceremonies. Mass was celebrated, and earnest prayers were addressed to Heaven that the work might be so performed as to meet the approbation of God. A fifth part of the plunder was set apart for the king of Spain, the Emperor, Charles the Fifth. Pizarro, as commander of the expedition, came next, and his share amounted to millions. De Soto was defrauded, not receiving half so much as Hernando Pizarro. Still, his share in this distribution and in another which soon took place, amounted to over five hundred thousand dollars. This was an enormous sum in those days. It [Pg 110] elevated him at once, in point of opulence, to the rank of the proudest grandees of Spain.

The great object of De Soto's ambition was accomplished. He had acquired fame and wealth beyond his most sanguine expectations. Thus he was prepared to return to Spain and demand the hand of Isabella. But his generous nature was troubled. He became very anxious for the fate of the Inca. His own honor was involved in his release, and day after day he became more importunate in his expostulations with Pizarro.

"Whatever the consequences may be," said De Soto, "the Inca must now be immediately set at liberty. He has your promise to that effect and he has *mine*; and my promise, come what will, shall not be violated."

Pizarro urged, in view of their peril, the delay of a few weeks. De Soto replied:

"Not a single week, not a day; if you do not liberate the prisoner, I will take that liberty on myself."

"To give him his freedom at this time," Pizarro replied, "would be certain destruction to us all."

"That may be," responded De Soto, "but that should have been considered before he was admitted to ransom."

"But since that agreement was made," said Pizarro, "I have received information which justifies me [Pg 111] in changing my intentions. Attahuallapa's officers, acting under his directions, are now engaged in exciting an insurrection for the extermination of the Spaniards."

De Soto had no faith whatever in this accusation. There was a long and angry controversy. Pizarro called in his interpreter Filipillo, who was undoubtedly bribed to testify according to the wishes of his master. He declared that the Inca was organizing this conspiracy. De Soto was unconvinced. He still regarded the accusation as a groundless calumny.

Finally they came to a compromise. The treacherous and wily Pizarro suggested that De Soto should take a party of dragoons and proceed to that section of the country, where it was said the conspirators were assembling in vast numbers, in preparation for their onset upon the Spaniards. If De Soto found no indication of such a movement, Pizarro gave his solemn pledge, that immediately upon his return, he would release Attahuallapa. De Soto agreed to the arrangement, and at once set out on the journey.

Pizarro had thus accomplished his object, of being relieved of the embarrassment of De Soto's presence, while he should lead the Inca to his execution. A sort of council of war was held, though Attahuallapa was not present, and nothing was heard in his [Pg 112] defence. It was necessary to proceed with the utmost expedition, as De Soto would soon return. The horrible verdict of the court was, that the captive should be burned to death at the stake. Pizarro himself, it is said, carried the terrible intelligence to the prisoner.

The Inca, a young man in the very prime of life, being but thirty years of age, was horror stricken, and for some time sat in silence, not uttering a word. And then turning to Pizarro, he said:

"Is it possible that you can believe in a God and fear him, and yet dare to commit such an act of injustice? What have I done to deserve death in any form, and why have you condemned me to a death so unusual and painful. Surely you cannot intend to execute this cruel sentence."

Pizarro assured him that the decree of the court was unalterable, and must immediately be carried into effect.

"Think of the wrong you have already done me," said the Inca, "and do not forget how much you are indebted to my kindness and forbearance. I could easily have intercepted you in the mountain passes, and made you all prisoners, or sacrificed you all justly to the offended laws of my country. I could have overpowered you with my armed warriors at Caxamarca. But I failed in my duty to my people in [Pg 113] receiving you as friends. You have robbed me of my kingdom and compelled me to insult my Deity, by stripping his temples to satisfy your avarice.

"Of all my possessions, you have left me nothing but my life, and that I supposed you would be willing to spare me, since you can gain nothing by taking it away. Consider how hard it is for me to die, so suddenly and without any warning of my danger. I have lived but thirty years, and until very lately, I had every reason to hope for a long and happy life. My prospects for happiness are blighted forever. But I will not complain of that, if you will permit me to live out the term which God and nature have allotted me."

The execution was to take place immediately. Pizarro waited only for the sun to go down, that darkness might shroud the fiendlike deed. As they were talking Pizarro's chaplain, Friar Vincent, came in to prepare the victim for the sacrifice. He was dressed in his ecclesiastical robes, and bore in his hand a large crucifix. Was he an unmitigated knave, or was he a fanatic? Who but God can tell.

"It is time for you," said he, "to withdraw your thoughts from earthly vanities and fix them upon the realities of the eternal world. You are justly condemned to death, for your infidelity and other sins. I call on you to accept the free gift of salvation which [Pg 114] I now offer you, so that you may escape the greater punishment of eternal fire."

The Inca seemed to pay little heed to these words, but with a gesture of impatience and anger, exclaimed:

"Oh, where is De Soto? He is a good man, and he is my friend. Surely he will not allow me to be thus murdered."

"De Soto," the priest replied, "is far away. No earthly help can avail you. Receive the consolations of the Church; kiss the feet of this image, and I will absolve you from your sins, and prepare you to enter the kingdom of Heaven."

"I worship the Maker of all things," the Inca firmly replied. "As much as I desire to live, I will not forsake the faith of my fathers to prolong my life."

Two hours after sunset, the sound of the trumpet assembled the Spanish soldiers by torchlight in the great square of Caxamarca. It was the evening of the twenty-ninth of August, 1533. The clanking of chains was heard as the victim, manacled hand and foot, toiled painfully over the stone pavement of the square. He was bound by chains to the stake; the combustible fagots were piled up around him. Friar Vincent then, it is said, holding up the cross before the victim, told him that if he would embrace [Pg 115] Christianity he should be spared the cruel death by the flames, and experience in its stead only the painless death of the garotte, and that the Inca did, while thus chained to the stake, abjure his religion and receive the rite of baptism. In reference to this representation Mr. Lambert A. Wilmer, in his admirable life of Ferdinand De Soto, says:

"As the traducers of the dead Inca were permitted to tell their own story without fear of contradiction, it is impossible to assign any limits to their fabrications. And their testimony is probable, only when it tends to criminate themselves. Perhaps the greatest injustice which these slanderers have done to Attahuallapa's memory, was by pretending that he became an apostate to his own religion and a convert to Catholicism just before his death.

"If this story were true, how could Pizarro justify himself, or how could the Pope and the king of Spain excuse him for putting a Christian to death on account of sins committed by an infidel. Surely the royal penitent, when he entered the pale of the Holy Catholic Church, would be entitled to a free pardon for those errors of conduct which were incidental to his unregenerate condition. We are told that when the Inca had consented to be baptized by Father Vincent, Pizarro graciously commuted his sentence, and allowed him to be strangled before his body was [Pg 116] reduced to ashes."

These fictions were doubtless contrived to illustrate Pizarro's clemency, and Father Vincent's apostolic success.

The probability is, as others state, that the Inca remained firm to the end; the torch was applied, and while the consuming flames wreathed around him, he uttered no cry. In this chariot of fire the spirit of this deeply outraged man was borne to the judgment of God.

De Soto soon returned. He was almost frantic with indignation when he learned of the crime which had been perpetrated in his absence, and perceived that his mission was merely an artifice to get him out of the way. His rage blazed forth in the most violent reproaches. Hastening to the tent of Pizarro, he rudely pushed aside a sentinel who guarded the entrance, and found the culprit seated on a low stool, affecting the attitude of a mourner. A large slouched hat was bent over his eyes.

"Uncover yourself;" said De Soto, "unless you are ashamed to look a human being in the face." Then with the point of his sword he struck off his hat, exclaiming:

"Is it not enough that I have disgraced myself in the eyes of the world by becoming your companion and confederate, making myself accessory to your crimes, and protecting you from the punishment you [Pg 117] deserve. Have you not heaped infamy enough upon me, without dishonoring me by the violation of my pledges, and exposing me to the suspicion of being connected with the most cruel and causeless murder that ever set human laws and divine justice at defiance? I have ascertained, what you well knew before I left Caxamarca, that the report of the insurrection was utterly false. I have met nothing on the road but demonstrations of good will. The whole country is quiet, and Attahuallapa has been basely slandered. You, Francisco Pizarro, are his slanderer, and you are his murderer.

"To prove that I have had no participation in the deed, I will make you accountable for his death. Craven and prevaricating villain as you are, you shall not escape this responsibility. If you refuse to meet me in honorable combat, I will denounce you to the king of Spain as a criminal, and will proclaim you to the whole world as a coward and an assassin."

Pizarro was both, an assassin and a coward. He stood in awe of his intrepid lieutenant. He did not dare to meet him in a personal rencontre, and he well knew that De Soto was not a man to be taken by force or guile, as he could immediately rally around him the whole body of his well-drilled dragoons. He therefore began to make excuses, admitted that he had acted hastily, and endeavored to throw the blame [Pg 118] upon others, declaring that by their false representations they had forced him to the act.

In the midst of the dispute, Pizarro's brothers—for there were two in the camp—entered the tent. De Soto, addressing the three, said:

"I am the champion of Attahuallapa. I accuse Francisco Pizarro of being his murderer." Then throwing his glove upon the floor, he continued:

"I invite any man who is disposed to deny that Francisco Pizarro is a coward and an assassin, to take it up."

The glove remained untouched. De Soto turned upon his heel contemptuously, and left the tent, resolved, it is said, no longer to have any connection whatever with such perfidious wretches. He immediately resigned his commission as lieutenant-general and announced his determination to return to Spain. But alas, for human frailty and inconsistency, he was to take with him the five hundred thousand dollars of treasure of which the Peruvians had been ruthlessly despoiled. Perhaps he reasoned with himself,

"What can I do with it. The Inca is dead. It would not be wise to throw it into the streets, and I surely am not bound to contribute it to the already enormous wealth of Pizarro."

Another source of embarrassment arose. Reinforcements to the number of two hundred men had just [Pg 119] arrived at Caxamarca, under Almagro. They had been sent forward from Panama, commissioned by the king of Spain to join the enterprise. The whole number of Spanish soldiers, assembled in the heart of the Peruvian empire, now amounted to about five hundred. Mountain ridges rose between them and the sea-coast, in whose almost impassable defiles a few hundred resolute men might arrest the advance of an army. The Peruvians had a standing force of fifty thousand soldiers. The whole population of the country was roused to the highest pitch of indignation. They were everywhere grasping their arms. Nothing but the most consummate prudence could rescue the Spaniards from their perilous position. The danger was imminent, that they would be utterly exterminated.

For De Soto, under these circumstances, to abandon his comrades, and retire from the field, would seem an act of cowardice. He had no confidence in the ability of the Pizarros to rescue the Spaniards. He therefore judged that duty to his king and his countrymen demanded of him that he should remain in Peru, until he could leave the army in a safe condition.

Pizarro did not venture to resent the reproaches and defiance of De Soto, but immediately prepared to avail himself of his military abilities, in a march of [Pg 120] several hundred miles south to Cuzco, the capital of the empire. With characteristic treachery, Pizarro seized one of the most distinguished nobles of the Peruvian court, and held him as a hostage. This nobleman, named Chalcukima, had occupied some of the highest posts of honor in the kingdom, and was greatly revered and beloved by the Peruvians. Pizarro sent far and wide the announcement, that upon the slightest movement of hostility on the part of the natives, Chalcukima would be put to death.

The Spaniards now set out on their long march. It was in the month of September, 1533, one of the most lovely months in that attractive clime. But for the rapine, carnage and violence of war, such a tour through the enchanting valley of the Cordilleras, in the midst of fruits and flowers, and bird songs, and traversing populous villages inhabited by a gentle and amiable people, would have been an enterprise full of enjoyment. But the path of these demoniac men was marked by the ravages of fiends. And notwithstanding the great embarrassments in which De Soto found himself involved, it is very difficult to find any excuse for him, in allowing himself to be one of their number.

Francisco Pizarro led the band. His brother Hernando, De Soto, and Almagro, were his leading captains. But it was the genius of De Soto alone, [Pg 121] with his highly disciplined dragoons, which conducted the enterprise to a successful issue. He led the advance; he was always sent to every point of danger; his sword opened the path, through which Pizarro followed with his vagabond and plundering crew.

In trembling solicitude for his own safety, Pizarro not only held Chalcukima as a hostage, but he also seized upon Topaxpa, the young, feeble and grief-stricken son of the murdered Attahuallapa, and declared him to be, by legitimate right, the successor to the throne. Thus he still had the Inca in his power. The Peruvians were still accustomed to regard the Inca with almost religious homage.

Topaxpa was compelled to issue such commands as Pizarro gave to him. Thus an additional element of embarrassment was thrown into the ranks of the Peruvians. Communication between different parts of the empire was extremely difficult and slow. There were no mails and no horses. This gave the mounted Spaniards a vast advantage over their bewildered victims.

For several days the Spanish army moved delightfully along, through a series of luxuriant valleys, where the secluded people had scarcely heard of their arrival in the country. The movement of the glittering host was one of the most wonderful pageants [Pg 122] which Peruvian eyes had ever beheld. A multitude of men, women and children, thronged the highway, gazing with curiosity and admiration upon the scene, and astonished by the clatter of the hoofs of the horses upon the flag-stones, with which the national road was so carefully paved. During these few days of peaceful travel the natives presented no opposition to the march, and the presence of De Soto seemed to restrain the whole army from deeds of ruffianly violence. Whenever Pizarro wished to engage in any of his acts of villany, he was always careful first to send De Soto away on some important mission.

They were now approaching a deep and rapid mountain stream, where the bridge had either been carried away by the recent flood or had been destroyed by the Peruvians. They were also informed that quite a large army was gathered upon the opposite bank to arrest, with the aid of the rushing torrent, the farther advance of the Spaniards. Pizarro immediately ordered a halt. De Soto, with a hundred horsemen, was sent forward to reconnoitre, and, if possible, to open the path. Almagro, with two hundred footmen, followed closely behind to support the cavalry.

De Soto, without paying much attention to his infantry allies, pressed so rapidly forward as soon to leave them far behind. He reached the river. It [Pg 123] was a swollen mountain torrent. Several thousand natives, brandishing their javelins and their war clubs, stood upon the opposite bank of the stream. De Soto and his horsemen, without a moment's hesitation, plunged into the stream, and some by swimming and some by fording, soon crossed the foaming waters. As the war horses, with their steel-clad riders, came rushing upon the Peruvians, their keen swords flashing in the sunlight, a large part of the army fled in great terror. It seemed to them that supernatural foes had descended for their destruction.

A few remained, and fought with the energies of despair. But they were powerless before the trampling horses and the sharp weapons of their foes. They were cut down mercilessly, and it was the genius of De Soto which guided in the carnage, and the strong arm of De Soto which led in the bloody fray. And we must not forget that these Peruvians were fighting for their lives, their liberty, their all; and that these Spaniards were ruthless invaders. Neither can we greatly admire the heroism displayed by the assailants. The man who is carefully gloved and masked can with impunity rob the bees of their honey. The wolf does not need much courage to induce him to leap into the fold of the lambs.

In the vicinity of this routed army there was a pagan temple; that is, a temple dedicated to the Sun, [Pg 124] the emblem of the God of the Peruvians. It was in those days thought that the heathen and all their possessions, rightly belonged to the Christians; that it was the just desert of the pagans to be plundered and put to death. Even the mind of De Soto was so far in accord with these infamous doctrines of a benighted age, that he allowed his troopers to plunder the temple of all its rich treasures of silver and of gold. A very large amount of booty was thus obtained. One of the principal ornaments of this temple was an artificial sun, of large size, composed of pure and solid gold.

Mr. Wilmer, speaking of this event, judiciously remarks:

"De Soto, finding his path once more unobstructed, pushed forward, evidently disposed to open the way to Cuzco without the assistance of his tardy and irresolute commander. It is a remarkable fact, and one which admits of no denial, that every important military movement of the Spaniards in Peru, until the final subjugation of the empire by the capture of the metropolis, was conducted by De Soto. Up to the time to which our narrative now refers, Pizarro had never fought a single battle which deserved the name. The bloody tragedy of Caxamarca, it will be remembered, was only massacre; the contrivance and execution of which required no [Pg 125] military skill and no soldier-like courage. Pizarro acquired the mastery of Peru by the act of a malefactor. And he was, in fact, a thief and not a conqueror. The *heroic* element of this conquest is represented by the actions of De Soto."

[Pg 126]

CHAPTER VIII.

De Soto Returns to Spain.

Dreadful Fate of Chalcukima.—His Fortitude.—Ignominy of Pizarro.—De Soto's Advance upon Cuzco.—The Peruvian Highway.—Battle in the Defile.—De Soto takes the Responsibility.—Capture of the Capital and its Conflagration.—De Soto's Return to Spain.—His Reception there.—Preparations for the Conquest of Florida.

Considering the relations which existed between De Soto and Pizarro, it is not improbable that each was glad to be released from the presence of the other. It is very certain that so soon as De Soto was gone, Pizarro, instead of hurrying forward to support him in the hazardous encounters to which he was exposed, immediately engaged, with the main body of his army, in plundering all the mansions of the wealthy and the temples on their line of march. And it is equally certain that De Soto, instead of waiting for the troops of Pizarro to come up, put spurs to his horse and pressed on, as if he were anxious to place as great a distance as possible between himself and his superior in command.

Though De Soto had allowed his troops to plunder the temple of Xauxa, he would allow no robbery of private dwellings, and rigidly prohibited the slightest [Pg 127] act of violence or injustice towards the persons of the natives.

It will be remembered that Pizarro had threatened to hold Chalcukima responsible for any act of hostility on the part of the Peruvians. He now summoned his captive before him, and charged him with treason; accusing him of having incited his countrymen to measures of resistance. Chalcukima, with dignity and firmness which indicate a noble character, replied:

"If it had been possible for me to communicate with the people, I should certainly have advised them to do their duty to their country, without any regard to my personal safety. But you well know that the vigilance with which you have guarded me, has prevented me from making any communication of the kind. I am sorry that it has not been in my power to be guilty of the fact with which you charge me."

The wretched Pizarro, utterly incapable of appreciating the grandeur of such a character, ordered him to be burned at the stake. The fanatic robber and murderer, insulting the cross of Christ, by calling himself a Christian, sent his private chaplain, Friar Vincent, to convert Chalcukima to what he called the Christian faith. The priest gave an awful description of the glooms of hell, to which the prisoner was destined as a heathen. In glowing colors he depicted [Pg 128] the splendors of the celestial Eden, to which he would be admitted the moment after his execution if he would accept the Christian faith. The captive coldly replied:

"I do not understand your religion, and all that I have seen of it does not impress me in its favor."

He was led to the stake. Not a cry escaped his lips, as the fierce flames consumed his quivering flesh. From that scene of short, sharp agony, we trust that his spirit ascended to be folded in the embrace of his Heavenly Father. It is a fundamental principle in the teachings of Jesus, that in every nation he that feareth God, and doeth righteousness, is accepted of him. But God's ways here on earth are indeed past all finding out. Perhaps the future will solve the dreadful mystery, but at present, as we contemplate man's inhumanity to man, our eyes are often blinded with tears, and our hearts sink despairingly within us.

De Soto pressed rapidly onwards, league after league, over sublime eminences and through luxuriant vales. The road was admirable: smooth and clean as a floor. It was constructed only for foot passengers, as the Peruvians had no animals larger than the lama or sheep. This advance-guard of the Spanish army, all well mounted, and inspired by the energies of their impetuous chief, soon reached a [Pg 129] point where the road led over a mountain by steps cut in the solid rock, steep as a flight of stairs. Precipitous cliffs rose hundreds of feet on either side. Here it was necessary for the troopers to dismount, and carefully to lead their horses by the bit up the difficult ascent.

The road was winding and irregular, leading through the most savage scenery. This pass, at its summit, opened upon smooth table-land, luxuriant and beautiful under the influence of a tropical sun and mountain showers and dews. About half way up this pass, upon almost inaccessible crags, several thousand Peruvians had assembled to make another attempt at resistance. Arrows and javelins were of but little avail. Indeed they always rebounded from the armor of the Spaniards as from the ledges of eternal rock.

But the natives had abundantly provided themselves with enormous stones to roll down upon the heads of men and horses. Quite a band of armed men were also assembled upon the open plain at the head of the pass. As the Spaniards were almost dragging their horses up the gorge, suddenly the storm of war burst upon them. Showers of stone descended from the cliff from thousands of unseen hands. Huge boulders were pried over and went thundering down, crashing all opposition before them. [Pg 130] It seems now incomprehensible why the whole squadron of horsemen was not destroyed. But in this awful hour the self-possession of De Soto did not for one moment forsake him. He shouted to his men:

"If we halt here, or attempt to go back, we must certainly perish. Our only safety is in pressing forward. As soon as we reach the top of the pass, we can easily put these men to flight."

Suiting his action to his words, and being at the head of his men, he pushed forward with almost frantic energy, carefully watching and avoiding the descending missiles. Though several horses and many men were killed, and others sorely wounded, the majority soon reached the head of the pass. They then had an unobstructed plain before them, over which their horses could gallop in any direction at their utmost speed.

Impetuously they fell upon the band collected there, who wielded only the impotent weapons of arrows, javelins and war clubs. The Spaniards, exasperated by the death of their comrades, and by their own wounds, took desperate vengeance. No quarter was shown. Their sabres dripped with blood. Few could escape the swift-footed steeds. The dead were trampled beneath iron hoofs. Night alone ended the carnage.

During the night the Peruvians bravely rallied [Pg 131] from their wide dispersion over the mountains, resolved in their combined force to make another attempt to resist their foes. They were conscious that should they fail here, their case was hopeless.

At the commencement of the conflict a courier had been sent back, by De Soto, to urge Almagro to push forward his infantry as rapidly as possible. By a forced march they pressed on through the hours of the night, almost upon the run. The early dawn brought them to the pass. Soon the heart of De Soto was cheered as he heard their bugle blasts reverberating among the cliffs of the mountains. Their banners appeared emerging from the defile, and two hundred well-armed men joined his ranks.

Though the Peruvians were astonished at this accession to the number of their foes, they still came bravely forward to the battle. It was another scene of slaughter for the poor Peruvians. They inflicted but little harm upon the Spaniards, while hundreds of their slain soon strewed the ground.

The Spanish infantry, keeping safely beyond the reach of arrow or javelin, could, with the deadly bullet, bring down a Peruvian as fast as they could load and fire, while the horsemen could almost with impunity plunge into the densest ranks of the foe. The Peruvians were vanquished, dispersed, and cut down, until the Spaniards even were weary with carnage. [Pg 132] This was the most important battle which was fought in the conquest of Peru.

The field was but twenty-five miles from the capital, to which the army could now advance by an almost unobstructed road. De Soto was anxious to press on immediately and take possession of the city. He however yielded to the earnest entreaties of Almagro, and consented to remain where he was with his band of marauders. This delay, in a military point of view, proved to be very unfortunate. Had they gone immediately forward, the vanquished and panic-stricken Peruvians would not have ventured upon another encounter. But Almagro was the friend of Pizarro, dependent upon him, and had been his accomplice in many a deed of violence. He was anxious that Pizarro should have the renown of a conqueror, and should enjoy the triumph of riding at the head of his troops into the streets of the vanquished capital.

This delay of several days gave the Peruvians time to recover from their consternation, and they organized another formidable line of defense in a valley which the Spaniards would be compelled to traverse, a few miles from the city. Pizarro was still several miles in the rear. De Soto dispatched a courier to him, informing him of the new encounter to which the army was exposed, and stating that the Peruvians [Pg 133] were well posted, and that every hour of delay added to their strength. Still Pizarro loitered behind; still Almagro expressed his decided reluctance to advance before Pizarro's arrival. To add to De Soto's embarrassments, he declared that De Soto was acting without authority and in direct opposition to the orders of his superior. After a little hesitancy De Soto resolved to take the responsibility and to advance. He said to Almagro:

"A soldier who is entrusted with an important command, is not bound in all cases to await the orders of his superior. Where there is manifestly an important advantage to be gained, he must be allowed to act according to his own discretion."

He then appealed to his own dragoons, saying to them:

"The whole success of our expedition now depends upon the celerity of our movements. While we are waiting for Pizarro, our best chance for victory will be lost."

With one united voice the dragoons of De Soto demanded to be led forward. Availing himself of this enthusiasm, De Soto put his troops in motion. The Peruvians were a few miles in advance, strongly posted in a deep and rugged ravine, where they hoped that the movements of the horses would be so impeded that they could accomplish but little. They [Pg 134] pressed forward, and the battle was immediately commenced. Both parties fought with great fury. In the midst of the conflict a large reinforcement of the natives came rushing upon the field, under the leadership of a young Peruvian noble, who displayed truly chivalric courage and energy. De Soto was ever where the blows fell thickest and where danger was most imminent.

Quite a number of the Peruvians were slain, and many dead horses were strewed over the field. At one time De Soto, separated from his comrades by the surging tides of the battle, found himself surrounded by twenty Peruvians, who, with arrows, javelins and battle clubs, assailed him with the utmost impetuosity. Javelins and arrows glanced harmless from the Spanish armor. But war clubs, armed with copper and wielded by sinewy arms, were formidable weapons even for the belted knight to encounter. De Soto, with his keen and ponderous sword, cut his way through his assailants, strewing the ground with the dead. The young Peruvian, who, it is said, was heir to the throne of the Inca, had assumed the general command.

He gazed with astonishment upon the exploits of De Soto, and said in despairing tones to his attendants: "It is useless to contend with such enemies! These men are destined to be our masters."

[Pg 135]

Immediately he approached De Soto, throwing down his arms, advancing alone, and indicating by gestures that he was ready to surrender. The battle at once ceased, and most of the Peruvian army rushed precipitately back towards the city. In a state of frenzy they applied the torch in all directions, resolved to thwart the avarice of the conqueror by laying the whole city and all its treasures in ashes. The inhabitants of Cuzco, almost without exception, fled. Each one seized upon whatever of value could be carried away. Volumes of smoke and the bursting flames soon announced to the Spaniards the doom of the city.

De Soto and his dragoons put spurs to their horses and hastened forward, hoping to extinguish the conflagration. Now that the battle was fought and the victory won, Francisco Pizarro, with his band of miscreants, came rushing on to seize the plunder.

"They came like wolves or jackals to fatten on the prey which never could have been attained by their own courage or prowess. The disappointment of Pizarro and his congenial associates, when they found that the principal wealth of the city had been carried off by the Peruvians, vented itself in acts of diabolical cruelty. They seized on the aged and sick persons who had been unable to escape, and put many of them to the torture to make them confess where

[Pg 136] the treasures of Cuzco were concealed. Either these unfortunate people could not give the information required, or they had sufficient firmness to endure agony and death rather than betray the consecrated treasures of their national monuments and altars into the hands of their enemies." [A]

It was late in the afternoon of a November day, 1533, when the dragoons of De Soto, closely followed by the whole Spanish army, entered the burning streets of Cuzco. They ran about eagerly in all directions searching for gold in the blazing palaces and temples. Thus an immense amount of spoil was found, which the Peruvians had been unable to remove. It is said that after one-fifth had been subtracted for the Spanish crown, and the officers had received their abundant shares, the common soldiers, four hundred and eighty in number, received each one a sum amounting to four thousand dollars.

Peru was conquered, but the victors had indeed gained a loss. Nearly all who were engaged in the enterprise perished miserably. Almagro was eventually taken captive by the Peruvians and strangled. Hernando Pizarro, returning to Spain, languished for weary years in a prison. The younger brother was beheaded. Friar Vincent, who had given the support of religion to many of the most atrocious of [Pg 137] these crimes, fell into an ambush with a small party, and they all were massacred. Francisco Pizarro himself fell a victim to a conspiracy among his own soldiers, and at mid-day was put to death in his own palace. But we must leave these wild men to their career of cruelty and crime, while we follow the footsteps of De Soto.

Early in the year 1534, De Soto took leave of his comrades in Peru, and embarked for Spain. He had left his native land in poverty. He now returned after an absence of about fifteen years, greatly enriched, prepared in opulence as well as in illustrious birth to take his stand with the proudest grandees of that then opulent realm. His last labors in Peru were spent in unavailing endeavors to humanize the spirit of his countrymen there, and to allay the bitter feuds which were springing up among them. But his departure seemed to remove from them all restraints, and Spaniards and Peruvians alike were whelmed in a common ruin.

No account has been transmitted to us of De Soto's return voyage. While he was in Peru, Don Pedro had died. His sick-bed was a scene of lingering agony, both of body and of mind. The proud spirit is sometimes vanquished and crushed by remorse; but it is never, by those scorpion lashes, subdued, and rendered humble and gentle and lovable. [Pg 138] The dying sinner, whose soul was crimsoned with guilt, was overwhelmed with "a certain fearful looking for of judgment and fiery indignation." The ecclesiastics, who surrounded his death-bed, assured him that such sins as he had been guilty of could only be expiated by the most liberal benefactions to the church. He had never forgiven Isabella for her pertinacious adherence to De Soto. In the grave he could not prohibit their nuptials. By bequeathing his wealth to the church, he could accomplish a double object. He could gratify his revenge by leaving his daughter penniless, and thus De Soto, if he continued faithful, would be compelled to receive to his arms a dowerless bride; and a miserable superstition taught him that he could thus bribe God to throw open to him the gates of paradise.

Don Pedro's eldest daughter, Maria, was engaged to be married to Vasco Nuñez, the very worthy governor who had preceded Don Pedro at Darien, and whom he had so infamously beheaded. She had spent fifteen years in her father's castle in the gloom and tears of this cruel widowhood. Don Pedro bequeathed nearly all his fortune to the endowment of a monastery, over which Maria was appointed abbess. Isabella was left unprovided for. Thus suddenly the relative position of the two lovers was entirely changed. De Soto found himself in possession of large wealth. [Pg 139] Isabella was reduced to poverty. We know not where to find, in the annals of history, the record of a more beautiful attachment than that which, during fifteen years of separation, trial, and sorest temptations, had united the hearts of De Soto and Isabella. Their love commenced when they were children, walking hand in hand, and playing in the bowers of Don Pedro's ancestral castle.

De Soto had now attained the age of thirty-five years. Isabella was only a few years younger. When we contemplate her youth, her beauty, the long years of absence, without even a verbal message passing between them, the deadly hostility of her father to the union, and the fact that her hand had been repeatedly solicited by the most wealthy of the Spanish nobility, this fidelity of Isabella to her youthful love is one of the most remarkable in the records of time.

"During the long separation," says Mr. Wilmer, "of these exemplary lovers, many important changes had taken place. Time and sorrow had somewhat dimmed the lustre of Isabella's beauty. But she was still the fairest among ten thousand, and De Soto was too deeply enamored and too justly appreciative to value her the less, because the rose had partially faded from her cheek."

Immediately upon De Soto's return to Spain, as [Pg 140] all obstacles to their union were removed, the nuptial ceremony was performed. The voice of fame had already proclaimed De Soto as the real conqueror of Peru. As such, he had not only enriched himself, but had also greatly enriched the Spanish crown. All eyes were fixed upon him. It is said that at once he became the most noted and most popular man in the kingdom. He and his bride were received at the Spanish court with the most flattering marks of distinction. In his style of living he assumed almost regal splendor. He had acquired his money very suddenly, and he lavished it with an unsparing hand. A contemporary annalist writes:

"He kept a steward, a gentleman usher, several pages, a gentleman of the horse, a chamberlain, a footman, and all other officers that the house of a nobleman requires."

One of the most splendid mansions in Seville he selected for his residence, and in less than two years he found that one-half of his princely fortune had melted away. They were two years of adulation, of self-indulgence, of mental intoxication. It was a delirious dream from which he suddenly awoke. Reflection taught him that he must immediately curtail his expenses, and very seriously, or engage in some new enterprise to replenish his wasting purse.

The region of North America called Florida, a [Pg 141] territory of undefined and boundless extent, was then attracting much attention as a fresh field for the acquisition of gold and glory. Several expeditions had touched upon the unknown coast, but from various causes had proved entire failures. Eight years before this De Narvaez had visited the country with three hundred adventurers. He found the natives far more warlike than the Peruvians, and the country more difficult of access. De Narvaez himself, and nearly all his band, fell before the fury of the Floridians. Five only escaped. One of these, Cabaca de Vaca, a man of glowing imagination, and who held the pen of a ready writer, wrote a Baron Munchausen account of the expedition. He descanted upon the delicious clime, the luxuriant soil, the populous cities, the architectural splendor of the edifices, and the inexhaustible mines of silver and of gold. There was no one to call his account in question. His extravagant stories were generally believed.

De Soto, who was in the prime of his vigorous manhood, having as yet only attained his thirty-seventh year, read this narrative and pondered these statements with enthusiasm. A couple of years of inaction in his luxurious saloons had inspired him with new zeal for romantic adventure; and to this there was added the powerful motive of the necessity of retrieving his fortunes. He believed that gold could be gathered in [Pg 142] Florida, even more abundantly than in Peru; that by the aid of the crown a numerous colony might be established where, under genial skies, every man could be put into possession of broad acres of the most luxuriant soil. And he felt fully confident that his long experience on the isthmus and in Peru, qualified him in the highest degree to be the leader of such an enterprise.

In these views he was sustained by the common sentiment of the whole community. De Soto applied to the king of Spain, the Emperor Charles Fifth, for permission to organize an expedition, at his own expense, for the conquest of Florida. He offered to the crown, as usual for its share, one-fifth of the plunder.

Eagerly the Emperor, who was always in need of money, accepted the proposition, "asking no questions, for conscience sake." The Emperor was very profuse in conferring honors and titles upon his heroic subject. He appointed him governor of the island of Cuba, which he was to make the base of his operations, investing him with almost dictatorial powers as both military and civil governor. He also granted him a private estate in Florida, with the title of marquis, in whatever part of the country he might choose. This magnificent estate was to consist of a region, ninety miles long and forty-five miles wide.

[Pg 143]

As soon as it was known throughout Spain that De Soto was about to embark on such an enterprise, volunteers began to flock to his standard. He would accept of none but the most vigorous young men, whom he deemed capable of enduring the extremes of toil and hardship. In a few months nine hundred and fifty men were assembled at San Lucar, eager to embark. Many of these were sons of the wealthy nobles, who were thoroughly equipped in splendid style, with costly armor, and accompanied by a train of servants.

Twenty-four ecclesiastics, of various grades, joined the expedition, whose arduous task it was to convert the natives to that religion of the Spaniards which allowed them to rob their houses and their temples, to maltreat their wives and daughters, to set fire to their villages, to hunt them down with bloodhounds, and to trample them under the iron hoofs of their fiery steeds.

Never before had an expedition set out so abundantly supplied. Not only was every necessity provided for, but luxury and even wasteful extravagance reigned through the armament. De Soto himself was a man of magnificent tastes. Many who were with him in Peru, and had become there enriched, had joined the enterprise. And the young nobles of Spain surrounded themselves with the conveniences and splendor which large wealth could furnish.

[Pg 144]

CHAPTER IX.

The Landing in Florida.

The Departure from Spain.—Arrival in Cuba.—Leonora and Tobar.—Isabella Invested with the Regency.—Sad Life of Isabella.—Sailing of the Expedition.—The Landing at Tampa Bay.—Outrages of Narvaez.—Noble Spirit of Ucita.—Unsuccessful Enterprises.—Disgrace and Return of Porcallo.

The brilliant armament spread its sails to a favorable breeze at the port of San Lucar, on the morning of the sixth of April, 1538. The squadron consisted of seven large ships, and three smaller vessels. It must have been an imposing and busy scene in that little bay, upon which the sun looked serenely down three hundred years ago.

In addition to the Floridian fleet, there was another squadron of twenty-six sail, at the same time weighing anchor, bound for Mexico. Bugle peals resounded from ship and shore, while salvoes of artillery swept over the waves and reverberated among the cliffs.

Isabella accompanied her husband, and quite an imposing train of attendants was attached to the governor's family. The sail of a fortnight brought them to the Canary Islands. The Count Gomera, a Spanish nobleman, was in command. No religious scruples [Pg 145] lent their restraints to his luxurious court. He had a very beautiful daughter, seventeen years of age, named Leonora. The father loved her tenderly. He was perhaps anxious to shield her from the deleterious influences with which she was surrounded. The high moral worth of Isabella impressed him; and arrangements were made for Leonora to accompany Isabella to Cuba, as a companion, to be treated in all respects as her own daughter.

On the twenty-fourth of April the fleet again set sail, and reached St. Jago de Cuba the latter part of May. This city was then the capital of the island. It was situated on the southern shore, at the head of a bay running inland about six miles. It was then quite populous, and was opulent with the wealth of which previous Spanish adventurers had robbed the unhappy Cubans. The whole city turned out with music, and banners and gorgeous processions, to give a suitable reception to their new governor.

A grand tournament was held on the occasion. Among the cavaliers who were contending for the prizes there was a young nobleman, Nuño de Tobar, who was De Soto's lieutenant-general. He was one of the most accomplished of the Spanish grandees, and bore off many of the prizes. The beauty of Leonora won his admiration. They were thrown much together, and he betrayed her. At the confessional [Pg 146] Leonora opened her heart to the priest. It is probable that he communicated with the governor. De Soto's indignation was thoroughly roused. He summoned the culprit before him. Tobar, deeming his offense a very trivial one, without hesitation acknowledged it, thinking, perhaps, that he might receive some slight reprimand. He was not a little surprised when the governor said in indignant tones:

"Leonora was placed under my care by her father. I pledged myself to protect her at the hazard of my own life. To-morrow morning you must meet me in single combat, where you will have a chance to protect the life you have justly forfeited."

There was no man probably, in the whole Spanish army, who could safely cross swords with De Soto in mortal strife. Tobar was appalled. He well knew that in such a rencontre death was his inevitable doom. Overwhelmed with confusion, he said:

"I have not committed a capital crime. If I had, I should not expect your Excellency to be my executioner. It is impossible for me to contend with you in single combat. By accepting your challenge, I doom myself to certain destruction."

De Soto replied: "Your crime is not a trivial one. You cannot evade the consequences by refusing to meet them. To say nothing of the wrong you have done this unhappy girl, your treachery to me [Pg 147] deserves the punishment of a traitor. You may choose whether you will die like a soldier, sword in hand, or like a criminal, under the axe of the executioner."

Tobar withdrew. He hastened to the room of the confessor. With him he called upon Leonora, and, taking a few witnesses, repaired to the church, where the marriage ceremony was immediately performed. Within an hour he returned to the governor and informed him that he had made all the reparation in his power. De Soto, his brow still clouded with severe displeasure, replied:

"You have saved your life, but you can never regain my confidence. You are no longer my lieutenant. That office can be held only by one whose honor is unsullied."

De Soto remained about three months in Cuba, making a tour of the island, establishing his government, purchasing horses, and making other preparations for the expedition to Florida. While thus engaged, he sent a vessel, with a picked crew, to coast along the shores of the land he was about to invade, in search of a commodious harbor, where his troops might disembark. After many perilous adventures, the vessel returned with a satisfactory report.

The fleet, and all the armament it was to bear, were rendezvoused at Havana, on the northern coast [Pg 148] of Cuba, where a fair wind in a few hours would convey them to the shores of Florida. On the twelfth of May, some authorities say the eighteenth, of the year 1539, the expedition set sail upon one of the most disastrous adventures in which heroic men ever engaged. Terrible as were the woes they inflicted upon the natives, no less dreadful were the calamities which they drew down upon themselves.

Isabella had been anxious to accompany her husband to Florida. But he, aware of the hardships and perils to which they would be exposed, would not give his consent. She consequently remained at Cuba, entrusted with the regency of the island. She never saw her husband again. Poor Isabella! In sadness she had waited fifteen years for her nuptials. Two short years had glided away like a dream in the night. And then, after three years of intense anxiety, during which she heard almost nothing of her husband, the tidings reached her of his death. It was a fatal blow to her faithful and loving heart. World-weary and sorrow-crushed, she soon followed him to the spirit-land. Such is life; not as God has appointed it, but as sin has made it.

The expedition consisted of eight large ships, a caraval, and two brigantines. They were freighted with everything which could be deemed needful to conquer the country, and then to colonize it. The [Pg 149] force embarked, in addition to the sailors who worked the ships, consisted of a thousand thoroughly armed men, and three hundred and fifty horses. Contrary winds gave them a slow passage across the gulf. On the twenty-fifth of May they entered the harbor of which they were in search. It was on the western coast of the magnificent peninsula. De Soto then gave it the name of Espiritu Santo. It is now however known as Tampa Bay.

As they entered the harbor beacon fires were seen blazing along the eminences, indicating that the natives had taken the alarm, and were preparing for resistance. Several days were employed in cautious sounding of the harbor and searching for a suitable landing-place, as it seemed probable that opposition was to be encountered. On the last day of May, a detachment of three hundred soldiers landed on the beach and took possession of the land in the name of Charles the Fifth. The serene day was succeeded by a balmy night.

Not an Indian was to be seen; and the bloom, luxuriance and fruitage of the tropics, spread enchantingly around them.

The hours of the night passed away undisturbed. But just before dawn a terrific war-whoop resounded through the forest, as from a thousand throats, and a band of Indian warriors came rushing down, hurling upon the invaders a shower of arrows and javelins. [Pg 150] The attack was so sudden and impetuous that the Spaniards were thrown into a panic. They rushed for their boats, and with loudest bugle peals, called for aid from their companions in the ships. The summons met with a prompt response. Boats were immediately lowered, and a large party of steel-clad men and horses were sent to their aid.

When Nuño Tobar was degraded, and dismissed from his office as lieutenant-general, a rich, hair-brained Spanish nobleman, by the name of Vasco Porcallo, took his place. He was a gay cavalier, brave even to recklessness, of shallow intellect, but a man who had seen much hard service in the battlefields of those days. He was very rich, residing at Trinidad in Cuba. He joined the enterprise for the conquest of Florida, influenced by an instinctive love of adventure, and by the desire to kidnap Indians to work as slaves on his plantations. The valiant Porcallo headed the party sent to the rescue of those on shore.

In such an adventure he was entirely in his element. Immediately upon landing he put spurs to his horse and, accompanied by only seven dragoons, with his sabre flashing in the air, plunged into the very thickest of the Indians. Soon they were put to flight. An Indian arrow, however, pierced his saddle and its housings, and reached the vitals of his horse. [Pg 151] The noble steed dropped dead beneath him. Porcallo was quite proud of his achievement, and boasted not a little that his arm had put the *infidels*, as he called the Indians, to flight, and that his horse was the first to fall in the encounter.

During the day all the troops were disembarked and encamped upon the shore. It was reported that there was quite a populous Indian town at the distance of about six miles from the place of landing. While the ammunition and commissary stores were being brought on shore, the little army marched for this village. It was the residence of the chief of the powerful tribe who occupied that region. His name was Ucita, and from him the village received the same appellation.

The Spaniards met with no opposition on their march. But when they reached the village they found it entirely deserted. It was quite a large town, the houses being built substantially of timber, thatched with palm leaves. Many of these edifices were large and commodious, containing several rooms. Their articles of household furniture were convenient, and some of them quite elegant. The dresses, especially those of the females, were artistic and often highly ornamental. Very beautiful shawls and mantillas were manufactured by them. Their finest fabrics were woven by the hand from the [Pg 152] fibrous bark of the mulberry-tree and hemp, which grew wild and in abundance. The natives had acquired the art of rich coloring, and the garments thus manufactured by them were often really beautiful. The walls of the houses of the wealthier citizens were hung with tapestry of very softly tanned and richly prepared buckskin; and carpets of the same material were spread upon the floors.

The Floridians were not acquainted with iron, that most indispensable article with nations of high enlightenment. But they had succeeded in imparting a temper to copper, so as to give many of their tools quite a keen edge. Though the inhabitants of Florida had not attained that degree of civilization which had been reached by the Peruvians, it will be seen that they were immeasurably in advance of the savages in the northern portion of the continent, and that their homes far surpassed those of the peasantry of Ireland, and were more tasteful and commodious than the log huts which European emigrants erect as their first home in the wilderness of the West. They cultivated the ground mainly for their subsistence, though hunting and fishing were resorted to, then as now, for recreation as well as for food.

De Soto took possession of the deserted village, and occupied the houses of the inhabitants as barracks for his soldiers. A few straggling Indians [Pg 153] were taken captive. From them he learned that he was doomed to suffer for the infamous conduct of the Spanish adventurer, Narvaez, who had preceded him in a visit to this region. This vile man had been guilty of the most inhuman atrocities. He had caused the mother of the chief Ucita to be torn to pieces by bloodhounds, and in a transport of passion had awfully mutilated Ucita himself, by cutting off his nose. Consequently, the chief and all his people were exasperated to the highest degree. The injuries they had received were such as could never be forgiven or forgotten.

De Soto was very anxious to cultivate friendly relations with the Indians. Whatever may have been his faults, his whole career thus far had shown him to be by nature a kind-hearted and upright man, hating oppression and loving justice. The faults of his character rather belonged to the age in which he lived, than to the individual man. No military leader has ever yet been able to restrain the passions of his soldiers. Wherever an army moves, there will always be, to a greater or less degree, plunder and violence. De Soto earnestly endeavored to introduce strict discipline among his troops. He forbade the slightest act of injustice or disrespect towards the Indians. Whenever a captive was taken, he treated him as a father would treat a child, and returned him to his [Pg 154] home laden with presents. He availed himself of every opportunity to send friendly messages to Ucita. But the mutilated chief was in no mood to be placated. His only reply to these kind words was,

"I want none of the speeches or promises of the Spaniards. Bring me their heads and I will receive them joyfully."

The energies of De Soto inspired his whole camp. The provisions and munitions of war were promptly landed and conveyed to Ucita. The place was strongly fortified, and a hardy veteran, named Pedro Calderon, was placed in command of the garrison entrusted with its defence. All the large ships were sent back to Cuba, probably to obtain fresh supplies of military stores; some say that it was to teach the army that, there being no possibility of escape, it now must depend upon its own valor for existence.

De Soto was very unwilling to set out for a march into the interior for discovery and in search of gold, while leaving so powerful a tribe as that over which Ucita reigned, in hostility behind him. He therefore sent repeated messages to Ucita expressing his utter detestation of the conduct of Narvaez; his desire to do everything in his power to repair the wrong which had been inflicted upon him, and his earnest wish to establish friendly relations with the deeply-injured chief.

[Pg 155]

These reiterated friendly advances, ever accompanied by correspondent action, at length in some slight degree mitigated the deadly rancor of Ucita, so that instead of returning a message of defiance and hate, he sent back the truly noble response:

"The memory of my injuries prevents me from returning a kind reply to your messages, and your courtesy is such that it will not allow me to return a harsh answer."

The man who, under these circumstances, could frame such a reply, must have been one of nature's noblemen. De Soto could appreciate the grandeur of such a spirit. While these scenes were transpiring, a man was brought into the camp, in Indian costume, who announced himself as a Spaniard by the name of Juan Ortiz. He had been one of the adventurers under Narvaez. In the extermination of that infamous band he had been taken captive and bound to the stake, to be consumed. He was then but eighteen years of age, tall and very handsome. As the tongues of torturing flame began to eat into his quivering flesh, cries of agony were extorted from him.

He was in the hands of a powerful chief, whose daughter is represented as a very beautiful princess, by the name of Uleleh. She was about sixteen years of age, and could not endure the scene. She threw her arms [Pg 156] around her father's neck, and with tears of anguish pleaded that his life might be saved. He was rescued; and though for a time he suffered extreme cruelty, he eventually became adopted, as it were, into the tribe, and for ten years had resided among the Indians, sometimes regarded as a captive, upon whom heavy burdens could be imposed, and again treated with great kindness. Juan Ortiz being thus familiar with the habits of the natives and their language, became an invaluable acquisition to the adventurers.

De Soto inquired very earnestly of him respecting the country and the prospect of finding any region abounding with silver and gold. Ortiz had but little information to give, save that, at the distance of about a hundred miles from where they then were, there was a great chief named Uribaracaxi, to whom all the adjacent chiefs were tributary. His realms were represented as far more extensive, populous, and rich than those of the surrounding chieftains. De Soto dispatched a band of sixty horsemen and sixty foot soldiers with presents and messages of friendship to Uribaracaxi. The object of the expedition was to explore the country and to make inquiries respecting gold.

A weary march of about forty miles brought the party to the village of Mucozo, where Ortiz had resided for some years. The chief of this tribe, whose name was also Mucozo, was brother-in-law to [Pg 157] Uribaracaxi. Mucozo received the Spaniards with great hospitality, and learning that they were on a friendly visit to Uribaracaxi, furnished them with a guide. Four days were occupied in a tedious march through a country where pathless morasses continually embarrassed their progress.

This expedition was under the command of Balthazar de Gallegos. He reached his point of destination in safety. But the chief, deeming it not prudent to trust himself in the hands of the Spaniards, whose renown for fiendish deeds had filled the land, had retired from his capital, and nearly all the inhabitants had fled with him. He left for his uninvited guests no message either of welcome or defiance. Gallegos found all his attempts to open any communications with him unavailing. There was no plunder in the city worth seizing, and De Soto's commands to the expedition were very strict, to treat the Indians with the utmost kindness and humanity.

Gallegos made earnest inquiries of the Indians whom he met, as to the provinces where gold and silver could be found. They told him that there was a country many leagues west of them, of marvellous luxuriance and beauty, where gold was found in such abundance that the warriors had massive shields and helmets made of that precious metal. The more shrewd of the Spaniards placed very little reliance [Pg 158] upon this testimony. They thought they saw evidence that the Indians were ready to fabricate any story by which they could rid themselves of their visitors.

Soon after the departure of Gallegos, De Soto received the intelligence that the chief Ucita had taken refuge in a forest, surrounded with swamps, not far from the Spanish camp. The vainglorious

Porcallo was exceedingly indignant that the Indian chief should presume to hold himself aloof from all friendly advances. He entreated De Soto to grant him the privilege of capturing the fugitive. De Soto complied with his request. The impetuous old man, fond of parade, and lavish of his wealth, selected a band of horsemen and footmen, all of whom were gorgeously apparelled for the occasion. He, himself, was mounted on a magnificent steed and cased in glittering armor.

It seems that the noble Ucita kept himself well informed of every movement of the invaders. With a spirit of magnanimity which would have done honor to the best Christian in the Spanish ranks, he sent a courier to meet Porcallo, and to say to him,

"You will only expose yourself to infinite peril from the rivers, morasses, and forests through which you will have to pass in your attempt to reach my retreat. My position is so secure that all your [Pg 159] attempts to take me will result only in your own loss. I do not send you this message from any fears on my own account, but because your leader, De Soto, has manifested so much forbearance in not injuring my territory or my subjects."

It is really refreshing to find here and there, among all these demoniac deeds of demoniac men, some remaining traces of that nobility of character which man had before the fall, when created in God's image he was but little lower than the angels. Man, as we see him developed in history, is indeed a ruin, but the ruin of a once noble fabric. When we think of what man might be, in all generous affections, and then think of what man is, it is enough to cause one to weep tears of blood.

Porcallo could not appreciate the magnanimity of Ucita. He regarded the message as one of the stratagems of war, dictated either by fear or cowardice. He therefore ordered the trumpets to sound the advance, his only fear being, that the chief might escape. Porcallo, a Quixotic knight, had no element of timidity in his character. He led his troops. He never said "Go," but "Follow." Pressing rapidly forward, the little band soon arrived upon the border of a vast and dismal morass, utterly pathless, stretching out many leagues in extent.

The hot-headed cavalier, thinking that the swamp [Pg 160] might be waded, put spurs to his horse and dashed forward. He had advanced but a few rods when the horse, struggling knee-deep through the mire, stumbled and fell. One of the legs of the rider was so caught beneath the animal as to pin him inextricably in the morass, covering him with water and with mud. The weight of his armor sank him deeper in the mire, and in the desperate struggles of the steed for extrication, he was in great danger of being suffocated. None could come to his aid without danger of being swallowed up in the bog.

The unfeeling and brutal soldiers stood upon the borders of the morass with shouts of merriment, as they witnessed the sudden discomfiture of their leader; a discomfiture the more ludicrous, in contrast with his gorgeous attire, and his invariably proud and lofty bearing. At length Porcallo extricated himself, and, drenched with water, and covered with mud, led his equally bemired steed to the land. He was humiliated and enraged. The derision of the soldiers stung him to the quick. He had embarked in the expedition to gain glory and slaves. He had encountered disgrace; and the prospect of kidnapping the natives, under such a leader as De Soto had proved himself to be, was very small.

It is probable that before this disaster he had seriously contemplated abandoning the expedition and [Pg 161] returning to his princely mansion in Trinidad. Ordering his men to face about, he sullenly and silently returned to the Spanish camp. Throwing up his commission with disgust, he embarked for Cuba, and we hear of him no more.

"His train of servants," writes Mr. Theodore Irving, "Spanish, Indian and negro, were embarked with all speed. But when the gallant old cavalier came to take leave of his young companions in arms, and the soldiers he had lately aspired to lead so vaingloriously, his magnificent spirit broke forth. He made gifts to the right and left, dividing among the officers and knights all the arms, accoutrements, horses and camp equipage, with which he had come so lavishly and so ostentatiously provided, and gave, for the use of the army, all the ample store of provisions and munitions brought for the use of himself and his retinue. This done, he bade farewell to campaigning and set sail for Cuba, much to the regret of the army, who lamented that so gallant a spirit should have burned out so soon." [B]

Indeed, it is stated in what is called "The Portuguese Narrative" of these events, that Porcallo and De Soto had already quarrelled so decisively that they were no longer on speaking terms. Porcallo, thoroughly destitute of moral principle, was a slave [Pg 162] hunter; a character whom De Soto thoroughly despised, and whose operations he would not on any account allow to be carried on in his army. Porcallo therefore found no difficulty in obtaining permission to retire from the service. Probably both the governor and his lieutenant were equally happy to be rid of each other.

[Pg 163]

CHAPTER X.

The March to Ochile.

The March Commenced.—The Swamps of Florida.—Passage of the Morass.—Heroism of Sylvestre.—Message to Acuera.—His Heroic Reply.—Fierce Hostility of the Indians.—Enter the Town of

Ocali.—Strange Incident.—Death of the Bloodhound.—Historical Discrepancies.—Romantic Entrance to Ochile.

The day after the departure of Porcallo, a courier from Captain Gallegos, accompanied by a small guard, came to the Spanish camp at Ucita. He informed De Soto that there was an ample supply of provisions at Uribaracaxi to sustain the army for several days; and that he had received information that at not a great distance from that place large quantities of gold could be obtained. De Soto and his companions were greatly elated by these tidings, trusting that they were about to enter upon another Peru. A garrison of forty horsemen and eighty foot soldiers, was left at Ucita, to protect the military and commissariat stores collected there, and to guard the three vessels still remaining in the bay. Captain Calderon, who was left in command, was strictly enjoined to treat the Indians with the utmost kindness, [Pg 164] and not to make war upon them, even if provoked by taunts and insults.

De Soto, then, with the main body of his army, set out on the march for Uribaracaxi. It was soon very evident to him that he was not in Peru. There was no smoothly-paved highway for his soldiers to traverse. The country was pathless, rough, apparently uninhabited, encumbered with tangled forests, and vast dismal swamps. It was a very arduous enterprise for soldiers burdened with heavy armor to force their way through such a wilderness, with the baggage essential to such a body of men.

One of the great objects of the governor, and a humane one, was to establish a colony in Florida. A herd of three hundred swine was kept in the line of march, as these animals were deemed the most advantageous stock for new settlers. After a toilsome march of two days they reached the native village of Mucozo, where the friendly chief of the same name resided. It is said that this place is now called Hichipuchsassa. The chief received them with great hospitality.

Pressing on without delay, they soon reached Uribaracaxi, which town it is supposed was situated near the head of the Hillsborough river, which stream empties into Tampa Bay. The chief was still absent, in his place of refuge, amidst the fastnesses of the forest. [Pg 165] All of De Soto's friendly endeavors to draw him from his retreat proved unavailing. The Spaniards were yet to traverse many leagues of this unknown country before they could enter the region where it was supposed the gold could be found.

Florida is emphatically a region of swamps. There is probably no section of our country which, in a state of nature, would be more difficult for the passage of an army. About nine miles from the village, directly on their line of march, extending far away to the east and the west, there was a vast bog three miles wide. It was a chaotic region of mud and water, with gigantic trees and entangling roots. After long search a passage was found through which, by the toilsome efforts of a whole day, the army forced its way. Beyond the swamp there opened before them a smooth, luxuriant flower-enamelled prairie. Rejoicingly the army pressed forward over this beautiful expanse, when suddenly they found their steps again arrested by a series of sluggish streams, stagnant bayous, and impenetrable bogs.

De Soto now took a hundred horse and a hundred foot soldiers, and leaving the remainder of the army safely encamped, set out to explore the country in search of a practicable route of travel. For three days he skirted the region of bogs, lakes and thickets, sending out his runners in different directions to find some [Pg 166] outlet. But there was no outlet for the journeyings of civilized men. They captured some Indians, who offered to guide them, but who treacherously led them to more difficult passes and into ambushes where many of their horses were slain. The dreadful punishment of these false guides was to be torn to pieces by bloodhounds. They bore their sufferings with amazing fortitude.

At length they found a very rude, difficult and dangerous path by which the Indians crossed these swamps. At one point, where the water could not be forded for a distance of nearly three hundred feet, the Indians had constructed a bridge by cutting down two large trees and uniting the space that still remained between them in this Stygian lake, by tying logs together, with cross-poles for flooring. To add to the embarrassments of the Spaniards, apparently innumerable small bands of Indians were hovering on their track, assailing them with their sharp-pointed arrows, wherever they could get a shot, and then escaping into the impenetrable region around. They were very careful never to come to an open conflict. Canoes, propelled by the paddle, would often dart out from the thickets, a shower of arrows be discharged, and the canoes disappear where no foot could follow them.

A very bold courier, on one of the fleetest horses, [Pg 167] was sent back to summon the main body of the army to march, under the command of Moscoso, and join the party of explorers which De Soto had led. This young man, by the name of Sylvestre, accomplished his feat through a thousand perils and hair-breadth escapes.

Three days De Soto's band had passed struggling through bog and brake, bramble and forest. Sylvestre was to find his path back travelling with all possible speed by night as well as by day. One attendant only was with him, Juan Lopez. They never could have found their path but through the sagacity of their horses. These noble animals seemed to be endowed for the time with the instinct of setter dogs. For in the darkness of the night they would puff and snort, with their noses close to the ground, ever, under the most difficult circumstances, finding the track. The distance over which they urged their horses exceeded thirty miles. For three days the poor creatures had not been unsaddled, and the bits had but occasionally been removed from their mouths that they might enjoy the brief refreshment of grazing.

"At times," writes Mr. Irving, "they passed within sight of huge fires, around which the savages were stretched in wild fantastic groups, or capering and singing, and making the forests ring with yells and howlings. These were probably celebrating their [Pg 168] feasts with war-dances. The deafening din they raised was the safeguard of the two Spaniards, as it prevented the savages noticing the clamorous barking of their dogs, and hearing the tramping of the horses as they passed." [C]

Immediately on the arrival of these two bold troopers, Moscoso dispatched supplies for the governor with an escort of thirty horsemen. In the mean time the troops under De Soto were nearly perishing with hunger. They were compelled to leave their encampment in search of food. Fortunately, at no great distance, they found a beautiful valley, waving luxuriantly with fields of corn or maize. Here they encamped and here were soon joined by the escort and their welcome supplies. In a few days Moscoso came also with the residue of the army. They were about sixty miles north of Uribaracaxi. It is supposed the place is now known by the old Indian name of Palaklikaha.

The chief, whose name was Acuera, and all his people had fled to the woods. De Soto sent Indian interpreters to him with friendly messages and the declaration that the Spaniards had no desire to do him any injury; but that it was their power, if the Indians resisted, to punish them with great severity. He also commissioned them to make the declaration, [Pg 169] which to him undoubtedly seemed perfectly just and reasonable, but which, to our more enlightened minds, seems atrocious in the extreme, that it was their only object to bring him and his people into obedience to their lawful sovereign, the king of Spain. With this end in view, he invited the chief to a friendly interview. It can hardly be doubted that in that benighted age De Soto felt that he was acting the part of a just and humane man, and of a Christian, in extending the *Christian* reign of Spain over the heathen realms of Florida. Acuera returned the heroic reply:

"Others of your accursed race have, in years past, poisoned our peaceful shores. They have taught me what you are. What is your employment? To wander about like vagabonds from land to land; to rob the poor; to betray the confiding; to murder in cold blood the defenceless. With such a people I want no peace—no friendship. War, never-ending, exterminating war, is all the boon I ask. You boast yourself valiant; and so you may be, but my faithful warriors are not less brave; and this, too, you shall one day prove, for I have sworn to maintain an unsparing conflict while one white man remains in my borders; not openly, in battle, though even thus we fear not to meet you, but by stratagem, and ambush, and midnight surprisals. I am king in my own land, and will never become the vassal of a mortal like myself. As [Pg 170] for me and my people, we choose death, yes a hundred deaths, before the loss of our liberty and the subjugation of our country."

This answer certainly indicates a degree of intelligence and mental culture far above what we should expect to find in the chief of a tribe of Florida Indians. The chivalric spirit of De Soto compelled him to admire the heroism it displayed. He consequently redoubled his efforts to gain the friendship of the chief, but all in vain. For twenty days De Soto remained in this encampment, recruiting his troops and making arrangements for a farther advance. The Indians made constant warfare upon him, lurking in the thickets which densely surrounded his camp. No Spaniard could wander one hundred steps without danger of being shot down by an invisible foe, whose deadly arrow was more noiseless in its flight than the sighing of the breeze through the tree tops. In this way, during these twenty days, fourteen Spaniards were killed and many more wounded. Fifty Indians also fell struck by the bullets of the invaders. De Soto allowed himself only in a war of self-defence. He strictly prohibited his followers from doing any injury to the villages or the property of the natives, or of engaging in the slightest act of violence towards any who were not in active hostility against them.

After twenty days of such repose as could be [Pg 171] found in this war harassed camp, De Soto resumed his march. He directed the steps of his army in a northeasterly direction towards a town called Ocali, about sixty miles from their encampment. It seems that in most, if not all of this region, the chief and his principal town bore the same name.

The path of the army led just over a dreary expanse of desert sands, about thirty miles broad. There was no underbrush, and over the smooth surface both men and horses could travel with the greatest ease. They then entered upon a beautiful region of fertility and luxuriance. Fields of corn waved their graceful leaves and bannered heads in the breeze. Farm houses and pleasant villages were scattered around, indicating that peace, with its nameless blessings, reigned there. They reached the central town, Ocali, and found it to consist of six hundred substantially built houses. This would give the place a population of probably not less than three thousand.

But the chief, Ocali, and his principal inhabitants, with their effects, had fled to the forests. The Spanish army immediately took up its quarters in the dwellings of Ocali. They found here an ample supply of provisions, which they seem without any questionings to have appropriated to their own use. The clime was balmy, the region beautiful, the houses commodious, the food abundant, and the few Indians [Pg 172] who remained behind manifested no hostility. The common soldiers, following the example of their leader, treated all with great kindness.

De Soto sent several Indian messengers daily to the retreat of the chief with proffers of peace and friendship. Though Ocali rejected all these overtures, it seems that they must have made an impression on the minds of some of his followers.

One day, four young Floridian warriors, gorgeously dressed and with nodding plumes, came to the Spanish camp. De Soto received them with great cordiality and invited them to a handsome collation with his principal officers. Mr. Irving, in his well authenticated narrative, gives the following account of the scene which there ensued:

"They sat down and appeared to be eating quietly, when perceiving the Spaniards to be off their guard, they rose suddenly and rushed full speed to the woods. It was in vain for the Spaniards to pursue them on foot, and there was no horse at hand. A hound of uncommon sagacity, however, hearing the cry of the Indians, and seeing them run, pursued them. Overtaking and passing by the first and second and third, he sprang upon the shoulders of the foremost and pulled him to the ground; as the next Indian passed on, the dog, leaving the one already down, sprang upon his successor and secured him in [Pg 173] the same way. In like manner he served the third and fourth, and then kept running from one to the other, pulling them down as fast as they rose, and barking so furiously that the Indians were terrified and confounded and the Spaniards were enabled to overtake and capture them. They were taken back to the camp and examined separately. For as they were armed, the Spaniards apprehended some treachery; but it appeared that their sudden flight was only by way of exploit, to show their address and fleetness." [D]

Ocali, after resisting for six days all friendly advances, was at length induced to visit the Spanish camp. He was received by De Soto with the greatest kindness, and every effort was made to win his confidence. There was a deep and wide river near the village which it was necessary for the Spaniards to cross in their advance. De Soto, accompanied by Ocali and several of his subjects, was walking on the banks of this stream to select a spot for crossing, by means of a bridge or raft, when a large number of Indians sprang up from the bushes on the opposite side, and assailing them with insulting and reproachful language, discharged a volley of arrows upon them, by which one of the Spaniards was wounded.

Upon De Soto's demanding of the chief the meaning [Pg 174] of this hostile movement, Ocali replied, that they were a collection of his mutinous subjects, who had renounced their allegiance to him, in consequence of his friendship for the Spaniards. The bloodhound, to which we have alluded, that had so sagaciously captured the four Floridians, was in the company held in a leash by one of the servants of the governor. The moment the ferocious animal heard the yells of the Indians, and witnessed their hostile actions, by a desperate struggle he broke from his keeper and plunged into the river. In vain the Spaniards endeavored to call him back. The Indians eagerly watched his approach, and as he drew near they showered upon him such a volley of arrows, that more than fifty pierced his head and shoulders. He barely reached the land, when he fell dead. The army mourned the loss of the sagacious, fearless and merciless brute as if he had been one of the most valiant of their warriors.

It soon became evident that Ocali had but slight influence over his tribe. De Soto, apprehensive that it might be thought that he detained him against his will, advised him to return to his people, assuring him that he would always be a welcome guest in the Spanish camp. He left, and they saw him no more.

Crossing the river by a rude bridge constructed by the Spanish engineers, De Soto took the lead with [Pg 175] a hundred horse and a hundred foot. After a monotonous march of three days over a flat country, they came to a very extensive province called Vitachuco, which was governed in common by three brothers. The principal village, Ochile, was rather a fortress than a village, consisting of fifty large buildings strongly constructed of timber. It was a frontier military post; for it seems that this powerful tribe was continually embroiled in war with the adjacent provinces. Mr. Williams, in his History of Florida, locates Ochile just south of what is called the Allachua prairie.

There are two sources of information upon which we are dependent for most of the facts here recorded. One is, the "History of Hernando De Soto," written by the Inca Garcilaso de la Vega. He was the son of a Spanish nobleman and of a Peruvian lady of illustrious rank. His narrative was written as related to him, by a friend who was one of the expedition. With some probable exaggerations it is generally deemed authentic. Mr. Southey describes the work as one of the most delightful in the Spanish language.

The other is what is called "The Portuguese Narrative." It is from the pen of an anonymous writer, who declares himself to have been a Spanish cavalier, and that he describes the scenes of which he was an [Pg 176] eye-witness. Though these two accounts generally harmonize, there is at times very considerable discrepancy between their statements. In the extraordinary events now to be chronicled, the writer has generally endeavored to give the narrative, as has seemed to him most probable, in comparing the two accounts, with the well-established character of De Soto.

The advance guard of the Spanish army marched all night, and just before the dawn of the morning, entered the silent streets of Ochile. Wishing to produce as deep an impression as possible upon the minds of the Indians, their drums were beat, and their trumpets emitted their loudest blasts, as one hundred horsemen with clattering hoofs, and one hundred footmen with resounding arms, startled the citizens from their repose. To these simple natives, it must have been a scene almost as astounding as if a legion of adventurers, from the star Sirius, were at midnight to make their appearance in the streets of a European city.

The house of the chief was centrally situated. It was a large mansion, nearly three hundred feet in length by one hundred and twenty in width. There were also connected with it quite a number of outbuildings of very considerable dimensions.

As a matter of course, immediately the whole [Pg 177] population was in the streets in a state of utter amazement. It was the object of De Soto to appear in such strength, and to take such commanding positions, as would prevent any assault on the part of the Indians, which would lead to bloodshed. He was well informed of the warlike reputation of the chief who resided there; and knew that in that fortress he was surrounded by a numerous band of warriors, ever armed and always ready for battle. The region around was densely populated. Should the chief escape, determined upon hostility, and rally his troops around him, it might lead to sanguinary scenes, greatly to be deplored.

De Soto immediately held an interview with the chief; treated him with the utmost kindness and assured him that he had no intention of inflicting any injury upon him or any of his subjects; that he sought only for permission to pass peaceably and unmolested through his realms. The soldiers were strictly enjoined to treat the natives in the most friendly manner, and not to allow themselves, by any provocation whatever, to be drawn into a conflict.

The chief was very narrowly watched, that he might not escape. Still he was unconscious of his captivity, for he was held by invisible chains.

During the following day the main body of the army entered Ochile with all the pomp which prancing [Pg 178] horses richly accoutred, gorgeous uniforms, bugle-blasts, waving banners, and glittering armor could present. Ocile, its chief, and his warriors were at the mercy of the Spaniards. But they had come not as conquerors, but as peaceful travellers, with smiles and presents, and kindly words. Still the power of these uninvited guests was very manifest, and it was very evident that any hostility on the part of the natives would bring down upon them swift destruction.

It so happened, that the youngest of the three brother chiefs resided at Ochile. At the suggestion of De Soto, he sent couriers to his two brothers, informing them of the arrival of the Spaniards, of their friendly disposition, and of their desire simply to pass through the country unmolested. At the same time he stated, by request of De Soto, that the strength of the Spaniards was such that they were abundantly able to defend themselves; and that should any attack be made upon them, it would lead to results which all would have occasion to deplore.

The capital of the second brother was not far distant. In three days he came to Ochile, decorated in gorgeous robes of state and accompanied by a retinue of his warriors, in their most showy costume. It is recorded that he had the bearing of an accomplished gentleman, and seemed as much at ease amidst the wondrous surroundings of the Spanish [Pg 179] camp, as if he had been accustomed to them all his days. He entered into the most friendly relations with De Soto and his distinguished officers, and seemed very cordially to reciprocate all their courteous attentions.

[Pg 180]

CHAPTER XI.

The Conspiracy and its Consequences.

The Three Brother Chieftains.—Reply of Vitachuco to his Brothers.—Feigned Friendship for the Spaniards.—The Conspiracy.—Its Consummation and Results.—Clemency of De Soto.—The Second Conspiracy.—Slaughter of the Indians.—March of the Spaniards for Osachile.—Battle in the Morass.

Of the three brothers who reigned over this extended territory the elder bore the same name with the province which he governed, which was Vitachuco. He was far the most powerful of the three, in both the extent and populousness of his domain. His two brothers had united in sending an embassy to him, earnestly enjoining the expediency of cultivating friendly relations with the Spaniards. The following very extraordinary reply, which he returned, is given by Garcilaso de la Vega. And though he says he quotes from memory, still he pledges his word of honor, that it is a truthful record of the message Vitachuco sent back. We read it with wonder, as it indicates a degree of mental enlightenment, which we had not supposed could have been found among those semi-civilized people.

"It is evident," said the chief to his brothers, [Pg 181] "that you are young and have neither judgment nor experience, or you would never speak as you have done of these hated white men. You extol them as virtuous men, who injure no one. You say that they are valiant; are children of the Sun, and merit all our reverence and service. The vile chains which they have hung upon you, and the mean and dastardly spirit which you have acquired during the short period you have been their slaves, have caused you to speak like women, lauding what you should censure and abhor.

"You remember not that these strangers can be no better than those who formerly committed so many cruelties in our country. Are they not of the same nation and subject to the same laws? Do not their manner of life and actions prove them to be the children of the spirit of evil, and not of the Sun and Moon—our Gods? Go they not from land to land plundering and destroying; taking the wives and daughters of others instead of bringing their own with them; and like mere vagabonds maintaining themselves by the laborious toil and sweating brow of others!

"Were they virtuous, as you represent, they never would have left their own country; since there they might have practised their virtues; planting and cultivating the earth, maintaining themselves, without [Pg 182] prejudice to others or injury to themselves, instead of roving about the world, committing robberies and murders, having neither the shame of men nor the fear of God before them. Warn them not to enter into my dominions. Valiant as they may be, if they dare to put foot upon my soil, they shall never go out of my land alive."

De Soto and his army remained eight days at Ochile. By unwearied kindness, he so won the confidence of the two brother chiefs, that they went in person to Vitachuco to endeavor by their united representations to win him to friendly relations with the Spaniards. Apparently they succeeded. Vitachuco either became really convinced that he had misjudged the strangers, or feigned reconciliation. He invited De Soto and his army to visit his territory, assigning to them an encampment in a rich and blooming valley. On an appointed day the chief advanced to meet them, accompanied by his two brothers and five hundred warriors, in the richest decorations and best armament of military art as then understood by the Floridians.

De Soto and Vitachuco were about of the same age and alike magnificent specimens of physical manhood. The meeting between them was as cordial as if they had always been friends. The Indian warriors escorted their guests from their encampment to the [Pg 183] capital. It consisted of two hundred spacious edifices, strongly built of hewn timber. Several days were passed in feasting and rejoicing, when Juan Ortiz informed the governor that some friendly

Indians had revealed to him that a plot had been formed, by Vitachuco, for the entire destruction of the Spanish army.

The chief was to assemble his warriors, to the number of about ten thousand, upon an extensive plain, just outside the city, ostensibly to gratify De Soto with the splendors of a peaceable parade. To disarm all suspicion, they were to appear without any weapons of war, which weapons were however previously to be concealed in the long grass of the prairie. De Soto was to be invited to walk out with the chief to witness the spectacle. Twelve very powerful Indians, with concealed arms, were to accompany the chief or to be near at hand. It was supposed that the pageant would call out nearly all the Spaniards, and that they would be carelessly sauntering over the plain. At a given signal, the twelve Indians were to rush upon De Soto, and take him captive if possible, or if it were inevitable, put him to death.

At the same moment the whole band of native warriors, grasping their arms, was to rush upon the Spaniards in overpowering numbers of ten to one. In this way it was supposed that every man could speedily [Pg 184] be put to death or captured. Those who were taken prisoners were to be exposed to the utmost ingenuity of Indian torture.

This seemed a very plausible story. De Soto, upon careful inquiry, became satisfied of its truth. He consulted his captains, and decided to be so prepared for the emergence, that should he be thus attacked, the Indian chief would fall into the trap which he had prepared for his victims.

The designated day arrived. The sun rose in a cloudless sky and a gentle breeze swept the prairie. Early in the morning, Vitachuco called upon De Soto, and very obsequiously solicited him to confer upon him the honor of witnessing a grand muster of his subjects. He said they would appear entirely unarmed, but he wished De Soto to witness their evolutions, that he might compare them with the military drill of European armies. De Soto, assuming a very friendly and unsuspicious air, assured the chief, that he should be very happy to witness the pageant. And to add to its imposing display, and in his turn to do something to interest the natives, he said he would call out his whole force of infantry and cavalry, and arrange them in full battle array on the opposite side of the plain.

The chief was evidently much embarrassed by this proposition, but he did not venture to present any obstacles. [Pg 185] Knowing the valor and ferocity of his troops, he still thought that with De Soto as his captive, he could crush the Spaniards by overwhelming numbers. Matters being thus arranged, the whole Spanish army, in its most glittering array, defiled upon the plain. De Soto was secretly well armed. Servants were ready with two of the finest horses to rush to his aid. A body-guard of twelve of his most stalwart men loitered carelessly around him.

At nine o'clock in the morning, De Soto and Vitachuco walked out, side by side, accompanied by their few attendants and ascended a slight eminence which commanded a view of the field. Notwithstanding the careless air assumed by De Soto, he was watching every movement of Vitachuco with intensest interest. The instant the Indian chief gave his signal, his attendants rushed upon De Soto, and his ten thousand warriors grasped their arrows and javelins, and with the hideous war-whoop rushed upon the Spaniards. But at the same instant a bugle blast, echoing over the plain, put the whole Spanish army in motion in an impetuous charge. The two signals for the deadly conflict seemed to be simultaneous. The body-guard of De Soto, with their far superior weapons, not only repelled the Indian assailants, but seized and bound Vitachuco as their captive. De Soto lost not a moment in mounting a horse, led to him by his servant. [Pg 186] But the noble animal fell dead beneath him, pierced by many arrows. Another steed was instantly at his side, and De Soto was at the head of his cavalry, leading the charge. Never, perhaps, before, did so terrible a storm burst thus suddenly from so serene a sky.

The natives fought with valor and ferocity which could not be surpassed even by the Spaniards. All the day long the sanguinary battle raged, until terminated by the darkness of the night. The field was bordered, on one side, by a dense forest, and on the other by a large body of water, consisting of two lakes. Some of the natives escaped into the almost impenetrable forest. Many were drowned. Several of the young men, but eighteen years of age, who were taken captive,—the sons of chiefs,—developed a heroism of character which attracted the highest admiration of De Soto. They fought to the last possible moment, and when finally captured, expressed great regret that they had not been able to die for their country. They said to their conqueror,

"If you wish to add to your favors, take our lives. After surviving the defeat and capture of our chieftain, we are not worthy to appear before him, or to live in the world."

It is said that De Soto was greatly moved with compassion in view of the calamity which had befallen these noble young men. He embraced them [Pg 187] with parental tenderness, and commended their valor, which he regarded as proof of their noble blood.

"For two days," writes Mr. Irving, "he detained them in the camp, feasting them at his table and treating them with every distinction; at the end of which time he dismissed them with presents of linen, cloths, silks, mirrors and other articles of Spanish manufacture. He also sent by them presents to their fathers and relations, with proffers of friendship."

De Soto had succeeded in capturing four of the most distinguished captains of Vitachuco. They had been ostensibly the friends of the Spaniard, had ate at his table and had apparently reciprocated all his kindly words and deeds. While thus deceiving him, they had coöperated with Vitachuco for his destruction. De Soto summoned them with their chief before him.

"He reproached them," says Mr. Irving "with the treacherous and murderous plot, devised against him and his soldiers, at a time when they were professing the kindest amity. Such treason, he observed, merited death; yet he wished to give the natives evidence of his clemency. He pardoned them, therefore, and restored them to his friendship; warning them, however, to beware how they again deceived him, or trespassed against the safety and welfare of [Pg 188] the Spaniards, lest they should bring down upon themselves dire and terrible revenge."

Vitachuco was now a captive. Yet notwithstanding the conspiracy which had led to such deplorable results, De Soto treated him with great kindness, giving him a seat at his own table, and endeavoring in all ways to obliterate the remembrance of the conflict. De Soto was in search of gold. He had heard of mountains of that precious metal far away in the interior. The natives had no wealth which he desired to plunder. Their hostility he exceedingly deprecated, as it deprived him of food, of comforts, and exposed his little band to the danger of being cut off and annihilated, as were the troops of Narvaez, who had preceded him. The past career of De Soto proves, conclusively, that he was by nature a humane man, loving what he conceived to be justice.

Under these circumstances, a wise policy demanded that he should do what he could to conciliate the natives before he advanced in his adventurous journey, leaving them, if hostile, disposed to cut off his return. It is said that nine hundred of the most distinguished warriors of Vitachuco were virtually enslaved, one of whom was assigned to each of the Spaniards, to serve him in the camp and at the table. Such at least is the story as it comes down to us. Vitachuco formed the plan again to assail the Spaniards [Pg 189] by a concerted action at the dinner-table. Every warrior was to be ready to surprise and seize his master, and put him to death. There is much in this narrative which seems improbable. We will, however, give it to our readers as recorded by Mr. Irving in his very carefully written history of the Conquest of Florida. We know not how it can be presented in a more impartial manner.

"Scarcely had Vitachuco conceived this rash scheme than he hastened to put it into operation. He had four young Indians to attend him as pages. These he sent to the principal prisoners, revealing his plan, with orders that they should pass it secretly and adroitly from one to another, and hold themselves in readiness, at the appointed time, to carry it into effect. The dinner hour of the third day was the time fixed upon for striking the blow. Vitachuco would be dining with the governor, and the Indians in general attending upon their respective masters.

"The cacique was to watch his opportunity, spring upon the governor and kill him, giving at the moment of assault a war-whoop which should resound throughout the village. The war-whoop was to be the signal for every Indian to grapple with his master or with any other Spaniard at hand and dispatch him on the spot.

"On the day appointed Vitachuco dined as usual [Pg 190] with the governor. When the repast was concluded, he sprang upon his feet, closed instantly with the governor, seized him with the left hand by the collar, and with the other fist dealt him such a blow in the face as to level him with the ground, the blood gushing out of eyes, nose and mouth. The cacique threw himself upon his victim to finish his work, giving at the same time his signal war-whoop.

"All this was the work of an instant; and before the officers present had time to recover from their astonishment, the governor lay senseless beneath the tiger grasp of Vitachuco. One more blow from the savage would have been fatal; but before he could give it a dozen swords and lances were thrust through his body, and he fell dead.

"The war-whoop had resounded through the village. Hearing the fatal signal, the Indians, attending upon their masters, assailed them with whatever missile they could command. Some seized upon pikes and swords; others snatched up the pots in which meal was stewing at the fire, and beating the Spaniards about the head, bruised and scalded them at the same time. Some caught up plates, pitchers, jars, and the pestles wherewith they pounded the maize. Others seized upon stools, benches and tables, striking with impotent fury, when their weapons had not the power to harm. Others snatched up [Pg 191] burning fire-brands, and rushed like very devils into the affray. Many of the Spaniards were terribly burned, bruised and scalded. Some had their arms broken."

This terrible conflict was of short duration. Though the Spaniards were taken by surprise, they were not unarmed. Their long keen sabres gave them a great advantage over their assailants. Though several were slain, and many more severely wounded, the natives were soon overpowered. The exasperated Spaniards were not disposed to show much mercy. In these two conflicts with the Indians, Vitachuco fell, and thirteen hundred of his ablest warriors.

De Soto had received so terrific a blow, that for half an hour he remained insensible. The gigantic fist of the savage had awfully bruised his face, knocking out several of his teeth. It was four days before he recovered sufficient strength to continue his march and twenty days elapsed before he could take any solid food. On the fifth day after this great disaster the Spaniards resumed their journeyings in a northwest direction, in search of a province of which they had heard favorable accounts, called Osachile. The first day they advanced but about twelve miles, encamping upon the banks of a broad and deep river, which is supposed to have been the Suwanee.

A band of Indians was upon the opposite side of [Pg 192] the stream evidently in hostile array. The Spaniards spent a day and a half in constructing rafts to float them across. They approached the shore in such strength, that the Indians took to flight, without assailing them. Having crossed the river they entered upon a prairie country of fertile soil, where the industrious Indians had many fields well filled with corn, beans and pumpkins. But as they journeyed on, the Indians, in small bands, assailed them at every point from which an unseen arrow or javelin could be thrown. The Spaniards, on their march, kept in quite a compact body, numbering seven or eight hundred men, several hundred of whom were mounted on horses gayly caparisoned, which animals, be it remembered, the Indians had never before seen.

After proceeding about thirty miles through a pretty well cultivated country, with scattered farm-houses, they came to quite an important Indian town called Osachile. It contained about two hundred houses; but the terrified inhabitants had fled, taking with them their most valuable effects, and utter solitude reigned in its streets.

The country was generally flat, though occasionally it assumed a little of the character of what is called the rolling prairie. The Indian towns were always built upon some gentle swell of land. Where this could not be found, they often constructed artificial [Pg 193] mounds of earth, sufficient in extent to contain from ten to twenty houses. Upon one of these the chief and his immediate attendants would rear their dwellings, while the more humble abodes of the common people, were clustered around. At Osachile De Soto found an ample supply of provisions, and he remained there two days.

It is supposed that Osachile was at the point now called Old Town. Here De Soto was informed by captive Indians that about thirty leagues to the west there was a very rich and populous country called Appalachee. The natives were warlike in the highest degree, spreading the terror of their name through all the region around. Gold was said to abound there. The country to be passed through, before reaching that territory, was filled with gloomy swamps and impenetrable thickets, where there was opportunity for ambuscades. De Soto was told that the Appalachians would certainly destroy his whole army should he attempt to pass through those barriers and enter their borders.

This peril was only an incentive to the adventurous spirit of the Spanish commander. To abandon the enterprise and return without the gold, would be not only humiliating, but would be his utter ruin. He had already expended in the undertaking all that he possessed. He had no scruples of conscience to retard [Pg 194] his march, however sanguinary the hostility of the natives might render it. It was the doctrine of the so-called church at Rome, that Christians were entitled to the possessions of the heathen; and though De Soto himself by no means professed to be actuated by that motive, the principle unquestionably influenced nearly his whole army.

But he did assume that he was a peaceful traveller, desiring to cultivate only friendly relations with the natives, and that he had a right to explore this wilderness of the new world in search of those precious medals of which the natives knew not the value, but which were of so much importance to the interest of all civilized nations.

For three days the Spaniards toiled painfully along over an arid, desert plain, beneath a burning sun. About noon on the fourth day they reached a vast swamp, probably near the Estauhatchee river. This swamp was bordered by a gloomy forest, with gigantic trees, and a dense, impervious underbrush, ever stimulated to wonderful luxuriance by an almost tropical sun and a moist and spongy soil. Through this morass the Indians, during generations long since passed away, had constructed a narrow trail or path about three feet wide. This passage, on both sides, was walled up by thorny and entangled vegetation almost as impenetrable as if it were brick or stone.

[Pg 195]

In the centre of this gloomy forest, there was a sheet of shallow water about a mile and a half in width and extending north and south as far as the eye could reach. The Indians had discovered a ford across this lake till they came to the main channel in the centre, which was about one hundred and twenty feet wide. This channel, in the motionless waters, was passed by a rude bridge consisting of trees tied together.

De Soto encamped on the borders of this gloomy region for a short time to become acquainted with the route and to force the passage. There were various spots where the Indians, familiar with the whole region, lay in ambush. From their unseen coverts, they could assail the Spaniards with a shower of arrows as they defiled through the narrow pass, and escape beyond any possibility of pursuit. Compelling some Indians to operate as guides, under penalty of being torn to pieces by bloodhounds, De Soto commenced his march just after midnight. Two hundred picked men on foot, but carefully encased in armor, led the advance in a long line two abreast. Every man was furnished with his day's allowance of food in the form of roasted kernels of corn. They pressed along through a path which they could not lose, and from which they could not wander, till they reached the lake. Here the guides led them along by a narrow [Pg 196] ford, up to their waists in water, till they reached the bridge of logs. The advance-guard had just passed over this bridge when the day dawned, and they were discovered by the Indians, who had not supposed they would attempt to cross the morass by night.

The Appalachian warriors, with hideous yells and great bravery, rushed into the lake to meet their foes. Here Spaniard and Floridian grappled in the death struggle up to their waists in water. The steel-clad Spaniards, with their superior arms, prevailed, and the natives repulsed, rushed into the narrow defile upon the other side of the lake. The main body of the army pressed on, though continually and fiercely assailed by the arrows of the Indians. Arriving at a point where there was an expanse of tolerably dry ground, De Soto sent into the forests around forty skirmishers to keep off the Indians, while a hundred and fifty men were employed in felling trees and burning brush, in preparation for an encampment for the night.

Exhausted by the toil of the march and of the battle; drenched with the waters of the lake; many of them suffering from wounds, they threw themselves down upon the hot and smouldering soil for sleep. But there was no repose for them that night. During all the hours of darkness, the prowling natives kept up a continuous clamor, with ever recurring assaults. [Pg 197] With the first dawn of the morning the Spaniards resumed their march, anxious to get out of the defile and into the open prairie beyond, where they could avail themselves of their horses, of which the Indians stood in great dread. As they gradually emerged from the impenetrable thicket into the more open forest, the army could be spread out more effectually, and the horsemen could be brought a little more into action. But here the valor of the natives did not forsake them.

"As soon as the Spaniards," writes Mr. Irving, "entered this more open woodland, they were assailed by showers of arrows on every side. The Indians, scattered about among the thickets, sallied forth, plied their bows with intense rapidity, and plunged again into the forest. The horses were of no avail. The arquebusiers and archers seemed no longer a terror; for in the time a Spaniard could make one discharge, and reload his musket or place another bolt in his cross-bow, an Indian would launch six or seven arrows. Scarce had one arrow taken flight before another was in the bow. For two long leagues did the Spaniards toil and fight their way forward through this forest.

"Irritated and mortified by these galling attacks and the impossibility of retaliating, at length they emerged into an open and level country. Here, overjoyed [Pg 198] at being freed from this forest prison, they gave reins to their horses, and free vent to their smothered rage, and scoured the plain, lancing and cutting down every Indian they encountered. But few of the enemy were taken prisoners, many were put to the sword."

[Pg 199]

CHAPTER XII.

Winter Quarters.

Incidents of the March.—Passage of the River.—Entering Anhayea.—Exploring Expeditions.—De Soto's desire for Peace.—Capture of Capafi.—His Escape.—Embarrassments of De Soto.—Letter of Isabella.—Exploration of the Coast.—Discovery of the Bay of Pensacola.—Testimony Respecting Cafachiqué.—The March Resumed.

The Spaniards now entered upon a beautiful and highly cultivated region, waving with fields of corn and adorned with many pleasant villages and scattered farm-houses. It seemed to be the abode of peace, plenty and happiness. It certainly might have been such, but for the wickedness of man. Wearied with their long march and almost incessant battle, the Spaniards encamped in the open plain, where their horsemen would be able to beat off assaults.

But the night brought them no repose. It was necessary to keep a large force mounted and ready for conflict. The natives, in large numbers, surrounded them, menacing an attack from every quarter, repeatedly drawing near enough in the darkness to throw their arrows into the camp, and keeping up an incessant and hideous howling. After a sleepless [Pg 200] night, with the earliest light of the morning they resumed their march along a very comfortable road, which led through extensive fields of corn, beans, pumpkins and other vegetables. The prairie spread out before them in its beautiful, level expanse, till lost in the distant horizon. All the day long their march was harassed by bands of natives springing up from ambush in the dense corn-fields which effectually concealed them from view. Many were the bloody conflicts in which the natives were cut down mercilessly, and still their ferocity and boldness continued unabated.

After thus toiling on for six miles the Spaniards approached a deep stream, supposed to be the river Uche. It was crossed by a narrow ford with deep water above and below. Here the natives had constructed palisades, and interposed other obstacles, behind which, with their arrows and javelins, they seemed prepared to make a desperate resistance. De Soto, after carefully reconnoitering the position, selected a number of horsemen, who were most effectually protected with their steel armor, and sent them forward, with shields on one arm, and with swords and hatchets to hew away these obstructions, which were all composed of wood. Though several of the Spaniards were slain and many wounded, they effected a passage, when the mounted horsemen plunged [Pg 201] through the opening, put the Indians to flight and cut them down with great slaughter.

Continuing their march, on the other side of the river, for a distance of about six miles through the same fertile and well populated region, they were admonished by the approach of night, again to seek an encampment. The night was dark and gloomy. All were deeply depressed in spirits. An incessant battle seemed their destiny. The golden mountains of which they were in pursuit were ever vanishing away. They were on the same path which had previously been traversed by the cruel but energetic Narvaez, and where his whole company had been annihilated, leaving but four or five to tell the tale of the awful tragedy.

Dreadful as were the woes which these adventurers had brought upon the Indians, still more terrible were the calamities in which they had involved themselves. They were now three hundred miles from Tampa Bay. Loud murmurs began to rise in the camp. Nearly all demanded to return. But, for De Soto, the abandonment of the enterprise was disgrace, and apparently irretrievable ruin. There was scarcely any condition of life more to be deplored than that of an impoverished nobleman. De Soto was therefore urged onward by the energies of despair.

[Pg 202] Again through all the hours of the night, they were exposed to an incessant assault from their unwearied foes. From their captives they learned that they were but six miles from the village of Anhayea, where their chief, Capafi, resided. This was the first instance in which they heard of a chief who did not bear the same name as the town in which he dwelt. Early in the morning, De Soto, with two hundred mounted cavaliers and one hundred footmen, led the advance, and soon entered the village, which consisted of two hundred and fifty houses, well built and of large size.

At one end of the village stood the dwelling of the chief, which was quite imposing in extent, though not in the grandeur of its architecture. The chief and all his men had fled, and the Spaniards entered deserted streets. The army remained here for several days, finding abundance of food. Still they were harassed, day and night, by the indomitable energy of the natives. Two well armed expeditions were sent out to explore the country on the north and the west, for a distance of forty or fifty miles, while a third was dispatched to the south in search of the ocean.

Anhayea, where the main body of the army took up its quarters, is supposed to have been near the present site of the city of Tallahassee. The two [Pg 203] first expeditions sent out, returned, one in eight and the other in nine days, bringing back no favorable report. The other, sent in search of the ocean, was absent much longer, and De Soto became very apprehensive that it had been destroyed by the natives.

Through many perilous and wild adventures, being often betrayed and led astray by their guides, they reached, after a fortnight's travel, the head of the bay now called St. Mark's. Here they found vestiges of the adventurers who had perished in the ill-fated Narvaez expedition. There was a fine harbor to which reinforcements and fresh supplies of ammunition might be sent to them by ships from Cuba, or from Tampa Bay. With these tidings they hurried back to Anhayea.

They had now reached the month of November, 1539. The winter in these regions, though short, had often days of such excessive cold that men upon the open prairie, exposed to bleak winds called northers, often perished from the severity of the weather. De Soto resolved to establish himself in winter-quarters at Anhayea. With his suite he occupied the palace of the chief. The other houses were appropriated to the soldiers for their barracks. He threw up strong fortifications and sent out foraging parties into the region around, for a supply of provisions. As we have no intimation that any payment was [Pg 204] made, this was certainly robbery. Whatever may be said of the necessities of his case, it was surely unjust to rob the Indians of their harvests. Still, De Soto should not be condemned unheard; and while we have no evidence that he paid the natives for the food he took from them, still we have no proof that he did not do so.

In accordance with his invariable custom, he made strenuous efforts to win the confidence of the natives. Through captive Indians he sent valuable presents to the chief Capafi in his retreat, and also assurances that he sought only friendly relations between them. The chief, however, was in no mood to give any cordial response to these advances. He had taken refuge in a dense forest, surrounded by dismal morasses, which could only be traversed by a narrow pass known only to the Indians, where his warriors in ambush might easily arrest the march of the whole army of Spaniards. The brutal soldiery of Narvaez had taught them to hate the Spaniards.

He kept up an incessant warfare, sending out from his retreat fierce bands to assail the invaders by day and by night, never allowing them one moment of repose. Many of the Spaniards were slain. But they always sold their lives very dearly, so that probably ten natives perished to one of the Spaniards. There was nothing gained by this carnage. [Pg 205] De Soto was anxious to arrest it. Every consideration rendered it desirable for him to have the good will of the natives. Peace and friendship would enable him to press forward with infinitely less difficulty in search of his imaginary mountains of gold and silver, and would greatly facilitate his establishment of a colony around the waters of some beautiful bay in the Gulf, whence he could ship his treasures to Spain and receive supplies in return.

Finding it impossible to disarm the hostility of Capafi by any kindly messages or presents, he resolved if possible to take him captive. In this way only could he arrest the cruel war. The veneration of the Indians for their chief was such that, with Capafi in the hands of the Spaniards as a hostage, they would cease their attacks out of regard to his safety.

It was some time before De Soto could get any clew to the retreat in which Capafi was concealed. And he hardly knew how to account for the fact, that the sovereign of a nation of such redoubtable ferocity, should never himself lead any of his military bands, in the fierce onsets which they were incessantly making. At length De Soto learned that Capafi, though a man of great mental energy, was incapacitated from taking the field by his enormous obesity. He was so fat that he could scarcely walk, [Pg 206] and was borne from place to place on a litter. He could give very energetic commands, but the execution of them must be left to others. He also ascertained that this formidable chief had taken up his almost unapproachable quarters about twenty-five miles from Anhayea; and that in addition to the tangled thickets and treacherous morasses with which nature had surrounded him, he had also fortified himself in the highest style of semi-barbarian art, and had garrisoned his little fortress with a band of his most indomitable warriors.

Notwithstanding the difficulty of the enterprise, De Soto resolved to attempt to capture him. This was too arduous a feat to be entrusted to the leadership of any one but himself. He took a select body of horsemen and footmen, and after a very difficult journey of three days, came to the borders of the citadel where the chief and his garrison were intrenched. Mr. Irving, in his admirable history of the Conquest of Florida, gives the following interesting account of the fortress, and of the battle in which it was captured:

"In the heart of this close and impervious forest, a piece of ground was cleared and fortified for the residence of the Cacique and his warriors. The only entrance or outlet, was by a narrow path cut through the forest. At every hundred paces, this path was [Pg 207] barricaded by palisades and trunks of trees, at each of which was posted a guard of the bravest warriors. Thus the fat Cacique was ensconced in the midst of the forest like a spider in the midst of his web, and his devoted subjects were ready to defend him to the last gasp.

"When the Governor arrived at the entrance to the perilous defile, he found the enemy well prepared for its defence. The Spaniards pressed forward, but the path was so narrow that the two foremost only could engage in the combat. They gained the first and second palisades at the point of the sword. There it was necessary to cut the osiers and other bands, with which the Indians had fastened the beams. While thus occupied they were exposed to a galling fire and received many wounds. Notwithstanding all these obstacles, they gained one palisade after the other until, by hard fighting, they arrived at the place of refuge of the Cacique.

"The conflict lasted a long time, with many feats of prowess on both sides. The Indians however, for want of defensive armor, fought on unequal terms, and were most of them cut down. The Cacique called out to the survivors to surrender. The latter, having done all that good soldiers could do, and seeing all their warlike efforts in vain, threw themselves on their knees before the Governor and offered [Pg 208] up their own lives, but entreated him to spare the life of their Cacique.

"De Soto was moved by their valor and their loyalty; receiving them with kindness, he assured them of his pardon for the past, and that henceforth he would consider them as friends. Capafi, not being able to walk, was borne in the arms of his attendants to kiss the hands of the Governor, who, well pleased to have him in his power, treated him with urbanity and kindness."

Severe as had been the conflict, De Soto returned to Anhayea with his captive, highly gratified by the result of his enterprise. He had strictly enjoined it upon his troops not to be guilty of any act of wanton violence. On the march he had very carefully refrained from any ravaging of the country. He now hoped that, the chief being in his power and being treated with the utmost kindness, all hostilities would cease. But, much to his disappointment, the warriors of Capafi, released from the care of their chief, devoted themselves anew to the harassment of the Spaniards in every possible way.

Capafi seemed much grieved by this their conduct, assuming to be entirely reconciled to his conqueror. He informed De Soto that his prominent warriors, who directed the campaign, had established their headquarters in a dense forest about thirty [Pg 209] miles from Anhayea. He said that it would be of no avail for him to send messengers to them, for they would believe that the messages were only such as De Soto compelled their chief to utter. He however offered to go himself to the camp of his warriors, accompanied by such a guard of Spanish troops as De Soto might deem it best to send with him. He expressed the assurance, that he should be enabled to induce his warriors to throw down their arms.

De Soto accepted the proposition. In the early morning a strong escort of infantry and cavalry left the village to conduct the chief to the encampment of the natives. Skillful guides accompanied them, so that they reached the vicinity of the encampment just as the sun was going down. The chief sent forward scouts immediately, to inform his friends of his approach. The Spaniards, weary of their long day's march, and convinced of the impossibility of the escape of the chief, who could scarcely walk a step, were very remiss in watchfulness. Though they established sentinels and a guard, in accordance with military usage, it would seem that they all alike fell asleep. It is probable that the wily chief had sent confidential communications to his warriors through his scouts.

The Spaniards were encamped in the glooms of [Pg 210] the forest. At midnight, when darkness, silence and solitude reigned, Capafi stealthily crept on his hands and knees, a few rods from his sleeping guard, into the thicket, where a band of Indian runners met him with a litter and bore him rapidly away beyond all chance of successful pursuit. The Spaniards never caught glimpse of their lost captive again. When they awoke their chagrin and dread of punishment were extreme. The sentinels, who had been appointed to watch the captive, solemnly averred, in excuse for their neglect, that during the night demoniac spirits had appeared, and had borne away the unwieldy chief through the air.

As all the band were implicated in the escape, all were alike ready to aver that, during the night, they had witnessed very strange sights and heard very strange sounds. When they carried back this report, the good-natured De Soto, convinced that fretting and fault-finding would do no good, appeased their alarm by saying, with a peculiar smile:

"It is not strange. These Indian wizards perform feats far more difficult than conjuring away a fat chief."

The winter passed slowly away. The natives were a very ferocious race; tall, strong, athletic, and delighting in war. Every day and every hour brought alarm and battle. The Indians conducted a harassing [Pg 211] and destructive warfare. In small bands they roamed through the forest, cutting off any who ventured to wander from the town. It required a large amount of food to supply the wants of the army in Anhayea. Not a native carried any provisions to the town, and it was necessary for De Soto to send out foraging expeditions, at whatever risk. The winter was cold. Fires were needed for warmth and cooking. But the sound of an axe could not be heard in the forest, without drawing upon the wood-cutters, a swarm of foes. De Soto found himself in what is called a false position; so that he deemed it necessary to resort to cruel and apparently unjustifiable expedients.

He took a large number of Indian captives. These he compelled to be his hewers of wood and drawers of water. He would send a party of Spaniards into the forests for fuel. Each man led an Indian as a servant to operate in the double capacity of a shield against the arrows of the natives, and a slave to collect and bring back the burden. To prevent the escape of these Indians, each one was led by a chain, fastened around his neck or waist. Sometimes these natives would make the most desperate efforts to escape; by a sudden twitch upon the chain they would endeavor to pull it from the hands of their guard, or to throw him down and, seizing any club [Pg 212] within their reach, would spring upon him with the ferocity of a tiger.

In various ways more than twenty Spaniards lost their lives, and many more were seriously wounded. It was indeed a melancholy winter for the army of De Soto. Their supplies were so far expended that it was needful for them to await the arrival of their vessels in the Bay of St. Marks. It will also be remembered, that De Soto had sent back an expedition to cut its way for a distance of three hundred miles through hostile nations to Ucita, and to summon the garrison there, to set out on a march to join him at Anhayea. Five months were thus spent in weary waiting.

It is estimated that De Soto's force in Anhayea, including the captives who were servants or slaves, amounted to about fifteen hundred persons. He had also over three hundred horses. The fertility of the region was however such, with its extended fields of corn, beans, pumpkins and other vegetables, that it was not necessary to send foraging parties to a distance of more than four or five miles from the village. On the 29th of December, 1539, the two brigantines, which had sailed from Tampa Bay, came into St. Marks, then called the Bay of Aute. For twelve days before the arrival of the ships, De Soto had kept companies of horse and foot marching and [Pg 213] countermarching between Anhayea and the Bay, to keep the communication open. They also placed banners on the highest trees, as signals to point out the place of anchorage.

Juan De Añasco, who had command of the vessels, left them well manned in the bay, and with the remainder of the ship's company marched to Anhayea, under escort of the troops sent him by De Soto.

Soon after this, Pedro Calderon arrived with his gallant little band of a hundred and twenty men. By a series of the wildest adventures and most heroic achievements they had cut their way through a wilderness thronging with foes, where an army of eight hundred men had with difficulty effected a passage. Fighting every step of the way and bearing along with them their wounded, their progress was necessarily slow. Several of their number were killed and many wounded. Of the wounded, twelve died soon after they reached Anhayea.

Their arrival in the village was a cause of great gratification to all there. De Soto received them as an affectionate father welcomes his son whom he had supposed to have been lost. The rumor had reached the Governor that all had been slain on the road.

Captain Calderon brought a letter to De Soto, from his wife Isabella. We find the following [Pg 214] interesting extract from this letter in the life of De Soto by Mr. Lambert A. Wilmer. It seems to bear internal evidence of authenticity, though we know not the source from which Mr. Wilmer obtained it. The spirit of the letter is in entire accord with the noble character which Mr. Washington Irving gives Isabella, in his life of Columbus and his companions.

"I have lately had some conversation with Las Casas, the Bishop of Chiapa. He has convinced me that the behavior of our people to the Indians is inexcusable in the sight of God, however it may be overlooked by men in high authority. The Bishop has proved to me that all who have taken part in the abuse of these harmless people, have been visited in this life with the manifest displeasure of heaven; and God grant that they may not be punished in the life to come according to the measure of their offense.

"I hope, my dearest husband that no considerations of worldly advantage will make you neglectful of the precepts of humanity and of the duties of religion. Be persuaded to return to me at once; for you can gain nothing in Florida which can repay me for the sorrow and anxiety I feel in your absence. Nor for all the riches of the country would I have you commit one act the remembrance of which would be painful to you hereafter. If you have [Pg 215] gained nothing I shall be better satisfied, because there may be the less cause for repentance. Whatever may have been your want of success or your losses, I implore you to come to me without delay; for any reverse of fortune is far better than the suspense and misery I now endure."

This letter must have caused De Soto great perplexity. But for reasons which we have above given he could not make up his mind to abandon the enterprise, and return to Cuba an unsuccessful and impoverished man.

De Soto now ordered the two vessels under Diego Maldonado to explore the coast to the westward, carefully examining every river and bay. It would seem also probable that at the same time he fitted out an expedition of fifty foot soldiers, to march along the coast on a tour of discovery. Maldonado, after a sail of about two hundred miles, entered the beautiful bay of Pensacola, then called Archusi. It was an admirable harbor, and with shores so steep and bold that ships could ride in safety almost within cable length of the land. No Spaniards had previously visited that region, consequently the natives were friendly. They came freely on board, bringing fruits and vegetables, and inviting the strangers to the hospitality of their homes.

Maldonado was allowed without molestation to [Pg 216] explore the bay in all directions, taking careful soundings. The vessels returned to the bay of Aute, after an absence of but eight weeks. De Soto was highly gratified with the results of the expedition. It seemed to him that the shores of the bay of Pensacola presented just the position he desired for the location of his colony. He had thus far failed, in his search for gold, but it seemed to him still possible that he might lay the foundation of a populous and powerful empire.

It was now the latter part of February, and an almost vertical sun was throwing down its rays upon them. Maldonado was dispatched with the brigantines to Havana, to return with a supply of clothing, ammunition and such other freight as was needful for the army in its isolated condition. He received orders to be back in the bay of Pensacola, by the first of October. In the mean time De Soto with his army was to make a long circuit through the country, in search of gold. De Soto had received information of a distant province called Cofachiqui, which was governed by a queen, young and beautiful. It was said that this nation was quite supreme over the adjacent provinces, from which it received tribute and feudal homage.

Two lads but sixteen years of age had come to Anhayea, from this province in company with some [Pg 217] Indian traders. So far as they could make themselves understood, though very unskilful interpreters, they represented the country as abounding in silver, gold and precious stones. In pantomime they described the process of mining and smelting the precious metals so accurately that experienced miners were convinced that they must have witnessed those operations.

In the month of March, 1540, De Soto left his comfortable quarters, and commenced his march for that province, in a northeasterly direction. Their path led first through an almost unpeopled wilderness many leagues in extent. Each soldier bore his frugal supper or food upon his back. It consisted mainly of roasted corn pounded or ground into meal.

An unobstructed but weary tramp of three days brought them through this desert region to a very singular village, called Capachiqui. In the midst of a vast morass, there was an island of elevated and dry ground. Here quite a populous village was erected, which commanded a wide spread view of the flat surrounding region. The village could only be approached by several causeways crossing the marsh, about three hundred feet in length. The country beyond was fertile and sprinkled with small hamlets. Eight hundred armed warriors, on the open plain, presented a force which the most valiant Indians would not venture to assail. The Spaniards entered [Pg 218] the village by these causeways unopposed, and found there a not inhospitable reception.

The day after their arrival, seven of De Soto's body-guard, thoughtless and rollicking young men, set out, without authority from their superior officers, to seek amusement in the neighboring hamlets. They had scarcely reached the main land, beyond the marsh, when the Indians, from an ambush, rushed upon them, and after a very fierce struggle all but one were slain, and that one, Aguilar, was mortally wounded. The soldiers in the village hastened to the relief of their comrades, but they were too late. Aguilar, in a dying condition, was carried back to the encampment. He had, however, sufficient strength left to make the following extraordinary statement:

"You must know that a band of more than fifty savages sprang out of the thickets to attack us. The moment, however, they saw that we were but seven, and without our horses, seven warriors stepped forth, and the rest retired to some distance. They began the attack, and as we had neither arquebus nor cross-bow, we were entirely at their mercy. Being more agile, and fleet of foot than our men, they leaped around us like so many devils, with horrid laughter, shooting us down like wild beasts without our being able to close with them. My poor comrades [Pg 219] fell one after the other, and the savages seeing me alone, all seven rushed upon me, and with their bows battered me as you have witnessed."

This singular event took place within the territory of Appalachee. It is said that the Spaniards not unfrequently met with similar instances, in which the natives disdained to avail themselves of superior numbers.

[Pg 220]

CHAPTER XIII.

Lost in the Wilderness.

Incidents at Achise—Arrival at Cofa.—Friendly Reception by Cofaqui.—The Armed Retinue.—Commission of Patofa.—Splendors of the March.—Lost in the Wilderness.—Peril of the Army.—Friendly Relations.—The Escape from the Wilderness.—They Reach the Frontiers of Cofachiqui.—Dismissal of Patofa.—Wonderful Reception by the Princess of Cofachiqui.

After a couple of days of rest and feasting, the Spanish army resumed its march. De Soto led the advance with forty horsemen and seventy foot soldiers. Ere long they entered the province of Attapaha, from which the river Attapaha probably takes its name. On the morning of the third day they approached a village called Achise. The affrighted natives had fled. Two warriors who had tarried behind, were captured as the dragoons came dashing into the streets. They were led into the presence of De Soto. Without waiting to be addressed by him, they haughtily assailed him with the question,

"What is it you seek in our land? Is it peace, [Pg 221] or is it war?" De Soto replied, through his interpreter,

"We seek not war with any one. We are in search of a distant province; and all that we ask for is an unobstructed passage through your country, and food by the way."

The answer seemed to them perfectly satisfactory, and they at once entered apparently into the most friendly relations. The captives were set at liberty and treated by the Spaniards, in all respects, as friends. Promptly the two warriors sent a message to their chief, informing him of the peaceful disposition of the Spaniards, and he accordingly issued orders to his people not to molest them.

In this pleasant village, and surrounded by this friendly people, De Soto spent three days. He then resumed his journey, in a northeasterly direction, along the banks of some unknown river, fringed with mulberry trees, and winding through many luxuriant and beautiful valleys. The natives were all friendly, and not the slightest collision occurred. For eleven days the army continued its movements, encountering nothing worthy of note.

They then entered a province called Cofa. De Soto sent couriers in advance to the chief with proffers of friendship. The chief, in return, sent a large number of Indians laden with food for the strangers. [Pg 222] With the provisions were sent rabbits, partridges, and a species of dog whose flesh was held in high esteem. The Spaniards suffered for want of meat; for though game in the forest was abundant, being constantly on the march, they had no time for hunting.

The chief of Cofa received the Spaniards in his metropolitan town with great hospitality. He assigned his own mansion to De Soto, and provided comfortable quarters for all his troops. The natives and the Spaniards mingled together without the slightest apparent antagonism. The province of Cofa was of large extent, populous and fertile. Here the Spaniards remained five days, entertained by the abounding hospitality of the chief.

De Soto had thus far brought with him a piece of ordnance, which had proved of very little service. It was heavy and exceedingly difficult of transportation. He decided to leave it behind him with this friendly people. To impress them, however, with an idea of its power as an engine of destruction, he caused it to be loaded and aimed at a large oak tree just outside of the village. Two shots laid the oak prostrate. The achievement filled both the chief and his people with amazement and awe.

Again the army resumed its march towards the next province, which was called Cofaqui whose [Pg 223] chief was brother of Cofa. The Spaniards were escorted by Cofa and a division of his army, during one day's journey. The friendly chief then took an affectionate leave of De Soto, and sent forward couriers to inform his brother of the approach of the Spaniards and to intercede for his kindly offices in their behalf. It required a march of six days to reach the territory of the new chieftain.

In response to Cofa's message, Cofaqui dispatched four of his subordinate chiefs, with a message of welcome to the Spaniards. He sent out his runners to bring him speedy intelligence of their approach. As soon as he received news that they were drawing near, he started himself, with a retinue of warriors in their richest decorations, to welcome the strangers. The meeting, on both sides, was equally cordial. Side by side, almost hand in hand, the Floridians and the Spaniards entered the pleasant streets of Cofaqui. The chief led De Soto to his own mansion, and left him in possession there while he retired to another dwelling.

The intercourse between these two illustrious men seemed to be as cordial as that between two loving brothers. The Floridian chief, with great frankness, gave De Soto information respecting the extent, population and resources of his domain. He informed him that the province of Cofachiqui, of [Pg 224] which he was in search, could only be reached by a journey of seven days, through a dreary wilderness. But he offered, should De Soto decide to continue his journey, to send a strong band of his army, to accompany him with ample supplies. De Soto afterwards ascertained that there was some duplicity in this proposal; or rather, that the chief had a double object in view. It appeared, that there had been long and hereditary antagonism between the province of Cofaqui, and that of Cofachiqui; and the chief availed himself of that opportunity to invade the territory of his rival.

Scouts were sent out in all directions to assemble the warriors, and De Soto was surprised to find an army of four thousand soldiers, and as many burden-bearers, ready to accompany him. The provisions, with which they were fully supplied, consisted mainly of corn, dried plums and nuts of various kinds. Indian hunters accompanied the expedition to search the forests for game.

The Spaniards at first were not a little alarmed in finding themselves in company with such an army of natives; outnumbering them eight to one, and they were apprehensive of treachery. Soon, however, their fears in that direction were allayed, for the chief frankly avowed the object of the expedition. Summoning before him Patofa, the captain of the [Pg 225] native army, he said to him, in presence of the leading Spanish officers in the public square:

"You well know that a perpetual enmity has existed between our fathers and the Indians of Cofachiqui. That hatred you know has not abated in the least. The wrongs we have received from that vile tribe still rankle in our hearts, unavenged. The present opportunity must not be lost. You, at the head of my braves, must accompany this chief and his warriors, and, under their protection, wreak vengeance on our enemies."

Patofa, who was a man of very imposing appearance, stepped forward, and after going through several evolutions with a heavy broadsword carved from wood, exceedingly hard, said:

"I pledge my word to fulfill your commands, so far as may be in my power. I promise, by aid of the strangers, to revenge the insults and deaths, our fathers have sustained from the natives of Cofachiqui. My vengeance shall be such, that the memory of past evils shall be wiped away forever. My daring to reappear in your presence will be a token that your commands have been executed. Should the fates deny my hopes, never again shall you see me, never again shall the sun shine upon me. If the enemy deny me death, I will inflict upon myself the punishment my cowardice or evil fortune will merit."

[Pg 226]

It was indeed a large army which then commenced its march, for it consisted of four thousand native warriors, and four thousand retainers to carry supplies and clothing, and between eight and nine hundred Spaniards. The Indians were plumed and decorated in the highest style of military display. The horses of the Spaniards were gayly caparisoned, and their burnished armor glittered in the sun. Silken banners waving in the breeze and bugle peals echoing over the plains, added both to the beauty and the sublimity of the scene.

The Spaniards conducted their march as in an enemy's country, and according to the established usages of war. They formed in squadrons with a van and rear guard. The natives followed, also in martial array; for they were anxious to show the Spaniards that they were acquainted with military discipline and tactics. Thus in long procession, but without artillery trains or baggage wagons, they moved over the extended plains and threaded the defiles of the forest. At night they invariably encamped at a little distance from each other. Both parties posted their sentinels, and adopted every caution to guard against surprise.

Indeed, it appears that De Soto still had some distrust of his allies, whose presence was uninvited, and with whose company he would gladly have dispensed. [Pg 227] The more he reflected upon his situation, the more embarrassing it seemed to him. He was entering a distant and unknown province, ostensibly on a friendly mission, and it was his most earnest desire to secure the good-will and coöperation of the natives. And yet he was accompanied by an army whose openly avowed object was to ravage the country and to butcher the people.

The region upon which they first entered, being a border land between the two hostile nations, was almost uninhabited, and was much of the way quite pathless. It consisted, however, of a pleasant diversity of hills, forests and rivers. The considerable band of hunters which accompanied the native army, succeeded in capturing quite an amount of game for the use of the troops. For seven days the two armies moved slowly over these widely extended plains, when they found themselves utterly bewildered and lost in the intricacies of a vast, dense, tangled forest, through which they could not find even an Indian's trail. The guides professed to be entirely at fault, and all seemed to be alike bewildered.

De Soto was quite indignant, feeling that he had been betrayed and led into an ambush for his destruction. He summoned Patofa to his presence and said to him:

[Pg 228]

"Why have you, under the guise of friendship, led us into this wilderness, whence we can discover no way of extricating ourselves? I will never believe that among eight thousand Indians there is not one to be found capable of showing us the way to Cofachiqui. It is not at all likely that you who have maintained perpetual war with that tribe, should know nothing of the public road and secret paths leading from one village to another."

Patofa made the following frank and convincing reply.

"The wars that have been waged between these two provinces, have not been carried on by pitched battles nor invasions of either party, but by skirmishes by small bands who resort to the streams and rivers we have crossed, to fish; and also by combats between hunting parties, as the wilderness we have traversed is the common hunting ground of both nations. The natives of Cofachiqui are more powerful and have always worsted us in fight. Our people were therefore dispirited and dared not pass over their own frontiers.

"Do you suspect that I have led your army into these deserts to perish? If so, take what you please. If my head will suffice, take it; if not you may behead every Indian, as they will obey my mandate to the death."

[Pg 229]

The manner of Patofa was in accordance with these feeling and manly words. De Soto no longer cherished a doubt of his sincerity, and became also convinced that their guides were utterly unable to extricate him. Under these circumstances nothing remained but blindly to press forward or to retrace his steps. They at length found some narrow openings in the forest through which they forced their way until they arrived, just before sunset, upon the banks of a deep and rapid stream which seemed to present an impassable barrier before them.

They had no canoes or rafts with which to cross the river; their food was nearly consumed, as it had been supposed that a supply for seven days would be amply sufficient to enable them to traverse the desert. To turn back was certain death by starvation; to remain where they were was equal destruction; to go forward seemed impossible, for they had not sufficient food to support them even while constructing rafts. It was the darkest hour in all their wanderings. Despair seemed to take possession of all hearts excepting that of De Soto. He still kept up his courage, assuming before his people an untroubled and even cheerful spirit.

The river afforded water to drink. A large grove of pine trees bordering the river, beneath whose fragrant shade they were encamped, sheltered them [Pg 230] from the sun. The level and extended plain, dry and destitute of underbrush, presented excellent camping-ground. Food only was wanting. But without this food in a few short days the whole army must perish.

De Soto, that very evening leaving the armies there, took a detachment of horse and foot and set off himself in search of some relief or path of extrication. Late in the night he returned, perplexed and distressed, having accomplished nothing. A council of war was held. It was promptly decided that the armies should remain where they were while detachments were sent in all directions in search of food or of some path of escape.

These detachments left early in the morning and returned late at night having discovered neither road nor corn-field, nor habitation. De Soto then organized four bands of horse and two of foot to go up and down the river, and to penetrate the interior, and to make as wide an exploration as possible within the limit of five days. Each band was accompanied by a large number of natives. Patofa himself went with one of these detachments. A thousand Indian warriors were scattered through the forest in search of a road and such game as could be found. The Governor remained on the banks of the river anxiously awaiting their return.

[Pg 231]

"The four thousand Indians," writes Mr. Irving, "who remained with him, sallied out every morning and returned at night, some with herbs and roots that were eatable, others with fish, and others again with birds and small animals killed with their bows and arrows. These supplies were, however, by no means sufficient for the subsistence of such a multitude.

"De Soto fared equally with his men in every respect; and, though troubled and anxious for the fate of his great expedition, he wore a sunny countenance to cheer up his followers. These chivalrous spirits appreciated his care and kindness, and to solace him they concealed their sufferings, assumed an air of contentedness, and appeared as happy as though revelling in abundance."

Most of the exploring parties suffered no less from hunger than did their companions who remained behind. Juan De Añasco, after traversing the banks of the river for three days, had his heart gladdened by the sight of a small village. From an eminence he saw that the country beyond was fertile, well cultivated and dotted here and there with hamlets. In the village, for some unexplained reason, he found a large amount of provisions accumulated, consisting mainly of corn. He immediately dispatched four horsemen back to De Soto with the joyful tidings. [Pg 232] They took with them such food as they could carry. This proved to be the first village in the long-sought-for province of Cofachiqui.

It will be remembered that Patofa, the commander-in-chief of the native army, had, with a large number of his warriors, accompanied Añasco. He had pledged his word to his chief that he would do everything in his power to harass, pillage and destroy their ancestral foes. Añasco encamped his band a little outside the village. At midnight Patofa and his warriors crept stealthily from the encampment, pillaged the temple which contained many treasures prized by the Indians, and killed and scalped every native whom they met, man, woman or child. When Añasco awoke in the morning and found what they had done, he was terrified. The outrage had been committed by troops under his own command. He was apprehensive that every man in the village, aided by such warriors as could be gathered from around, would rush upon him in revenge, and that he and his enfeebled followers would be destroyed. Immediately he commenced a retreat to meet De Soto, who he doubted not would be promptly on the move to join him.

The four couriers reached the camp in one day, though in their slow exploring tour it had required three days to accomplish the forty miles which they [Pg 233] had traversed. The troops were overjoyed at the glad tidings, and immediately prepared to resume their march. Several of their detachments had not yet returned. In order to give them information of the direction which the army had taken, De Soto wrote a letter, placed it in a box, and buried it at the foot of a tree. Upon the bark of the tree, he had these words conspicuously cut: "Dig at the root of this pine, and you will find a letter."

The half famished troops, inspired with new energies, reached the village in a day and a half, where their hunger was appeased. The scattered detachments arrived a few days after. The force of De Soto was too strong for the natives to attack him, notwithstanding the provocation they had received. He found, however, much to his chagrin, that he was utterly unable to restrain the savage propensities of his allies. For seven days the Spaniards sojourned in this frontier village of Cofachiqui. Warlike bands were continually stealing out, penetrating the region around, killing and scalping men, women and children, and committing every conceivable outrage of barbaric warfare.

De Soto could endure this no longer. He called Patofa before him, and told him in very emphatic terms that he must return to his own province. He thanked the chieftain very cordially for his friendly [Pg 234] escort, made him a present of knives, clothing, and other valuables, and dismissed him and his followers. Patofa was not unwilling to return. He was highly gratified with the presents he had received, and still more gratified that he had been permitted to wreak vengeance on his hereditary foes.

Two days after his departure, the Spanish army was again in motion, along the banks of the river. Every step they took revealed to them the awful ravages committed by the bands of Patofa. They passed many dwellings and many small hamlets, where the ground was covered with the scalpless bodies of the dead. The natives had fled in terror to the woods, so that not a living being was encountered. There was, however, a plentiful supply of food in the villages, and the army again enjoyed abundance.

The heroic Añasco was sent in advance to search out the way and, if possible, to capture some Indians as guides. He took with him a small band of thirty foot-soldiers, who were ordered to move as noiselessly as possible, that they might, perchance, come upon the natives by surprise. There was quite a broad, good road leading along the banks over which the band advanced. Night came upon them when they were about six miles ahead of the army. They were moving in profound silence and with noiseless [Pg 235] step through a grove, when they heard, just before them, the sounds of a village. The barking of dogs, the shouts of children, and the voices of men and women, reached their ears. Pressing eagerly forward, hoping to capture some Indians in the suburbs, they found that there was a sudden turn in the river and that they stood upon the banks of its deep and swiftly flowing flood, with the village on the other side. There was no means of crossing, neither would it have been prudent to have crossed with such small numbers, not knowing the force they might encounter there.

They dispatched couriers back in the night, to inform De Soto of their discovery. By the break of day, the army was again in motion, De Soto himself taking the lead, with one hundred horse and one hundred foot. When he reached the banks, and the natives upon the opposite shore caught sight of his glittering dragoons, on their magnificent steeds, they were struck with amazement and consternation.

It would seem that the language of these different tribes must have been essentially the same, for Juan Ortiz was still their interpreter. He shouted across the river, assuring the natives of the friendly intentions of the Spaniards, and urging them to send some one over to convey a message to their chief. After some little hesitation and deliberation, the Indians [Pg 236] launched a large canoe, in which six Indians of venerable appearance took their seats, while quite a number of lusty men grasped the oars. Very rapidly the canoe was driven through the water.

De Soto, who had watched these movements with deep interest, perceived that he was about to be visited by men of much importance. He had therefore brought forward and placed upon the banks a very showy throne, or chair of state, which he always carried with him for such purposes. Here he took his seat, with his retinue of officers around him.

The native chieftains landed without any apparent fear, approached him with three profound reverences, and then with much dignity inquired, "Do you come for peace or for war?"

"I come for peace," De Soto replied, "and seek only an unmolested passage through your land. I need food for my people, and implore your assistance, by means of canoes and rafts, to cross the river."

The Indians replied, that they were themselves somewhat destitute of provisions; that a terrible pestilence the preceding year had swept off many of their inhabitants; and that others in their consternation had fled from their homes, thus neglecting to cultivate the fields.

They said that their chieftain was a young princess who had recently inherited the government, and [Pg 237] that they had no doubt that she would receive them with hospitality, and do everything in her power, to promote their welfare. Having thus concluded this friendly interview, the chiefs returned to the other side of the river.

Very soon the Spaniards, who eagerly watched every movement, perceived a decided commotion in the village. A large and highly decorated canoe appeared upon the banks; then quite a gorgeous palanquin was seen borne by four men, descending towards the stream; then several other canoes of imposing structure seemed to be preparing for an aquatic procession. From the palanquin a graceful girl, showily dressed, entered the state canoe and reclined upon cushions in the stern under a canopy. Eight female attendants accompanied her.

The six ambassadors, who had already visited De Soto, took seats in the canoe which led the van, driven as before by a large number of sinewy arms. The royal barge was attached to this canoe and was towed by it. Several other boats, filled with distinguished men, followed in the rear, completing the imposing show.

As the young princess stepped on shore, all the Spaniards were deeply impressed with her dignity, grace and beauty. To their eyes, she was in form and feature as perfect as any image which Grecian [Pg 238] artist ever sculptured. Her attendants brought with them a chair of state upon which she took her seat after courteously bowing to the Governor. Through an interpreter they immediately entered into conversation. The princess confirmed the statement of her ambassadors in reference to the pestilence, but offered to do everything in her power to provide them with food. She offered one-half of her own residence to De Soto for his accommodation, and one-half of the houses in her village as barracks for the soldiers. She also promised that by the next day rafts and canoes should be in readiness to transport the Spaniards across the river.

The generous soul of De Soto was deeply touched, and he assured her of his lasting friendship and that of his sovereign. At the close of the interview the princess rose, and as a present, suspended a string of costly pearls around the neck of De Soto. The Governor then rose and presented her with a ring of gold set with a ruby, which she placed upon one of her fingers. Thus terminated this extraordinary interview. What a difference between peace and war!

"Were half the power that fills the world with terror,
Were half the wealth bestowed on camps and courts,
Given to redeem the human mind from error,
There were no need for arsenals or forts.

[Pg 239] "The warrior's name would be a name abhorred;
And every nation that should lift again
Its hand against a brother, on its forehead
Would wear forevermore the curse of Cain."

[Pg 240]

CHAPTER XIV.

The Indian Princess.

Crossing the River.—Hospitable Reception.—Attempts to visit the Queen Mother.—Suicide of the Prince.—Futile search for Gold.—The Discovery of Pearls.—The Pearl Fishery.—The Princess a Captive.—Held in Silken Chains.—Her Escape.—Location of Cutifachiqui.—The March Resumed.

The next day after the extraordinary interview which we have described in the last chapter, the princess ordered several large rafts to be constructed, and with these, aided by a number of canoes, the army crossed the rapid stream. Four horses, in attempting to swim the swift river, were carried away and drowned. These animals were so precious that the loss was deplored by the whole army.

When the troops had all crossed, they found very pleasant accommodations provided for them. Some were lodged in the village. For the rest commodious wigwams were erected just outside of the village in a beautiful mulberry grove on the river banks. The province of Cofachiqui was found to be very fertile and quite densely populated. The natives were in [Pg 241] complexion nearly as white as the Spaniards. They had agreeable features, graceful forms, and were very frank and amiable in disposition. They did not seem to be fond of war, though often involved in conflicts with their neighbors. According to the custom of the times, all prisoners of war were enslaved and were employed in servile labor. To prevent their escape the cruel expedient was adopted of cutting the main tendon of one leg just above the heel.

The mother of the princess of this tribe was a widow, residing in a retired home about thirty-six miles down the river. De Soto, who was anxious to secure the firm friendship of this interesting people, expressed an earnest desire to see the queen mother. The princess immediately dispatched twelve of her chieftains to urge her mother to visit her, that she might be introduced to the strange visitors, and see the wonderful animals on which they rode.

She however declined the invitation, expressing her very decided disapproval of the conduct of her daughter, as both inexpedient and indelicate, in entering into such friendly relations with utter strangers, of whose ulterior designs she could know nothing. This message, greatly increased the desire of De Soto to have an interview with the queen mother, that he might conciliate her friendship. He therefore dispatched Juan De Añasco, who was alike distinguished [Pg 242] for bravery and prudence, with thirty companions on foot, to convey to her presents and friendly messages, and very earnest requests that she would visit them at the court of her daughter.

The princess sent a near relative of the family as guide to this party—a young man about twenty-one years of age, and exceedingly attractive both in person and character. He was richly habited in garments of soft deerskin, beautifully fringed and embroidered, with a head-dress of various colored plumes.

"In his hand he bore a beautiful bow, so highly polished as to appear as if finely enamelled. At his shoulder hung a quiver full of arrows. With a light and elastic step and an animated and gallant air his whole appearance was that of an ambassador, worthy of the young and beautiful princess whom he served."

The morning was somewhat advanced, ere they left the village. It was a beautiful day in a lovely clime. Their route led down the banks of the river through luxuriant and enchanting scenery. After a pleasant walk of ten or twelve miles, they rested in the shade of a grove, for their noonday meal. Their young guide had been very social all the way, entertaining them with information of the region through which they were passing, and of the people. As they were partaking of their refreshments, suddenly [Pg 243] the aspect of their young companion became greatly altered. He was silent, thoughtful and apparently deeply depressed. At length he quietly took the quiver from his shoulder, and slowly and seemingly lost in deep reflection, drew out the arrows one by one. They were very beautiful, of the highest possible finish, keenly pointed, and triangularly feathered.

The Spaniards took them up, admired them greatly, and passed them from hand to hand. At length he drew out an arrow barbed with flint, long, and sharp, and shaped like a dagger. Casting an anxious glance around, and seeing the attention of the Spaniards engrossed in examining his weapons, he plunged the keen pointed arrow down his throat, severing an artery, and almost immediately fell dead. The soldiers were shocked and bewildered, not being able to conceive of any reason for the dreadful occurrence. There were several Indian attendants in the company, who seemed to be overwhelmed with distress, uttering loud cries of grief over the corpse.

It subsequently appeared, that the young guide was a great favorite with the queen mother; that he knew that she was very unwilling to have any acquaintance with the Spaniards, and he apprehended that it was their object to seize her and carry her off by violence. The thought that he was guiding them to her retreat overwhelmed him. He could [Pg 244] not endure the idea of meeting her, and perhaps of being reproached as her betrayer.

On the other hand, the queen, whom he revered and loved, had commissioned him to conduct the Spaniards to her mother's abode. He did not dare to disobey her commands. Either alternative was more to be dreaded by him than death. The ingenuous young man had, therefore, endeavored to escape from the dilemma by self-destruction.

Juan De Añasco was not only deeply grieved by the fate of his young friend, but also greatly perplexed as to the course he was then to pursue. None of the Indian attendants knew where the widow was concealed. He took several natives prisoners, and anxiously inquired of them respecting the residence of the queen mother. But either they could not, or would not, give him any information. After wandering about fruitlessly until noon of the next day, he returned to the camp, much mortified in reporting to De Soto the utter failure of his expedition.

Two days after his return, an Indian came to him and offered to conduct him down the river in a canoe, to the dwelling of the queen mother. Eagerly he accepted the proposition. Two large canoes, with strong rowers, were prepared. Añasco, with twenty companions, set out on this second expedition. The [Pg 245] queen heard of his approach, and, with a few attendants, secretly fled to another retreat far away. After a search of six days, the canoes returned, having accomplished nothing. De Soto relinquished all further endeavors to obtain an interview with the widow.

In the meantime, while Añasco was engaged in these unsuccessful enterprises, De Soto was making very anxious inquiries respecting the silver and the gold which he had been informed was to be found in the province. The princess listened to his description of the yellow metal and the white metal of which he was in search, and said that they were both to be found in great abundance in her territories. She immediately sent out some Indians, to bring him specimens. They soon returned laden with a yellow metal somewhat resembling gold in color, but which proved to be nothing but an alloy of copper. The shining substance which he had supposed was silver, was nothing but a worthless species of mica, or quartz. Thus again, to his bitter disappointment, De Soto awoke from his dreams of golden treasure, to the toils and sorrows of his weary life.

The princess seemed to sympathize with her guest in the bitterness of his disappointment. In her attempts at consolation, she informed him that [Pg 246] at the distance of about three miles from where they were, there was a village called Talomeco, which was the ancient capital of the realm; that here there was a vast sepulchre, in which all the chieftains and great warriors had been buried; that their bodies were decorated with great quantities of pearls.

De Soto, with a large retinue of his own officers and of the household of the princess, visited this mausoleum. Much to his surprise, he found there an edifice three hundred feet in length, and one hundred and twenty in breadth, with a lofty roof. The entrance was decorated with gigantic statuary of wood. One of these statues was twelve feet in height. In the interior many statues and carved ornaments were found.

A large number of wooden chests or coffins contained the decaying bodies of the illustrious dead. By the side of each of these there was another smaller chest, containing such valuables as it was probably supposed the chief would need in the spirit-land. Both the Inca and the Portuguese narrative agree in the account of the almost incredible number of pearls there found. It is said that the Spaniards obtained fourteen bushels, and that the princess assured them, that by visiting the mausoleums of the various villages, they could find enough pearls to load down all the horses of the army.

[Pg 247]

The Spaniards generally were greatly elated at the discovery of these riches. Pearls were estimated at a value almost equal to diamonds. It is said that Queen Cleopatra possessed a single pearl which was valued at three hundred and seventy-five thousand dollars. Philip II. of Spain received as a present a pearl, about the size of a pigeon's egg, valued at one hundred and sixty thousand dollars.

De Soto was urged to establish his colony upon this river, which has variously been conjectured to have been the St. Helena, the Oconee, the Ogeechee, and the Savannah. The country was beautiful and fertile; the climate delightful; and apparently an inexhaustible pearl fishery near. It was urged that an agricultural colony could be established on the fertile banks of the river, while from the seaport at its mouth a lucrative trade could be carried on with the mother country for all the rich productions of Spain.

But the persistent spirit of De Soto was not to be turned from its one great all-absorbing object, the search for gold. He urged, and with great show of reason, that, in consequence of the recent pestilence, there was not sufficient provision in the country, to support the army for a month; that by continuing their march they might enter far richer provinces, and might find mines of gold. Should [Pg 248] they be disappointed, they could easily return; and in the meantime, the Indians having replanted their land, the fields would wave with abundant golden harvests.

In an army of eight or nine hundred Spanish adventurers, there would of course be many worthless characters, difficult of restraint. De Soto had been in this village several weeks. Notwithstanding all his endeavors to promote peace and friendship, several broils had arisen between the natives and some of the low and degraded of his soldiery. The conduct of these vile men had produced a general feeling of ill-will among the natives. Even the princess herself manifested estrangement. She had become distant and reserved, and was evidently desirous that her no longer welcome guests should take their speedy departure. There were some indications that the princess so far distrusted the Spaniards that, like her more prudent mother, she was about secretly to escape from them by flight.

This would leave the Spaniards in a very embarrassed condition. They needed guides to conduct them through the extended territory of the princess. Heavily armed as they were, they needed porters to carry their burdens of extra clothing and provisions. The flight of the princess would be the signal for the natives, all over the territory, to rise in a war of [Pg 249] attempted extermination. The queen mother would doubtless do everything in her power to rouse and stimulate this hostility. The Spaniards thus assailed on every side, destitute of guides, without porters to carry their baggage, and with but little food, would find themselves compelled in self-defence, to cut their way, with blood-dripping sabres, through their foes, to rob their granaries, and to leave behind them a path strown with the dead, and filled with misery.

Again De Soto found himself in a false position. Again he felt constrained to do that which his own conscience told him was unjust. The only possible way, as it seemed to him, by which he could obtain extrication from these awful difficulties, was to seize the person of the princess, his friend and benefactor, and hold her as a captive to secure the good behavior of her subjects. He knew that their love for her was such that so long as she was in his power, they would not enter upon any hostile movement which might bring down vengeance upon her head.

If De Soto had accepted the spirit of the noble letter from Isabella, and had said, "I will no longer persevere in this invasion of the lands of others, which is always plunging me more and more deeply into difficulties,"—had he said frankly to the friendly [Pg 250] princess, "I have decided to return to my home, and I solicit your friendly coöperation to assist me on my way;" and had he made her a present, in token of his gratitude, of some of those articles with which he could easily have parted, and which were of priceless value to her, he might doubtless have retired unmolested. Instead of this he followed the infamous example which Pizarro had set him in Peru.

He appointed a guard, who were directed to keep a constant watch upon the princess, so that she could by no possibility escape; at the same time he informing her, in the most courteous tones, that the protection of his army and of her own people rendered it necessary that she should accompany him on his march. He held her in silken chains, treating her with the utmost delicacy and deference. The princess had sufficient shrewdness to affect compliance with this arrangement. It certainly accomplished the desired effect. All strife between the natives and the Spaniards ceased, a sufficient body of porters accompanied the army, and its march was unimpeded. A beautiful palanquin was provided for the princess, and the highest honors were lavished upon her.

Colonel A. J. Pickett, in his interesting and very carefully prepared History of Alabama, speaking of the locality of this village where De Soto tarried [Pg 251] so long, and encountered so many adventures, says:

"He entered the territory of the present Georgia at its southwestern border, and successively crossing the Ockmulgee, Oconee, and Ogeechee, finally rested on the banks of the Savannah, immediately opposite the modern Silver Bluff. On the eastern side was the town of Cutifachiqui, where lived an Indian queen, young, beautiful, and unmarried, and who ruled the country around to a vast extent. In 1736 George Golphin, then a young Irishman, established himself as an Indian trader at this point, and gave the old site of Cutifachiqui the name of Silver Bluff. The most ancient Indians informed him that this was the place where De Soto found the Indian princess; and this tradition agrees with that preserved by other old traders, and handed down to me."

According to this statement the village of Cutifachiqui was on the eastern bank of the Savannah river, in Barnwell county, in the State of South Carolina. On the morning of the 4th of May, 1540, De Soto again put his army in motion, taking with him the beautiful queen and her retinue of plumed warriors. All this country was then called Florida. The army advanced rapidly up the eastern bank of the Savannah river, where [Pg 252] they forded the stream, and, again entering the present State of Georgia, traversed nearly its whole breadth until they reached the head waters of the Coosa river. Here, at the confluence of the Oostanaula and Etowa rivers, they found a large Indian town called Chiaha, near the present site of Rome.

While on the march across the State of Georgia, the queen, probably dreading to be carried captive beyond her own domain, and aided by an understanding with her retinue, leaped from the palanquin and disappeared in a dense forest through which they were passing. De Soto never saw her or heard from her again. Undoubtedly a band of her warriors were in rendezvous there to receive her.

For five days the adventurers pressed along as rapidly as possible, over a hilly country about sixty miles in breadth. Though well watered, and abounding in beautiful valleys, luxuriant with mulberry groves and rich prairies, it seemed to be quite uninhabited.

Having crossed this mountainous region, they reached a populous district called Guachule. The chief had received an intimation of the approach of the Spaniards, and that they came as messengers of peace and not of war. When De Soto and his band, led by native guides whom they had picked up by the way, had arrived [Pg 253] within two miles of the village of the chief, they discovered him approaching them with a retinue of five hundred plumed warriors, adorned with glittering robes and weapons in the highest style of semi-barbaric display. The chief was unembarrassed, dignified, and courtly in his address. He received De Soto with truly fraternal kindness, escorted him to his village, which consisted of three hundred spacious houses, in a beautiful valley of running streams at the base of adjacent hills.

The dwelling of the chief was upon a spacious artificial mound, the summit of which was sufficiently broad for the large edifice, leaving a terrace all around it about twelve feet in breadth. Here De Soto remained four days, enjoying the hospitality of the friendly Cacique.

Resuming their journey, the army marched down the banks of a large stream, supposed to be the Etowa, which empties into the Coosa. For five days they continued their march through an uninteresting country, almost destitute of inhabitants, until, having traversed, as they supposed, about ninety miles, they came in sight of a large village, called Chiaha.

De Soto, having arrived opposite the great town of Chiaha, which probably occupied the present [Pg 254] site of Rome, crossed the Oostanaula in canoes, and upon rafts made of logs, prepared by the Indians, and took up his quarters in the town. The noble young chief received De Soto with unaffected joy, and made him the following address:

"Mighty Chief:—Nothing could have made me so happy as to be the means of serving you and your warriors. You sent me word from Guaxule to have corn collected to last your army two months. Here I have twenty barns full of the best which the country can afford. If I have not met your wishes respect my tender age, and receive my good-will to do for you whatever I am able."

The Governor responded in a kind manner, and was then conducted to the chief's own house, prepared for his accommodation. The confluence of the Oostanaula and Etowa at this point forms the Coosa. Here De Soto remained for a fortnight, recruiting his wearied men and his still more exhausted horses. It was bright and balmy summer, and the soldiers encamping in a luxuriant mulberry grove a little outside of the town, enjoyed, for a season, rest and abundance. De Soto, as usual, made earnest inquiries for gold. He was informed that about thirty miles north of him there were mines of copper, and also of some [Pg 255] metal of the color of copper, but finer, brighter, and softer; and that the natives sometimes melted them together in their manufacture of barbs, spearheads, and hatchets.

This intelligence excited De Soto with new hopes. He had occasionally met on his way natives with hatchets composed of copper and gold melted together. As the province, which was called Chisca, was separated from Chiaha by a pathless wilderness which horses could not traverse, De Soto sent two of his most trusty followers on an exploring tour through the region, conducted by Indian guides. After an absence of ten days they returned with the disappointing report that they found nothing there but copper of different degrees of purity.

The rivers in the vicinity of Chiaha seem to have abounded with pearl oysters, and large numbers of beautiful pearls were obtained. The natives nearly spoiled them all by boring them through with a red-hot rod, that they might string them as bracelets. One day the Cacique presented De Soto with a string of pearls six feet in length, each pearl as large as a filbert. These gems would have been of almost priceless value but for the action of fire upon them.

De Soto expressed some curiosity to see how [Pg 256] the pearls were obtained. The Cacique immediately dispatched forty canoes down the river to fish during the night for pearl oysters. In the morning De Soto accompanied the Cacique to the banks of the river where the oysters were collected. Large fires were built, and the oysters placed upon the glowing coals. The heat opened them, and the pearls were sought for. From some of the first thus opened ten or twelve pearls were obtained, about the size of peas. They were all, however, more or less injured by the heat. Col. Pickett says that the oyster mentioned was the muscle, to be found in all the rivers of Alabama.

Again De Soto commenced his journey, leaving the friendly chief and his people well contented with the presents he made them of gayly colored cloths, knives, and other trinkets. Following the banks of the Coosa to the west they soon entered what is now the State of Alabama, and on the second of July came to a large native town named Acoste. The tribe, or nation, inhabiting this region, was famed for its martial prowess. The Cacique, a fierce warrior, did not condescend to advance to meet De Soto, but at the head of fifteen hundred of his soldiers, well armed and gorgeously uniformed, awaited in the public square the approach of the Spanish chief. De Soto encamped [Pg 257] his army just outside of the town, and, with a small retinue, rode in to pay his respects to the Cacique.

Some of the vagabond soldiers straggled into the city, and were guilty of some outrages, which led the natives to fall upon them. De Soto, with his accustomed presence of mind, seized a cudgel and assisted the natives in fighting the Spaniards, while at the same moment he dispatched a courier to summon the whole army to his rescue. Peace was soon established, but there was some irritation on both sides. The next morning De Soto was very willing to leave the neighborhood, and the chief was not unwilling to have him.

De Soto crossed the river Coosa to the eastern banks, and journeying along in a southerly direction, at the rate of about twelve miles a day, passed over a fertile and populous region, nearly three hundred miles in extent. It is supposed his path led through the present counties of Benton, Talladega, Coosa, and Tallapoosa, in Alabama. Throughout the whole route they were treated by the natives with the most profuse hospitality, being fed by them liberally, and supplied with guides to lead them from one village to another. The province which De Soto was thus traversing, and which was far-famed for its beauty and fertility, was called Coosa.

[Pg 258]

"With a delightful climate, and abounding in fine meadows and beautiful little rivers, this region was charming to De Soto and his followers. The numerous barns were full of corn, while acres of that which was growing bent to the warm rays of the sun and rustled in the breeze. In the plains were plum trees, peculiar to the country, and others resembling those of Spain. Wild fruit clambered to the tops of the loftiest trees, and lower branches were laden with delicious Isabella grapes." [E]

This is supposed to have been the same native grape, called the Isabella, which has since been so extensively cultivated.

[Pg 259]

CHAPTER XV.

The Dreadful Battle of Mobila.

The Army in Alabama.—Barbaric Pageant.—The Chief of Tuscaloosa.—Native Dignity.—Suspected Treachery of the Chief.—Mobila, its Location and Importance.—Cunning of the Chief.—The Spaniards Attacked.—Incidents of the Battle.—Disastrous Results.

On the 15th of July, 1540, the army came in sight of the metropolitan town of the rich and populous province through which it was passing. The town, like the province, bore the name of Coosa. The army had travelled slowly, so that the native chief, by his swift footmen, had easily kept himself informed of all its movements. When within a mile or two of Coosa, De Soto saw in the distance a very splendid display of martial bands advancing to meet him. The friendly greeting he had continually received disarmed all suspicion of a hostile encounter.

The procession rapidly approached. At its head was the chief, a young man twenty-six years of age, of admirable figure and countenance, borne in a chair palanquin upon the shoulders of four of his warriors. A thousand soldiers, in their most gaudy [Pg 260] attire, composed his train. As they drew near, with the music of well-played flutes, with regular tread, their mantles and plumes waving in the breeze, all the Spaniards were alike impressed with the beauty of the spectacle. The chief himself was decorated with a mantle of rich furs gracefully thrown over his shoulders. His diadem was of plumes very brilliantly colored. He addressed De Soto in the following speech:

"Mighty chief, above all others of the earth. Although I come now to receive you, yet I received you many days ago deep in my heart. If I had the whole world it would not give me as much pleasure as I now enjoy at the presence of yourself and your incomparable warriors. My person, lands, and subjects are at your service. I will now march you to your quarters with playing and singing." [F]

De Soto made a suitable response. Then the two armies, numbering, with their attendants, more than two thousand men, commenced their march toward the town. The native chief was borne in his palanquin, and De Soto rode on his magnificent charger by his side. The royal palace was assigned to De Soto, and one-half of the houses in the town were appropriated to the soldiers for their lodgings.

The town of Coosa, which consisted of five hundred [Pg 261] houses, was situated on the east bank of the river of the same name, between two creeks now known as Talladega and Tallasehatchee. During a residence of twelve days in this delightful retreat, some slight disturbance arose between some of the natives and some of the Spanish soldiers. It was, however, easily quelled by the prudence and friendly disposition of the chief and the Governor. Indeed, the native chief became so attached to De Soto as to urge him to establish his colony there. Or if he could not consent to that arrangement, at least to spend the winter with him.

"But De Soto," writes Mr. Irving, "was anxious to arrive at the bay of Achusi, where he had appointed Captain Diego Maldonado to meet him in the autumn. Since leaving the province of Xuala he had merely made a bend through the country, and was now striking southerly for the sea-coast."

On the 20th of August the Spanish army, after having spent twenty-five days at Coosa, was again in movement. The chief of Coosa, and a large body of his warriors, accompanied De Soto to their frontiers, evidently as a friendly retinue. The Portuguese Narrative makes the incredible assertion that they were all prisoners, compelled to follow the army for its protection and as guides. With much more probability it is represented that one of the chief's [Pg 262] subordinate officers on the frontier was in a state of insurrection, and that upon that account the chief gladly accompanied the

Spaniards, hoping to overawe his refractory subjects by appearing among them with such formidable allies.

The Spaniards now entered the territory of Tuscaloosa, who was the most warlike and powerful chieftain of all the southern tribes. His domain comprised nearly the whole of the present States of Alabama and Mississippi. The Tuscaloosa, or Black Warrior river, flowed through one of the richest of his valleys. Though there were no mails or telegraphs in those days, Indian runners conveyed all important intelligence with very considerable rapidity. The chief had heard of the approach of the Spaniards, and the annalists of those days say, we know not with what authority, that he hesitated whether to receive them as friends or foes. Whatever may have been his secret thoughts, he certainly sent his son, a young man of eighteen, with a retinue of warriors, to meet De Soto with proffers of friendship.

The young ambassador was a splendid specimen of manhood, being taller than any Spaniard or Indian in the army, and admirably formed for both strength and agility. In his bearing he was self-possessed and courteous, appearing like a gentleman [Pg 263] accustomed to polished society. De Soto was much impressed by his appearance and princely manners. He received him with the utmost kindness, made him several valuable presents, and dismissed him with friendly messages to his father, stating that he cordially accepted of his friendship, and would shortly visit him.

De Soto then crossed the river Tuscaloosa, or Black Warrior, having first taken an affectionate leave of the Cacique of Coosa, who had accompanied him to this frontier river. A journey of two days brought the Spaniards to within six miles of the large village where the chief of Tuscaloosa was awaiting their arrival. As they reached this spot in the evening, they encamped for the night in a pleasant grove. Early the next morning De Soto sent forward a courier to apprise the chief of his arrival, and set out soon after himself, accompanied by a suitable retinue of horsemen.

The chief had, however, by his own scouts, kept himself informed of every movement of the Spaniards. He had repaired with a hundred of his nobles, and a large band of warriors, to the summit of a hill, over which the route of the Spaniards led, and which commanded a magnificent prospect of the country for many leagues around. He was seated on a chair of state, and a canopy of parti-colored [Pg 264] deerskin, very softly tanned, and somewhat resembling a large umbrella, was held over his head. His chief men were arranged respectfully and in order near him, while at a little distance his warriors were posted in martial bands. The whole spectacle, crowning the smooth and verdant hill, presented a beautiful pageant.

The Cacique was about forty years of age, and of gigantic proportions, being, like his son, nearly a head taller than any of his attendants. He was well-formed, and his countenance indicated perfect self-possession, intelligence, and great firmness. The sight of the cavaliers approaching with their silken banners, their glittering armor, and bestride their magnificent steeds, must have been astounding in the highest degree to one who had never seen a quadruped larger than a dog. But the proud chief assumed an air of imperturbable gravity and indifference.

One would have supposed that he had been accustomed to such scenes from his childhood. He did not deign even to look upon the horsemen, though some of them endeavored to arrest his attention by causing the animals to prance and rear. Without taking the slightest notice of the cavaliers who preceded De Soto, his eye seemed instantly to discern the Governor. As he approached, the chief [Pg 265] courteously arose, and advanced a few steps to meet him. De Soto alighted from his horse, and with Spanish courtesy embraced the chieftain, who, with great dignity, addressed him in the following words:

"Mighty chief, I bid you welcome. I greet you as I would my brother. It is needless to talk long. What I have to say can be said in a few words. You shall know how willing I am to serve you. I am thankful for the things you have sent me, chiefly because they were yours. I am now ready to comply with your desires."

This interview, it is supposed, took place in the present county of Montgomery, Alabama. The whole party then returned to the village, De Soto and the chief walking arm in arm. A spacious house was assigned to De Soto and his suite by the side of that occupied by the Cacique.

After a rest of two days in the village, enjoying the rather cold and reserved, but abundant hospitality of the chief, the Spaniards continued their march. The chief, either for his own pleasure or by persuasion, was induced to accompany him. The most powerful horse in the army was selected to bear his herculean frame; and yet it is said that when the Cacique bestrode him his feet almost touched the ground. De Soto had made him a present of a dress and mantle of rich scarlet cloth [Pg 266] Thus habited and mounted, with his towering plumes, he attracted all eyes. The two chieftains rode side by side. Their route led through the counties of Montgomery, Lowndes, and the southeastern part of Dallas, until they came to a large town called Piache, upon the Alabama river. This stream they passed on rafts of log and cane, probably in the upper part of the county of Wilcox. The expedition then turned in a southerly direction, following down the western bank of the Alabama through Wilcox county.

The Indian chief continued proud and distant; was observed to be frequently consulting with his principal men, and often dispatching runners in different directions. De Soto was led to suspect that some treachery was meditated. Two of the Spaniards, who had wandered a little distance in the woods, disappeared, and were never heard of again. It was suspected that they had been killed by the natives. The Cacique being questioned upon the subject, angrily and contemptuously replied:

"Why do you ask me about your people? Am I their keeper?"

These suspicions led De Soto to keep a close watch upon the chief. This was done secretly, while still friendly relations were maintained between them. It was more than probable that the [Pg 267] chief was himself a spy in the Spanish camp, and that he was treacherously gathering his powerful armies at some favorable point where he could effectually annihilate the Spaniards, and enrich himself with all their possessions of armor and horses. It was therefore a matter of prudence, almost a vital necessity, for De Soto to throw an invisible guard around the chieftain, that all his movements might be narrowly observed, and that he might not take to sudden flight. With him in their hands as a hostage, the hostility of his warriors might, perhaps, be effectually arrested.

They were now approaching the town of Mobila, which was the capital of the Tuscaloosa kingdom. This town was probably situated at a place now called Choctaw Bluff, on the north or western side of the Alabama river, in the county of Clarke. At that point the Spaniards were at a distance of about twenty-five miles above the confluence of the Alabama and the Tombigbee, and about eighty-five miles from the bay of Pensacola. The town was beautifully situated upon a spacious plain, and consisted of eighty very large houses; each one of which, it was stated, would accommodate a thousand men.

As they approached this important place, De Soto sent forward some very reliable couriers, to observe [Pg 268] if there were any indications of conspiracy. Early in the morning of the eighteenth of October, 1540, De Soto with the advance guard of his army, consisting of one hundred footmen, all picked men, accompanied by the Cacique, entered the streets of Mobila. Mr. Irving gives the following interesting account of this important capital:

"This was the stronghold of the Cacique, where he and his principal men resided. It stood in a fine plain, and was surrounded by a high wall, formed of huge trunks of trees driven into the ground, side by side, and wedged together. These were crossed, within and without, by others, small and longer, bound to them by bands made of split reeds and wild vines. The whole was thickly plastered over with a kind of mortar, made of clay and straw trampled together, which filled up every chink and crevice of the wood-work, so that it appeared as if smoothed with a trowel. Throughout its whole circuit, the wall was pierced at the height of a man with loopholes, whence arrows might be discharged at an enemy, and at every fifty paces, it was surmounted by a tower capable of holding seven or eight fighting men."

As De Soto and the chief, accompanied by the advance guard of the Spanish army, and a numerous train of Indian warriors, approached the walls, a [Pg 269] large band of native soldiers, in compact martial array, and as usual gorgeously decorated, emerged from one of the gates. They were preceded by a musical band, playing upon Indian flutes, and were followed by a group of dancing girls, remarkably graceful and beautiful. As we have mentioned, De

Soto, and the Cacique in his scarlet uniform, rode side by side. Traversing the streets, the whole band arrived in the central square. Here they alighted, and all the horses were led outside the walls to be tethered and fed.

The chief then, through Juan Ortiz, the interpreter, pointed out to De Soto one of the largest houses for the accommodation of himself and suite. Another adjoining house was appropriated to the servants and attendants. Cabins were also immediately reared just outside the walls for the accommodation of the main body of the army.

De Soto was somewhat anxious in view of this arrangement. It was effectually separating him from his soldiers, and was leaving the Cacique entirely at liberty. Some words passed between the chief and the Governor, which led to an angry reply on the part of the Cacique, who turned upon his heel and retired to his own palace. The main body of the army had not yet come up, and if the chief [Pg 270] meditated treachery, the moment was very favorable for an attack upon the advance guard only.

Soon after the Cacique had left in an angry mood, one of the cavaliers whom De Soto had sent forward to examine into the state of affairs, entered with the announcement that many circumstances indicated a dark and treacherous plot. He said that more than ten thousand warriors, all evidently picked men, and thoroughly armed, were assembled in the various houses. Not a child was to be found in the town, and scarcely a woman, excepting the few dancing girls who had formed a part of the escort.

The Governor was much alarmed by these tidings. He dispatched orders to all the troops who were with him to be on the alert, and to hold themselves in readiness to repel an assault. At the same time he sent back a courier to inform Luis De Moscoso, who was master of the Spanish camp, of the dangerous posture of affairs. Unfortunately, relying upon the friendly spirit of the natives, he had allowed his men to scatter widely from the camp, hunting and amusing themselves. It was some time before they could be collected.

De Soto, anxious to avert a rupture, wished to get the person of the Cacique in his power. They had been accustomed since they met to eat together. [Pg 271] As soon as the attendants of the Governor had prepared some refreshments for him, he sent Juan Ortiz to invite the Cacique to join him in the repast. The interpreter was not permitted to enter the palace, but after a little delay, a messenger announced that the Cacique would come pretty soon.

The Governor waited some time, and again sent Ortiz to repeat the invitation. Again the interpreter returned with the same response. After another interval of waiting, and the Cacique not appearing, Ortiz was sent for the third time. Approaching the door of the palace, he shouted out, in a voice sufficiently loud to be heard by all within, "Tell the chief of Tuscaloosa to come forth. The food is upon the table, and the Governor is waiting for him."

Immediately one of the principal attendants of the Cacique rushed out in a towering passion, and exclaimed:

"Who are these robbers, these vagabonds, who keep calling to my chief of Tuscaloosa, 'come out! come out!' with as little reverence as if he were one of them? By the sun and moon, this insolence is no longer to be borne! Let us cut them to pieces on the spot, and put an end to their wickedness and tyranny!"

Uttering these words, he threw off his superb [Pg 272] mantle of marten skins, and seizing a bow from the hands of an attendant, drew an arrow to the head, aiming at a group of Spaniards in the public square. But before the arrow left the bow, a steel-clad cavalier, who had accompanied the interpreter, with one thrust of his sword laid the Indian dead at his feet. The son of the dead warrior, a vigorous young savage, sprang forward and let fly upon the cavalier six or seven arrows, as fast as he could draw them. But they all fell harmless from his armor. He then seized a club and struck him three or four blows over the head with such force that the blood gushed from beneath his casque.

All this was done in an instant, when the cavalier, recovering from his surprise, with two sword-thrusts, laid the young warrior dead in his blood by the side of his father. It seemed as though instantaneously the war-whoop resounded from a thousand throats.

The concealed warriors, ten thousand in number, with hideous yells, like swarming bees, rushed into the streets. De Soto had but two hundred men to meet them. But these were all admirably armed, and most of them protected by coats of mail. He immediately placed himself at the head of his troops, and slowly retreating, fighting fiercely every inch of the way, with his armored men facing the foe, succeeded [Pg 273] in withdrawing through the gate out upon the open plain, where his horsemen could operate to better advantage. In the retreat five of the Spaniards were killed and many severely wounded, De Soto being one of the number.

The Indians came rushing out upon the plain in a tumultuous mass, with yells of defiance and victory. But the dragoons soon regained their horses, which had been tethered outside the walls, and whose bodies were much protected from the arrows of the natives; and then, in a terrific charge, one hundred steel-clad men, cutting to the right hand and to the left, maddened by the treachery of which they had been the victims, plunged into the densest masses of their foes, and every sabre-blow was death to a half-naked Indian. The slaughter was awful. Brave as the Indians were, they were thrown into a panic, and fled precipitately into the town.

In the retreat from the town, about twenty of the Spaniards had been cut off from their comrades, and had taken refuge in the house assigned to the Governor. Here they valiantly defended themselves against fearful odds. The bold storming of the place by the Spanish troops rescued them from their perilous position. But now all the warriors of both parties crowded together in the public square, fought [Pg 274] hand to hand with a ferocity which could not be surpassed. Though the natives were far more numerous than their foes, and were equally brave and strong, still the Spaniards had a vast superiority over them in their bucklers, their impenetrable armor, and their long, keen sabres of steel.

De Soto, conscious that the very existence of his army depended upon the issue of the conflict, was ever in the thickest of the battle, notwithstanding the severity of the wound from which he was suffering. At length, to drive his foes from the protection of their houses, the torch was applied in many places. The timber of which they were built was dry almost as tinder. Soon the whole place was in flames, the fiery billows surging to and fro like a furnace. All alike fled from the conflagration. The horsemen were already upon the plain, and they cut down the fugitive Indians mercilessly.

The sun was then sinking; Mobila was in ruins, and its flaming dwellings formed the funeral pyre of thousands of the dead. The battle had lasted nine hours. To the Spaniards it was one of the most terrible calamities. Eighty-two of their number were slain. Nearly all the rest were more or less severely wounded. Forty-five horses had been shot—an irreparable loss which all the army deeply mourned.

[Pg 275]

In entering the city, they had piled their camp equipage against the walls. This was all consumed, consisting of clothing, armor, medicines, and all the pearls which they had collected. The disaster to the natives was still more dreadful. It is estimated that six thousand of their number perished by the sword or the flames. The fate of the chieftain is not with certainty known. It is generally supposed that he was slain and was consumed in the flames of his capital.

The situation of the Spanish army that night was distressing in the highest degree. They were hungry, exhausted, dejected, and seventeen hundred dangerous wounds demanded immediate attention. There was but one surgeon of the expedition who survived, and he was a man of but little skill.

De Soto forgot himself and his wound in devotion to the interests of his men. Foraging parties were sent in all directions to obtain food for the sufferers, and straw for bedding. Here the army was compelled many days to remain to recruit from the awful disaster with which it had been so suddenly overwhelmed.

[Pg 276]

CHAPTER XVI.

Days of Darkness.

The Melancholy Encampment.—The Fleet at Pensacola.—Singular Resolve of De Soto.—Hostility of the Natives.—Beautiful Scenery.—Winter Quarters on the Yazoo.—Feigned Friendship of the Cacique.—Trickery of Juan Ortiz.—The Terrible Battle of Chickasaw.—Dreadful Loss of the Spaniards.

For twenty-three days the Spaniards remained in their miserable quarters, nursing the sick and the wounded. As nearly all their baggage had been consumed in the flames, they were in a condition of extreme destitution and suffering. Parties, of those who were least disabled, were sent on foraging expeditions, penetrating the country around to a distance of about twelve miles. They found the villages deserted by the terror-stricken inhabitants. But they obtained a sufficient supply of food to meet their immediate wants. In the thickets and ravines they found the bodies of many Indians, who had died of their wounds, and had been left unburied by their companions. They also found in many of the deserted hamlets, wounded Indians, who could go no farther, and who were in a starving and dying condition. [Pg 277] De Soto kindly ordered that their wounds should be dressed, and that they should be fed and nursed just as tenderly as his own men. Several captives were taken. De Soto inquired of them if another attack were meditated. They replied that all their warriors were slain; that none were left to renew the battle; that their chief had sent his son to watch the movements of the Spaniards, and had summoned his warriors from a great distance for their extermination. Nearly all were to be slain. The survivors were to be held as slaves. All their possessions and especially the magnificent animals they rode, were to be divided as the spoils of the conqueror. They said that their chief, upon the arrival of De Soto with his advance guard, was holding a council with his officers, to decide whether they should immediately attack those who had already arrived, or wait until the whole army was within their power. The passion and imprudence of one of their generals had precipitated the conflict.

The loss of the natives was even greater than De Soto had at first imagined. The thousands of Indian warriors who were within the spacious houses, shooting their arrows through windows, doors and loopholes, were many of them cut off from all escape, by the devouring flames. Bewildered, blinded, [Pg 278] stifled by the smoke, and encircled by the billowy fire, they miserably perished.

While De Soto was thus encamped around the smouldering ruins of Mobila, he heard of the arrival of his fleet at Pensacola, then called the bay of Achusi. As he was but about one hundred miles from that point, an easy march of a few days would bring him to reinforcements and abundant supplies. The tidings of their arrival at first gave him great satisfaction. His determined spirit was still unvanquished. He immediately resolved to establish his colony on the shores of Pensacola Bay, whence he could have constant water communication with Cuba and with Spain. Having obtained a fresh supply of military stores and recruits from the ships, he would recommence his pursuit after gold.

While one cannot but condemn his persistence in a ruinous course, the invincible spirit it develops wins admiration. Indeed if we accept the facts of the affair at Mobila, as above described, and those facts seem to be fully corroborated by a careful examination of all the reliable annalists of those days, impartial history cannot severely condemn De Soto in that dreadful occurrence. But it cannot be denied that he would have acted much more wisely, had he followed the counsel of Isabella, previously given, [Pg 279] and withdrawn from scenes thus fraught with violence, cruelty and blood.

As De Soto was conversing with some of his officers, of his plan of still prosecuting his journey in search of gold, he was told, not a little to his dismay, that his soldiers would not follow him. It was said that they were all thoroughly disheartened, and anxious to return to their homes, and that immediately upon reaching their ships, they would insist upon reembarking, and abandoning a land where they had thus far encountered only disasters.

The thought of returning to Cuba an impoverished man, having utterly failed in his expedition, surrounded by ragged and clamorous followers, and thus in disgrace, was to De Soto dreadful. Not making sufficient allowance for the difference in those respects between himself and his followers, he found it difficult to credit the representations which had been made to him. He therefore dressed himself in a disguise, and secretly wandered about by night among the frail huts of the soldiers, and soon found, by listening to their conversation, his worst fears confirmed. It became clear to his mind that immediately on his return to the ships, his present followers would disband and shift for themselves, while it would be in vain for him to attempt to raise another army.

[Pg 280]

Speaking of the distress with which these considerations oppressed the mind of De Soto, Mr. Irving well says, referring in confirmation of his statement, both to the account given by the Portuguese Narrative, and that by the Inca:

"Should his present forces desert him, therefore, he would remain stripped of dignity and command, blasted in reputation, his fortune expended in vain, and his enterprise, which had caused so much toil and trouble, a subject of scoffing rather than renown. The Governor was a man extremely jealous of his honor; and as he reflected upon these gloomy prospects, they produced sudden and desperate resolves. He disguised his anger and his knowledge of the schemes he had overheard, but he determined to frustrate them by turning back upon the coast, striking again into the interior, and never seeking the ships nor furnishing any tidings of himself, until he had crowned his enterprise gloriously by discovering new regions of wealth like those of Peru and Mexico.

"A change came over De Soto from this day. He was disconcerted in his favorite scheme of colonization, and had lost confidence in his followers. Instead of manifesting his usual frankness, energy and alacrity, he became a moody, irritable, discontented man. He no longer pretended to strike out any grand undertaking, went recklessly wandering from place to [Pg 281] place, apparently without order or object, as if careless of time and life, and only anxious to finish his existence."

On the morning of the 15th of November, 1540, the troops, much to their consternation, received orders to commence their march to the north, instead of to the south. The established habits of military discipline, and the stern manner of De Soto, repelled all audible murmurs. Each soldier took with him two days' provision, which consisted mainly of roasted corn pounded into meal. It was not doubted that in the fertile region of that sunny clime they would find food by the way. But winter was approaching which, though short, would certainly bring with it some days and nights of such severe cold that an unsheltered army would almost perish.

After traversing a very pleasant country for five days, without meeting any adventure of any especial interest, they came to a river wide and deep, with precipitous banks, which is supposed to have been the Tuscaloosa, or Black Warrior. The point at which they touched this stream, upon whose banks they had already encamped, was probably near the present site of Erie, in Greene County. Here they found upon the farther banks of the river, a populous village called Cabusto. De Soto as usual sent a courier with a friendly message to the chief, saying [Pg 282] "that he came in friendship and sought only an unobstructed path through his realms."

The chief returned the defiant reply—

"We want no peace with you. War only we want; a war of fire and blood."

As De Soto, troubled by this message, moved cautiously forward, he found an army of fifteen hundred natives drawn up on the banks of the stream to prevent the passage; while the opposite banks were occupied by between six and seven thousand warriors, extending up and down the river for a distance of six miles. There was nothing for the Spaniards to do but to press forward. To turn back, in sight of their foes, was not to be thought of. After a pretty sharp skirmish, in which the Spaniards attacked their opponents, the natives sprang into their canoes, and some by swimming crossed the river and joined the main body of the Indians upon the opposite bank.

Here they were obviously prepared, to make a desperate resistance. Night came on, dark and chill. The Spaniards bivouacked on the open plain, awaiting the morning, when, with but about seven hundred men, they were to assail eight thousand warriors, very strongly posted on bluffs, with a deep and rapid river flowing at their feet. The Indians gave the Spaniards no repose. During the darkness they [Pg 283] were continually passing the river at different points in their canoes, and then uniting in one band, with hideous outcries assailing the weary travellers. The military genius of De Soto successfully beat them off through the night. He then intrenched himself so as to bid defiance to their attacks, and employed one hundred of his most skilful workmen in building, under the concealment of a neighboring grove, two very large flat boats.

Twelve days passed before these barges were finished. By the aid of men and horses, they were brought to the river and launched. In the morning, before the dawn, ten mounted horsemen and forty footmen embarked in each boat, the footmen to ply the oars as vigorously as possible in the rapid passage of the river to a designated spot, where the horsemen were immediately to spur their steeds upon the shore, and with their sabres open a passage for the rest of the troops. De Soto was anxious to pass in the first boat, but his followers entreated him not to expose his life, upon which everything depended, to so great a peril.

The moment the boats were dimly seen by the watchful natives, a signal war-whoop rang along the bank for miles. Five hundred warriors rushed to the menaced spot, to prevent the landing. Such a shower of arrows was thrown upon the boat that [Pg 284] every man was more or less wounded. The moment the bows touched the beach, the steel-clad horsemen plunged upon the foe, and cut their way through them with blood-dripping sabres. Other native warriors were however hurrying to the assistance of their comrades. In the meantime the boats had with great rapidity recrossed the river, and brought over another detachment of eighty men with De Soto himself at their head. After a sanguinary conflict the Spaniards obtained complete possession of the landing place. Though unimportant skirmishes were kept up through the day, the remaining troops were without difficulty brought across the river. At nightfall not an Indian was to be seen. They had all withdrawn and fortified themselves with palisades in a neighboring swamp.

The Spaniards found opening before them a beautiful and fertile country, well cultivated, with fields of corn and beans, and with many small villages and comfortable farm-houses scattered around. They broke up their boats for the sake of the nails, which might prove of priceless value to them in their future operations. Leaving the Indians unmolested in their fortress, they journeyed on five days in a westerly direction, when they reached the banks of another large river, which is supposed to have been the Tombigbee.

[Pg 285]

Here De Soto found hostile Indians arrayed on the opposite bank, ready to oppose his passage. Anxious to avoid, if possible, any sanguinary collision with the natives, he tarried for two days, until a canoe had been constructed by which he could send a friendly message across to the chief. A single unarmed Indian was dispatched in the canoe with these words of peace. He paddled across the river, and as soon as the canoe touched the shore the savages rushed upon him, beat out his brains with their war-clubs, and raising yells of defiance, mysteriously disappeared.

There being no longer any foe to oppose the passage, the troops were easily conveyed across on rafts. Unassailed, they marched tranquilly on for several days, until, on the 18th of December, they reached a small village called Chickasaw. It was pleasantly situated on a gentle eminence, embellished with groves of walnut and oak trees, and with streams of pure water running on either side. It is supposed that this village was on the Yazoo river, in the upper part of the State of Mississippi, about two hundred and fifty miles northwest of Mobile.

It was midwinter, and upon those high lands the weather was intensely cold. The ground was frequently encumbered with snow and ice, and the troops, unprovided with winter clothing, suffered [Pg 286] severely. De Soto decided to take up his winter quarters at Chickasaw, there to await the returning sun of spring. There appears to have been something senseless in the wild wanderings in which De Soto was now persisting, which have led some to suppose that care, exhaustion, and sorrow had brought on some degree of mental derangement. However that may be, he devoted himself with great energy to the promotion of the comfort of his men. Foraging parties were dispatched in all directions in search of food and of straw for bedding, while an ample supply of fuel was collected for their winter fires.

There were two hundred comfortable houses in this village, and De Soto added a few more, so that all of his men were well sheltered. So far as we can judge from the narratives given, the native inhabitants, through fear of the Spaniards, had abandoned their homes and fled to distant parts. De Soto did everything in his power to open friendly relations with the Indians. He succeeded, through his scouts, in capturing a few, whom he sent to their chief laden with presents, and with assurances of peace and friendship.

The Cacique returned favorable replies, and sent to De Soto in return fruit, fish, and venison. He, however, was very careful not to expose his person to [Pg 287] the power of the Spaniards. His warriors, in gradually increasing numbers, ventured to enter the village, where they were treated by De Soto with the greatest consideration.

He had still quite a large number of swine with him, for they had multiplied wonderfully on the way. The Indians, having had a taste of pork, found it so delicious that they began to prowl around the encampment by night to steal these animals. It is said that two Indians who were caught in the act were shot, and as this did not check the thievery, a third had both his hands chopped off with a hatchet, and thus mutilated was sent to the chief as a warning to others.

It is with great reluctance that we give any credence to this statement. It certainly is not sustained by any evidence which would secure conviction in a court of justice. It is quite contrary to the well-established humanity of De Soto. There can be no possible excuse for such an act of barbarity on the part of any civilized man. If De Soto were guilty of the atrocity, it would, indeed, indicate that his reason was being dethroned.

The chief had taken up his residence about three or four miles from the village. Four of the Spanish soldiers one night, well armed, stole from their barracks, in direct violation of orders, and repairing to the dwelling of the Cacique, robbed him of some rich [Pg 288] fur mantles, and other valuable articles of clothing. With that even-handed justice which has thus far characterized De Soto, he who had ordered two Indians to be shot for stealing his swine, now ordered the two ringleaders in this robbery of the Indian chief to be put to death.

The priests in the army, and most of the officers, earnestly implored De Soto to pardon the culprits. But he was inflexible. He would administer equal justice to the Indian and the Spaniard. The culprits were led into the public square to be beheaded. It so happened that, just at that time, an embassage arrived from the Cacique with complaints of the robbery, and demanding the punishment of the offenders. Juan Ortiz, the interpreter, whose sympathies were deeply moved in behalf of his comrades about to be executed, adopted the following singular and sagacious expedient to save them:

He falsely reported to the Governor that the chief had sent his messengers to implore the forgiveness of the culprits—to say that their offence was a very slight one, and that he should regard it as a personal favor if they were pardoned and set at liberty. The kind-hearted De Soto, thus delivered from his embarrassment, gladly released them.

On the other hand, the tricky interpreter sent word to the Cacique that the men who had robbed [Pg 289] him were in close imprisonment, and that they would be punished with the utmost severity, so as to serve as a warning to all others.

Many circumstances led De Soto to the suspicion that the chief was acting a treacherous part; that he was marshalling an immense army in the vicinity to attack the Spaniards; that his pretended friendliness was intended merely to disarm suspicion, and that the warriors who visited the village were spies, making preparation for a general assault. In this judgment subsequent events proved him to be correct.

Early in the month of March there was a dark and stormy night, and a chill north wind swept the bleak plains. The sentinels were driven to seek shelter; no one dreamed of peril. It was the hour for the grand assault. Just at midnight the Cacique put his martial bands in motion. They were in three powerful divisions, the central party being led by the chief in person. These moccasoned warriors, with noiseless tread, stealthily approached their victims. Suddenly the air resounded with war-whoops, blasts of conch shells, and the clangor of wooden drums, rising above the roar of the storm, when the savages, like spirits of darkness, rushed upon the defenceless village. They bore with them lighted matches, made of some combustible substance twisted [Pg 290] in the form of a cord, which, being waved in the air, would blaze into flame. The village was built of reeds, with thatch of dried grass. The torch was everywhere applied; the gale fanned the fire. In a few minutes the whole village was a roaring furnace of flame.

What pen can describe the scene which ensued of tumult, terror, blood, and woe! What imagination can conceive of the horrors of that night, when uncounted thousands of savages, fierce as demons, rushed upon the steel-clad veterans of Spain, not one of whom would ask for quarter! every one of whom would fight with sinewy arm and glittering sabre to the last possible gasp.

Nothing could throw the veteran Spaniards into a panic. They always slept prepared for surprise. In an instant every man was at his post. De Soto, who always slept in hose and doublet, drew his armor around him, mounted his steed ever ready, and was one of the first to dash into the densest of the foe. Twelve armored horsemen were immediately at his side. The arrows and javelins of the natives glanced harmless from helmet and cuirass, while every flash of the long, keen sabres was death to an Indian, and the proud war-horses trampled the corpses beneath their feet.

The fierce conflagration soon drove all alike out [Pg 291] into the plain. Many of the Spaniards could not escape, but perished miserably in the fire. Several of the splendid horses were also burned. Soon all were engaged hand to hand, fighting in a tumultuous mass by the light of the conflagration. There was, perhaps, alike bravery on either side. But the natives knew that if defeated they could flee to the forests; while to the Spaniards defeat was certain death, or captivity worse than death to every one.

De Soto observed not far from him an Indian chief of herculean strength, who was fighting with great success. He closed in upon him, and as he rose in his saddle, leaning mainly upon the right stirrup, to pierce him with his lance, the saddle, which in the haste had not been sufficiently girded, turned beneath him, and he was thrown upon the ground in the midst of the enemy. His companions sprang to the rescue. Instantly he remounted, and was again in the thickest of the foe. The battle was fierce, bloody, and short. So many of the horsemen had perished during their long journey that many of the foot soldiers were protected by armor. At length the savages were put to flight. Pursued by the swift-footed horses, they, in their terror, to add speed to their footsteps, threw away their weapons, and thus fell an easy prey to the conqueror.

The Spaniards, justly exasperated in being thus [Pg 292] treacherously assailed by those who had assumed the guise of friendship, pursued the fugitives so long as they could be distinguished by the light of the conflagration, and cut them down without any mercy. A bugle-blast then sounded the recall. The victors returned to an awful scene of desolation and misery. Their homes were all in ashes, and many of the few comforts they had retained were consumed. Forty Spaniards had been slain, besides many more wounded. Fifty horses had perished in the flames, or had been shot by the natives.

Their herd of swine, which they prized so highly, and which they regarded as an essential element in the establishment of their colony, had been shut up in an enclosure roofed with straw, and nearly every one had perished in the flames.

This disaster was the most severe calamity which had befallen them. Since landing at Tampa Bay, over three hundred men had fallen from the attacks of the natives. De Soto was thrown into a state of the deepest despondency. All hope seemed to be extinguished. World-weary, and in despair, he apparently wished only to die. Distress was all around him, with no possibility of his affording any relief. Sadly he buried the dead of his own army, while he left the bodies of the natives thick upon the plain, a prey for wolves and vultures. The smouldering [Pg 293] ruins of Chickasaw were abandoned, and an encampment was reared of logs and bark at a distance of about three miles; where they passed a few weeks of great wretchedness. Bodily discomfort and mental despondency united in creating almost intolerable gloom.

Terribly as the natives had been punished they soon learned the extent of the calamity they had inflicted upon the Spaniards. Through their spies they ascertained their diminished numbers, witnessed their miserable plight, and had the sagacity to perceive that they were very poorly prepared to withstand another attack. Thus they gradually regained confidence, marshalled their armies anew, and commenced an incessant series of assaults, avoiding any general action, and yet wearing out the Spaniards with the expectation of such action every hour of every night.

In the daytime, De Soto sent out his horsemen to scour the country around in all directions for a distance of ten or twelve miles. They would return with the declaration that not a warrior was to be found. But before midnight the fleet footed savages would be swarming around the encampment, with hideous yells, often approaching near enough to throw in upon it a shower of arrows. Occasionally these skirmishes became hotly contested. In one [Pg 294] of them forty Indians were slain, while two of the horses of the Spaniards were killed and two severely wounded.

In their thin clothing the Spaniards would have suffered terribly from the severe cold of the nights, but for the ingenuity of one of their number, who invented a soft, thick, warm matting or coverlet which he wove from some long grass that abounded in the vicinity. Every soldier was speedily engaged in the manufacture of these beds or blankets. They were made several inches in thickness and about six feet square. One half served as a mattress, and the other folded over, became a blanket. Thus they were relieved from the cold, which otherwise would have been almost unendurable.

The foraging parties succeeded in obtaining a supply of corn, beans, and dried fruit. Here De Soto was compelled to remain, to heal his wounded, for the remainder of the month of March. He was very anxious to escape from the hostile region as soon as possible. As an illustration of the scenes which were occurring almost every night during this sad encampment, we may mention the following.

The night was cold and dark. The defiant war-cries of the savages were heard in all directions and no one could tell how great their numbers, or upon what point their attack would fall. Several camp-fires [Pg 295] were built, around which horsemen were assembled ready to meet the foe from whatever point, in the darkness, he might approach. Juan De Gusman was the leader of one of these bands. He was a cavalier of high renown. In figure, he was delicate, almost feminine, but he had the soul of a lion.

By the light of the blazing fagots, he discerned a numerous band of Indians stealthily approaching. Leaping upon his horse, and followed by five companions, and a few armored footmen, he plunged into the midst of them. He aimed his javelin, at apparently the leader of the savages, a man of gigantic stature. The Indian wrenched the lance from his hand, seized him by the collar, and hurled him from his saddle to the ground. Instantly the soldiers rushed in, with their sabers, cut the savage to pieces and after a short conflict in which a large number of the natives were slain, put the rest to flight.

It may seem strange that so few of the Spaniards were killed in these terrible conflicts, in which they often cut down hundreds and even thousands of their foes. But it should be remembered that their coats of mail quite effectually protected them from the flint pointed arrows of the Indians. The only vulnerable point was the face, and even this was sometimes shielded by the visor. But the bodies of the natives, thinly clad, were easily cut down by the steel blades of the cavaliers.

[Pg 296]

CHAPTER XVII.

The Discovery of the Mississippi.

The Fortress of Hostile Indians.—Its Capture.—The Disastrous Conflict.—The Advance of the Army.—Discovery of the Mississippi River.—Preparations for Crossing.—Extraordinary Pageants.—Unjustifiable Attack.—The passage of the River.—Friendly Reception by Casquin.—Extraordinary Religious Festival.

On the first day of April, 1541, the army broke up its encampment, and again set out languidly on its journey to the westward. No sounds of joy were heard, for there was no longer hope to cheer. The indomitable energy of De Soto dragged along the reluctant footsteps of his troops. The first day they travelled about twelve miles, through a level and fertile country with many villages and farm houses to charm the eye. At night they encamped beyond the territory of Chickasaw, and consequently supposed that they would no longer be molested, by those hostile Indians.

A well armed party of cavalry and infantry was sent out on a foraging expedition. They accidently approached a strong fortress where a large number of Indian warriors was assembled, prepared to resist [Pg 297] their march. They were very fantastically clothed, and painted in the highest style of barbaric art, so as to render them as hideous as possible. Immediately upon catching sight of the Spaniards they rushed out upon them with ferocious cries. Añasco, who was in command of the Spanish party, seeing such overwhelming numbers coming upon him, retreated to an open field, where he drew up his horses and placed his cross-bow men in front with their bucklers, to protect the precious animals. At the same time he sent hastily back to De Soto for reinforcements.

The Indians came rushing on, clashing their weapons, beating wooden drums and raising the war-whoop, till they arrived within reach of the arrows of the cross-bow men. Then, somewhat appalled by the formidable military array of the Spaniards glittering in steel armor, they stopped and taunted their foes from the distance, with cries of defiance and gestures of insolence and insult.

The hot-headed Añasco found it hard to restrain his impatience. Soon De Soto himself came, with all his force, except a few left to guard the camp. Carefully he scrutinized the fortress where these savages had gathered their strength to crush him. It was indeed a formidable structure: consisting of a quadrangle twelve hundred feet square. There were three entrance gates, purposely so low that mounted men [Pg 298] could not enter. In the rear of the fortress there was a deep and rapid river with steep banks, probably the Yazoo; in the county of Tallahatchee. The fort was called the Alabama. Across this stream, frail bridges were constructed, over which the Indians, in case of necessity, could retreat, and easily destroy the bridges behind them. Directly in the rear of the front entrance, there was a second wall, and in the rear of that a third; so that if the outer wall were gained, the garrison could retreat behind one and the other.

De Soto very carefully reconnoitred the fort. He judged that the slightest appearance of timidity, on his part, would so embolden the savages as to expose him to great peril. Should he avoid the conflict, to which he was challenged, and endeavor to escape, by fleeing before his enemies, he would draw them down upon him with resistless fury. Thus again he found himself impelled to rouse all the energies of his army for the slaughter of the poor savages.

He formed his attacking force in three columns, to seize the three entrances. The Indians, carefully noting these preparations, made a simultaneous rush upon the Spaniards, pouring in upon them an incessant volley of flint-pointed arrows. Notwithstanding the armor, many of the Spaniards were wounded, the savages taking careful aim at those parts which were least protected. The three storming columns [Pg 299] pressed vigorously on, while two bands of horsemen, twenty in each, De Soto leading one of them, attacked the tumultuous foe on each flank. The assault was resistless. The panic-stricken savages fled to the fortress. The entrances were clogged by the crowd, and horsemen and footmen, with their long sharp sabres cut down their foes with enormous slaughter.

In the heat of the conflict an arrow, thrown by the sinewy arm of an Indian, struck the steel casque of De Soto with such force that it rebounded some sixteen feet in the air. The blow was so severe that it almost unhorsed the Governor, and seemingly caused, as he afterwards said, the fire to flash from his eyes. As the savages rushed pell-mell into the fortress, their pursuers were at their heels, cutting them down. The Spaniards were exasperated. They had sought peace, and had found only war. De Soto had wished, in a friendly spirit, to traverse their country, and they were hedging up his way and pursuing him with relentless ferocity. He assumed that it was necessary, for the salvation of his army, to teach them a lesson which they would not soon forget.

The carnage within the fortress was dreadful. All was inextricable confusion. It was a hand-to-hand fight. Wooden swords fell harmless upon helmet, [Pg 300] cuirass and buckler. But the keen and polished steel of the Spaniards did fearful execution upon the almost naked bodies of the Indians. Some climbed the palisades and leaped down into the plain, where they were instantly slain by the mounted troops. Others crowded through the fort and endeavored to escape by the narrow bridges. Many were jostled off, and in the swift current were drowned. But a few moments elapsed ere the fort was in the hands of the Spaniards. Its floor was covered by the gory bodies of the slain. Still, not a few had escaped, some by swimming, some by the bridges. They immediately formed in battle array upon the opposite bank of the river, where they supposed they were beyond the reach of the Spaniards.

Again they raised shouts of defiance and insult. De Soto was not in a mood to endure these taunts. Just above the fort he found a ford. Crossing with a squadron of horsemen, they rushed with gleaming sabres upon the savages, and put them instantly to flight. For more than three miles they pursued them over the plain, till wearied with slaughter. They then returned, victors, slowly and sadly to their encampment. Peace and friendship would have been far preferable to this war and misery. Even their victory was to the Spaniards a great disaster, for several of the men were slain, and many severely [Pg 301] wounded. Of the latter, fifteen subsequently died. De Soto remained four days in the encampment, nursing the wounded, and then resumed his weary march.

He still directed his footsteps in a westerly direction, carefully avoiding an approach to the sea, lest his troops should rise in mutiny, send for the ships, and escape from the ill-starred enterprise. This certainly indicates, under the circumstances, an unsound, if not a deranged mind. For four days the troops toiled along through a dismal region, uninhabited, and encumbered with tangled forests and almost impassable swamps.

At length they came to a small village called Chisca, upon the banks of the most majestic stream they had yet discovered. Sublimely the mighty flood, a mile and a half in width, rolled by them. The current was rapid and bore upon its bosom a vast amount of trees, logs, and drift-wood, showing that its sources must be hundreds of leagues far away, in the unknown interior. This was the mighty Mississippi, the 'father of waters.' The Indians, at that point, called it Chucagua. Its source and its embouchure were alike unknown to De Soto. Little was he then aware of the magnitude of the discovery he had made.

"De Soto," says Mr. Irving, "was the first European [Pg 302] who looked out upon the turbid waters of this magnificent river; and that event has more surely enrolled his name among those who will ever live in American history, than if he had discovered mines of silver and gold."

The Spaniards had reached the river after a four days' march through an unpeopled wilderness. The Indians of Chisca knew nothing of their approach, and probably had never heard of their being in the country. The tribe inhabiting the region of which Chisca was the metropolis, was by no means as formidable, as many whom they had already encountered. The dwelling of the Cacique stood on a large artificial mound, from eighteen to twenty feet in height. It was ascended by two ladders, which could of course be easily drawn up, leaving the royal family thus quite isolated from the people below.

Chisca, the chieftain, was far advanced in years, a feeble, emaciate old man of very diminutive stature. In the days of his prime, he had been a renowned warrior. Hearing of the arrival of the Spaniards, he was disposed to regard them as enemies, and seizing his tomahawk, he was eager to descend from his castle and lead his warriors to battle.

The contradictory statements are made that De Soto, weary of the harassing warfare of the winter, was very anxious to secure the friendship of these [Pg 303] Indians. Unless he were crazed, it must have been so, for there was absolutely nothing to be gained, but everything to be imperilled, by war. On the other hand, it is said that the moment the Spaniards descried the village, they rushed into it, plundering the houses, seizing men and women as captives. Both statements may have been partially true. It is not improbable that the disorderly troops of De Soto, to his great regret, were guilty of some outrages, while he personally might have been intensely anxious to repress this violence and cultivate only friendly relations with the natives.

But whatever may have been the hostile or friendly attitude assumed by the Spaniards, it is admitted that the Cacique was disposed to wage war against the new comers. The more prudent of his warriors urged that he should delay his attack upon them until he had made such preparations as would secure successful results.

"It will be best first," said they, "to assemble all the warriors of our nation, for these men are well armed. In the meantime, let us pretend friendship and not provoke an attack until we are strong enough to be sure of victory."

The irascible old chief was willing only partially to listen to this advice. He delayed the conflict, but did not disguise his hostility. De Soto sent to him [Pg 304] a very friendly message, declaring that he came in peace and wished only for an unmolested march through his country. The Cacique returned an angry reply, refusing all courteous intercourse.

The Spaniards had been but three hours in the village when, to their surprise, they perceived an army of four thousand warriors, thoroughly prepared for battle, gathered around the mound upon which was reared the dwelling of the chief. If so many warriors could be assembled in so short a time, they feared there must be a large number in reserve who could be soon drawn in. The Spaniards, in their long marches and many battles, had dwindled away to less than five hundred men. Four thousand against five hundred were fearful odds; and yet the number of their foes might speedily be doubled or even quadrupled. In addition to this, the plains around the city were exceedingly unfavorable for the movements of the Spanish army, while they presented great advantages to the nimble-footed natives, for the region was covered with forests, sluggish streams and bogs.

By great exertions, De Soto succeeded in effecting a sort of compromise. The Cacique consented to allow the Spaniards to remain for six days in the village to nurse the sick and the wounded. Food was to be furnished them by the Cacique. At the [Pg 305] end of six days the Spaniards were to leave, abstaining entirely from pillage, from injuring the crops, and from all other acts of violence.

The Cacique and all the inhabitants of the village abandoned the place, leaving it to the sole occupancy of the Spaniards. April, in that sunny clime, was mild as genial summer. The natives, with their simple habits, probably found little inconvenience in encamping in the groves around. On the last day of his stay, De Soto obtained permission to visit the Cacique. He thanked the chief cordially for his kindness and hospitality, and taking an affectionate leave, continued his journey into the unknown regions beyond.

Ascending the tortuous windings of the river on the eastern bank, the Spaniards found themselves, for four days, in almost impenetrable thickets, where there were no signs of inhabitants. At length they came to quite an opening in the forest. A treeless plain, waving with grass, spread far and wide around them. The Mississippi river here was about half a league in width. On the opposite bank large numbers of Indians were seen, many of them warriors in battle array, while a fleet of canoes lined the shore.

De Soto decided, for some unexplained reason, to cross the river at that point, though it was evident that the Indians had in some way received tidings [Pg 306] of his approach, and were assembled there to dispute his passage. The natives could easily cross the river in their canoes, but they would hardly venture to attack the Spaniards upon the open plain, where there was such a fine opportunity for the charges of their cavalry.

Here De Soto encamped for twenty days, while all who could handle tools were employed in building four large flat boats for the transportation of the troops across the stream. On the second day of the encampment, several natives from some tribe disposed to be friendly, on the eastern side of the river, visited the Spaniards. With very much ceremony of bowing and semi-barbaric parade, they approached De Soto, and informed him that they were commissioned by their chief to bid him welcome to his territory, and to assure him of his friendly services. De Soto, much gratified by this message, received the envoys with the greatest kindness, and dismissed them highly pleased with their reception.

Though this chief sent De Soto repeated messages of kindness, he did not himself visit the Spanish camp, the alleged reason being, and perhaps the true one, that he was on a sick bed. He, however, sent large numbers of his subjects with supplies of food, and to assist the Spaniards in drawing the timber to construct their barges. The hostile Indians [Pg 307] on the opposite bank frequently crossed in their canoes, and attacking small bands of workmen, showered upon them volleys of arrows, and fled again to their boats.

One day the Spaniards, while at work, saw two hundred canoes filled with natives, in one united squadron, descending the river. It was a beautiful sight to witness this fleet, crowded with decorated and plumed warriors, their paddles, ornaments, and burnished weapons flashing in the sunlight. They came in true military style: several warriors standing at the bows and stern of each boat, with large shields of buffalo hides on their left arms, and with bows and arrows in their hands. De Soto advanced to the shore to meet them, where he stood surrounded by his staff. The royal barge containing the chief was paddled within a few rods of the bank. The Cacique then rose, and addressed De Soto in words which were translated by the interpreter as follows:

"I am informed that you are the envoy of the most powerful monarch on the globe. I have come to proffer to you friendship and homage, and to assure you of my assistance in any way in which I can be of service."

De Soto thanked him heartily for his offers, and entreated him to land, assuring him he should meet [Pg 308] only the kindest reception. The following extraordinary account of the termination of this interview, a termination which seems incredible, is given in the "Conquest of Florida:"

"The Cacique returned no answer, but sent three canoes on shore with presents of fruit, and bread made of the pulp of a certain kind of plum. The Governor again importuned the savage to land, but perceiving him to hesitate, and suspecting a treacherous and hostile intent, marshalled his men in order of battle. Upon this the Indians turned their prows and fled.

"The cross-bowmen sent a flight of arrows after them, and killed five or six of their number. They retreated in good order, covering the rowers with their shields. Several times after this they landed to attack the soldiers, as was supposed, but the moment the Spaniards charged upon them they fled to their canoes."

If this account be true, the attack by the Spaniards was as inexcusable as it was senseless. At the end of twenty days the four barges were built and launched. In the darkness of the night De Soto ordered them to be well manned with rowers and picked troops of tried prudence and courage. The moment the bows touched the beach the soldiers sprang ashore, to their surprise encountering no resistance. [Pg 309] The boats immediately returned for another load. Rapidly they passed to and fro, and before the sun went down at the close of that day, the whole army was transported to the western bank of the Mississippi. The point where De Soto and his army crossed, it is supposed, was at what is called the lowest Chickasaw Bluff.

"The river in this place," says the Portuguese Narrative, "was a mile and a half in breadth, so that a man standing still could scarcely be discerned from the opposite shore. It was of great depth, of wonderful rapidity, and very turbid, and was always filled with floating trees and timber, carried down by the force of the current."

The army having all crossed, the boats were broken up, as usual, to preserve the nails. It would seem that the hostile Indians had all vanished, for the Spaniards advanced four days in a westerly direction, through an uninhabited wilderness, encountering no opposition. On the fifth day they toiled up a heavy swell of land, from whose summit they discerned, in a valley on the other side, a large village of about four hundred dwellings. It was situated on the fertile banks of a stream, which is supposed to have been the St. Francis.

The extended valley, watered by this river, presented a lovely view as far as the eye could reach, [Pg 310] with luxuriant fields of Indian corn and with groves of fruit trees. The natives had received some intimation of the approach of the Spaniards, and in friendly crowds gathered around them, offering food and the occupancy of their houses. Two of the highest chieftains, subordinate to the Cacique, soon came with an imposing train of warriors, bearing a welcome from their chief and the offer of his services.

De Soto received them with the utmost courtesy, and in the interchange of these friendly offices, both Spaniards and natives became alike pleased with each other. The adventurers remained in this village for six days, finding abundant food for themselves and their horses, and experiencing in the friendship and hospitality of the natives, joys which certainly never were found in the horrors of war. The province was called by the name of Kaska, and was probably the same as that occupied by the Kaskaskias Indians.

Upon commencing anew their march they passed through a populous and well cultivated country, where peace, prosperity and abundance seemed to reign. In two days, having journeyed about twenty miles up the western bank of the Mississippi, they approached the chief town of the province where the Cacique lived. It was situated, as is supposed, in the region now called Little Prairie, in the extreme [Pg 311] southern part of the State of Missouri, not far from New Madrid. Here they found the hospitable hands of the Cacique and his people extended to greet them.

The residence of the chief stood upon a broad artificial mound, sufficiently capacious for twelve or thirteen houses, which were occupied by his numerous family and attendants. He made De Soto a present of a rich fur mantle, and invited him, with his suite, to occupy the royal dwellings for their residence. De Soto politely declined this offer, as he was unwilling thus to incommode his kind entertainer. He, however, accepted the accommodation of several houses in the village. The remainder of the army were lodged in exceedingly pleasant bowers, skilfully, and very expeditiously constructed by the natives, of bark and the green boughs of trees, outside the village.

It was now the month of May. The weather was intensely hot, and these rustic bowers were found to be refreshingly cool and grateful. The name of this friendly chief was Casquin. Here the army remained for three days, without a ripple of unfriendly feeling arising between the Spaniards and the natives.

It was a season of unusual drouth in the country, and on the fourth day the following extraordinary incident occurred: Casquin, accompanied by quite [Pg 312] an imposing retinue of his most distinguished men, came into the presence of De Soto, and stepping forward, with great solemnity of manner, said to him,—

"Señor, as you are superior to us in prowess and surpass us in arms, we likewise believe that your God is better than our God. These you behold before you are the chief warriors of my dominions. We supplicate you to pray to your God to send us rain, for our fields are parched for the want of water."

De Soto, who was a reflective man, of pensive temperament and devoutly inclined, responded,—

"We are all alike sinners, but we will pray to God, the Father of mercies, to show his kindness to you."

He then ordered the carpenter to cut down one of the tallest pine trees in the vicinity. It was carefully trimmed and formed into a perfect, but gigantic cross. Its dimensions were such, that it required the strength of one hundred men to raise and plant it in the ground. Two days were employed in this operation. The cross stood upon a bluff, on the western bank of the Mississippi. The next morning after it was reared, the whole Spanish army was called out to celebrate the erection of the cross, by a solemn religious procession. A large number of the natives, with apparent devoutness, joined in the festival.

[Pg 313]

Casquin and De Soto took the lead, walking side by side. The Spanish soldiers and the native warriors, composing a procession of more than a thousand persons, walked harmoniously along as brothers, to commemorate the erection of the cross—the symbol of the Christian's faith. The Cross! It should be the emblem of peace on earth and good will among men. Alas! how often has it been the badge of cruelty and crime.

The priests, for there were several in the army, chanted their Christian hymns, and offered fervent prayers. The Mississippi at this point is not very broad, and it is said that upon the opposite bank twenty thousand natives were assembled, watching with intensest interest the imposing ceremony, and apparently, at times, taking part in the exercises. When the priests raised their hands in prayer, they, too, extended their arms and raised their eyes, as if imploring the aid of the God of heaven and of earth.

Occasionally a low moan was heard wafted across the river—a wailing cry, as if woe-stricken children were imploring the aid of an Almighty Father. The spirit of De Soto was deeply moved to tenderness and sympathy as he witnessed this benighted people paying such homage to the emblem of man's redemption. After several prayers were offered, the whole procession, slowly advancing two by two, knelt [Pg 314] before the cross, as in brief ejaculatory prayer, and kissed it. All then returned with the same solemnity to the village, the priests chanting the grand anthem, "Te Deum Laudamus."

Thus more than three hundred years ago the cross, significant of the religion of Jesus, was planted upon the banks of the Mississippi, and the melody of Christian hymns was wafted across the silent waters, and was blended with the sighing of the breeze through the tree-tops. It is sad to reflect how little of the spirit of that religion has since been manifested in those realms in man's treatment of his brother man.

It is worthy of especial notice that upon the night succeeding this eventful day clouds gathered, and the long-looked-for rain fell abundantly. The devout Las Casas writes:

"God, in his mercy, willing to show these heathen that he listeneth to those who call upon him in truth, sent down, in the middle of the ensuing night, a plenteous rain, to the great joy of the Indians."

[Pg 315]

CHAPTER XVIII.

Vagrant Wanderings.

Trickery of Casquin.—The March to Capaha.—The Battle and its Results.—Friendly Relations with Capaha.—The Return Journey.—The Marsh Southward.—Salt Springs.—The Savages of Tula.—Their Ferocity.—Anecdote.—Despondency of De Soto.

It is painful to recall the mind from these peaceful, joy-giving, humanizing scenes of religion, to barbaric war—its crime, carnage, and misery. It is an affecting comment upon the fall of man, that far away in this wilderness, among these tribes that might so have blessed and cheered each other by fraternal love, war seems to have been the normal condition. After a residence of nine days in this village, beneath truly sunny skies, in the enjoyment of abundance, and cheered by fruits, flowers, and bird-songs, the Spanish army again commenced its march in the wild and apparently senseless search for gold.

The Cacique, Casquin, was about fifty years of age. He begged permission to accompany De Soto to the next province, with his whole army in its best military array, and with a numerous band of attendants [Pg 316] to carry provisions and to gather wood and fodder for the encampments. De Soto cheerfully accepted this friendly offer. But he soon found that it was hatred, not love, which was the impelling motive; that the chief was incited by a desire to make war, not to cultivate peace. The chief of the next province was a redoubtable warrior named Capaha. His territories were extensive; his subjects numerous and martial. Time out of mind there had been warfare between these two provinces, the subjects of each hating each other implacably.

Capaha had in recent conflicts been quite the victor, and Casquin thought this a good opportunity, with the Spaniards for his powerful allies, to take signal vengeance upon his foe. Of this De Soto, at the time, knew nothing.

The army commenced its march. There were five thousand native warriors who accompanied him, plumed, painted, and armed in the highest style of savage art. There were three thousand attendants, who bore the supplies, and who were also armed with bows and arrows. Casquin, with his troops, took the lead; wishing, as he said, to clear the road of any obstructions, to drive off any lurking foes, and to prepare at night the ground for the comfortable encampment of the Spaniards. His troops were in a good state of military discipline, and marched in well [Pg 317] organized array about a mile and a half in advance of the Spaniards.

Thus they travelled for three uneventful days, until they reached an immense swamp, extending back unknown miles from the Mississippi. This was the frontier line which bordered the hostile provinces of Casquin and Capaha. Crossing it with much difficulty, they encamped upon a beautiful prairie upon the northern side. A journey of two days through a sparsely inhabited country brought them to the more fertile and populous region of the new province. Here they found the capital of the Cacique. It was a well fortified town of about five hundred large houses, situated upon elevated land, which commanded an extensive view of the country around. One portion of the town was protected by a deep ditch, one hundred and fifty feet broad. The higher portion was defended by a strong palisade. The ditch, or canal, connected with the Mississippi river, which was nine miles distant.

Capaha, hearing suddenly of the arrival of so formidable a force, fled down the canal in a curve, to an island in the river, where he summoned his warriors to meet him as speedily as possible. Casquin, marching as usual a mile and a half in advance, finding the town unprotected, and almost abandoned, entered and immediately commenced all the ravages [Pg 318] of savage warfare. One hundred men, women and children, caught in the place, were immediately seized, the men killed and scalped, the women and boys made captives. To gratify their vengeance, they broke into the mausoleum, held so sacred by the Indians, where the remains of all the great men of the tribe had been deposited. They broke open the coffins, scattered the remains over the floor and trampled them beneath their feet.

It is said that Casquin, would have set fire to the mausoleum, and laid it and the whole village in ashes, but that he feared that he might thus incur the anger of De Soto. When the Governor arrived and saw what ravages had been committed by those who had come as his companions, friends and allies, he was greatly distressed. Immediately he sent envoys to Capaha on the island, assuring him of his regret in view of the outrages; that neither he, nor his soldiers, had in the slightest degree participated in them, and that he sought only friendly relations with the Cacique.

Capaha, who was a proud warrior, and who had retired but for a little time that he might marshal his armies to take vengeance on the invaders, returned an indignant and defiant answer; declaring that he sought no peace; but that he would wage war to the last extremity.

[Pg 319]

Again De Soto found himself in what may be called a false position. The chief Capaha and his people were exasperated against him in the highest degree. The nation was one of the most numerous and powerful on the Mississippi. Should the eight thousand allies, who had accompanied him from Kaska, and who had plunged him into these difficulties, withdraw, he would be left entirely at the mercy of these fierce warriors. From ten to twenty thousand might rush upon his little band, now numbering but about four hundred, and their utter extermination could hardly be doubtful. Under these circumstances he decided to attempt to conquer a peace. Still he made other efforts, but in vain, to conciliate the justly enraged chieftain. He then prepared for war. However severely he may be censured for this decision, it is the duty of the impartial historian to state those facts which may in some degree modify the severity of judgment.

A large number of canoes were prepared, in which two hundred Spaniards and three thousand Indians embarked to attack Capaha upon his island, before he had time to collect a resistless force of warriors. They found the island covered with a dense forest, and the chief and his troops strongly intrenched. The battle was fought with great fury, the Spanish soldiers performing marvellous feats of bravery, [Pg 320] strength and endurance. The warriors of Capaha, who fought with courage equal to that of the Spaniards, and struck such dismay into the more timid troops of Casquin, that they abandoned their allies and fled tumultuously to their canoes, and swiftly paddled away.

De Soto, thus left to bear the whole brunt of the hostile army, was also compelled to retreat. He did this in good order, and might have suffered terribly in the retreat but for the singular and, at the time, unaccountable fact that Capaha withdrew his warriors and allowed the Spaniards to embark unmolested. It would seem that the sagacious chieftain, impressed by the wonderful martial prowess displayed by the Spaniards, and by the reiterated proffers of peace and friendship which had been made to him, and despising the pusillanimity of the troops of Casquin, whom he had always been in the habit of conquering, thought that by detaching the Spaniards from them he could convert De Soto and his band into friends and allies. Then he could fall upon the Indian army, and glut his vengeance, by repaying them tenfold for all the outrages they had committed.

Accordingly, the next morning, four ambassadors of highest rank visited the Spanish encampment. De Soto and Casquin were together. The ambassadors [Pg 321] bowed to De Soto with profound reverence, but disdainfully took no notice whatever of Casquin. The speaker then said,—

"We have come, in the name of our chief, to implore the oblivion of the past and to offer to you his friendship and homage."

De Soto was greatly relieved by the prospect of this termination of the difficulties in which he had found himself involved. He treated the envoys with great affability, reciprocated all their friendly utterances, and they returned to Capaha highly pleased with their reception.

Casquin was very indignant. He did everything in his power to excite the hostility of De Soto against Capaha, but all was in vain. The Governor was highly displeased with the trick Casquin had played upon him, in setting out on a military expedition under the guise of an honorary escort. He despised the cowardice which Casquin's troops had evinced in the battle, and he respected the courage which Capaha had exhibited, and the frankness and magnanimity of his conduct. He therefore issued orders to his own and the native army that no one should inflict any injury whatever, either upon the persons or the property of the natives of the province.

He allowed Casquin to remain in his camp and under his protection for a few days, but compelled [Pg 322] him to send immediately home the whole body of his followers, retaining merely enough vassals for his personal service.

The next morning Capaha himself, accompanied by a train of one hundred of his warriors, fearlessly returned to his village. He must have had great confidence in the integrity of De Soto, for by this act he placed himself quite in the power of the Spaniards. Immediately upon entering the village, he visited the desecrated mausoleum of his ancestors, and in silent indignation repaired, as far as possible, the injury which had been done. He then proceeded to the headquarters of De Soto. The Spanish Governor and Casquin were seated together.

Capaha was about twenty-six years of age, of very fine person and of frank and winning manners. With great cordiality he approached De Soto, reiterating his proffers of friendship, and his earnest desire that kindly feelings should be cherished between them. Casquin he treated with utter disdain, paying no more attention to him than if he had not been present. For some time the Indian Cacique and the Spanish Governor conversed together with perfect frankness and cordiality. A slight pause occurring in their discourse, Capaha fixed his eyes sternly for a moment upon Casquin and said, in tones of strong indignation,—

[Pg 323]

"You, Casquin, undoubtedly exult in the thought that you have revenged your past defeats. This you never could have done through your own strength. You are indebted to these strangers for what you have accomplished. Soon they will go on their way. But we shall be left in this country as we were before. We shall then meet again. Pray to the gods that they may send us good weather."

De Soto humanely did everything in his power to promote reconciliation between the hostile chieftains. But all was in vain. Though they treated each other with civility, he observed frequent interchanges of angry glances.

The Spaniards found, in this town, a great variety of valuable skins of deer, panthers, buffalo and bears. Taught by the Indians, the Spaniards made themselves very comfortable moccasons of deerskin, and also strong bucklers, impervious to arrows, of buffalo hide.

After making minute and anxious inquiries for gold, and ascertaining that there was none to be found in that direction, De Soto turned his desponding steps backwards to Kaska. Here he remained for four days, preparing for a march to the southward. He then continued his progress nine days down the western bank of the river, until, on the fourth of August, he reached a province called Quigate. [Pg 324] His path had led him through a populous country, but the Indians made no attempt to molest his movements. It is supposed that Quigate must have been on the White river, about forty or fifty miles from its mouth. Here De Soto learned that, faraway in the northwest there was a range of mountains, and there he thought might perhaps be the gold region of which he had so long been in search.

Immediately he put his soldiers in motion, led by a hope which was probably rejected by every mind in the army, except his own. A single Indian guide led them on a weary tramp for many days, through dreary morasses and tangled forests. They at length came to a village called Coligoa, which is supposed to have been upon the banks of White river. The natives at first fled in terror at their approach, but as no hostility was manifested by the Spaniards, they soon gained confidence, and returned with kind words and presents. But there was no gold there, and no visions of gold in the distance.

The chief informed De Soto that there was a very rich and populous province about thirty miles to the south, where the inhabitants were in the enjoyment of a great abundance of the good things of life. Again the Spaniards took up their line of march in that direction. They found a fertile and quite thickly inhabited country on their route. The Indians [Pg 325] were friendly, and seemed to have attained a degree of civilization superior to that of most of the tribes they had as yet visited. The walls of the better class of houses were hung with deerskins, so softly tanned and colored that they resembled beautiful tapestry. The floors were also neatly carpeted with richly decorated skins.

The Spaniards seem to have travelled very slowly, for nine days were occupied in reaching Tanico, in the Cayas country, which was situated probably upon Saline river, a branch of the Washita. Here they found some salt springs, and remained several days to obtain a supply of salt, of which they were greatly in need. Turning their steps towards the west, still groping blindly, hunting for gold, they journeyed four days through a barren and uninhabited region, when suddenly they emerged upon a wide and blooming prairie.

In the centre, at the distance of about a couple of miles, between two pleasant streams, they saw quite a large village. It was mid-day, and the Governor encamped his army in the edge of the grove, on the borders of the plain. In the afternoon, with a strong party of horse and foot, he set out upon a reconnoitering excursion. As he approached the village the inhabitants, men and women, sallied forth and attacked him with great ferocity. De Soto was [Pg 326] not a man ever to turn his back upon his assailants. The Spaniards drew their sabres, and, all being in armor, and led by charges of the horsemen, soon put the tumultuous savages to flight, and pursued them pell-mell into the village.

The natives fought like tigers from doors, windows, and house-tops. The exasperated Spaniards, smarting with their wounds, and seeing many of their comrades already slain, cut down their foes remorselessly. The women fell before their blows as well as the men, for the women fought with unrelenting fierceness which the Spaniards had never seen surpassed. Night came on while the battle still raged, with no prospect of its termination. De Soto withdrew his troops from the village, much vexed at having allowed himself to be drawn into so useless a conflict, where there was nothing to be gained, and where he had lost several valuable men in killed, while many more were wounded.

The next morning De Soto put his whole army in motion and advanced upon the village. They found it utterly abandoned. Strong parties were sent out in all directions to capture some of the natives, that De Soto might endeavor to enter into friendly relations with them. But it seemed impossible to take any one alive. They were as untamable and as savage as bears and wolves, fighting against [Pg 327] any odds to the last gasp. Both women and men were exceedingly ill-looking, with shapeless heads, which were said to have been deformed by the compression of bandages in infancy. The province was called Tula, and the village was situated, it is supposed, between the waters of the upper Washita and the little Missouri.

The Spaniards remained in the village four days, when suddenly, in the darkness of midnight, the war-whoop resounded from three different directions, and three large bands of native warriors, who had so stealthily approached as to elude the vigilance of the sentinels, plunged into the village in a simultaneous attack. Egyptian darkness enveloped the combatants, and great was the confusion, for it was almost impossible to distinguish friend from foe. The Spaniards, to avoid wounding each other, incessantly shouted the name of the Virgin. The savages were armed with bows and arrows and with javelins, heavy, sharp-pointed, and nine or ten feet in length, which could be used either as clubs or pikes. Wielded by their sinewy arms, in a hand-to-hand fight, the javelin proved a very formidable weapon.

The battle raged with unintermitted fury till the dawn of the morning. The savages then, at a given signal, fled simultaneously to the woods. The Spaniards did not pursue them. Thoroughly armored as [Pg 328] they were, but four of their number were killed, but many were severely wounded. It was nearly twenty days before the wounded were so far convalescent that the army could resume its march. The following incident illustrates the almost unexampled ferocity of these barbaric warriors:

The morning after the battle a large number of the Spanish soldiers, thoroughly armed, were exploring the fields around the village, on foot and on horseback. Three foot soldiers and two mounted men were in company. One of them saw in a thicket an Indian raise his head and immediately conceal it. The foot soldier ran up to kill him. The savage rose, and with a ponderous battle-axe which he had won from the Spaniards the day before, struck the shield of the Spaniard with such force as to cut it in two, at the same time severely wounding his arm. The blow was so violent and the wound so severe, that the soldier was rendered helpless. The savage then rushed upon another of the foot soldiers, and in the same way effectually disabled him.

One of the horsemen, seeing his companions thus roughly handled, put spurs to his steed and charged upon the Indian. The savage sprang to the trunk of an oak tree, whose low hanging branches prevented the near approach of the trooper. Watching his opportunity, he sprang forth and struck the [Pg 329] horse such a terrible blow with his axe as to render the animal utterly incapable of moving. Just at this moment the gallant Gonsalvo Sylvestre came up. The Indian rushed upon him, swinging his battle-axe in both hands; but Sylvestre warded the blow so that the axe glanced over his shield and buried its edge deeply in the ground.

Instantly the keen sabre of Sylvestre fell upon the savage, laying open his face and breast with a fearful gash, and so severing his right hand from the arm that it hung only by the skin. The desperate Indian, seizing the axe between the bleeding stump and the other hand, attempted to strike another blow. Again Sylvestre warded off the axe with his shield, and with one blow of his sword upon the waist of the naked Indian so nearly cut his body in two that he fell dead at his feet.

During the time the Spaniards tarried in Tula many foraging excursions were sent out to various parts of the province. The region was populous and fertile, but it was found impossible to conciliate in any degree the hostile inhabitants.

Again the soldiers were in motion. They directed their steps towards the northwest, towards a province named Utiangue, which was said to be situated on the borders of a great lake, at the distance of about two hundred and forty miles. They hoped [Pg 330] that this lake might prove an arm of the sea, through which they could open communications with their friends in Cuba, and return to them by water. The journey was melancholy in the extreme, through a desolate country occupied by wandering bands of ferocious savages, who were constantly assailing them from ambuscades by day and by night.

At length they reached the village of Utiangue, the capital of the province. It was pleasantly situated on a fine plain upon the banks of a river, which was probably the Arkansas. Upon the approach of the Spaniards the inhabitants had abandoned the place, leaving their granaries well stocked with corn, beans, nuts, and plums. The meadows surrounding the town offered excellent pasturage for the horses. As the season was far advanced, De Soto decided to take up his winter quarters here. He fortified the place, surrounding it with strong palisades. To lay in ample stores for the whole winter, foraging parties were sent out, who returned laden with dried fruits, corn, and other grain.

Deer ranged the forests in such numbers that large quantities of venison were obtained. Rabbits also were in abundance. The Cacique, who kept himself aloof, sent several messengers to De Soto, but they so manifestly came merely as spies, and always in the night, that De Soto gave orders that [Pg 331] none should be admitted save in the daytime. One persisting to enter was killed by a sentinel. This put an end to all intercourse between De Soto and the chief; but the Spaniards were assaulted whenever the natives could take any advantage of them on their foraging expeditions.

Here the Spaniards enjoyed on the whole, the most comfortable winter they had experienced since they entered Florida. Secure from attack in their fortified town, sheltered from the weather in their comfortable dwellings, and with a sufficient supply of food, they were almost happy, as they contrasted the comforts they then enjoyed with the frightful sufferings they had hitherto experienced. During the winter, the expedition met with a great loss from the death of its intelligent interpreter, Juan Ortiz. In reference to his services, Mr. Pickett says:

"Understanding only the Floridian language, he conducted conversations through the Indians of different tribes who understood each other and who attended the expedition. In conversing with the Chickasaws, for instance, he commenced with the Floridian, who carried the word to a Georgian, the Georgian to the Coosa, the Coosa to the Mobilian, and the latter to the Chickasaw. In the same tedious manner the reply was conveyed to him and reported to De Soto."

[Pg 332]

During the winter at Utiangue, the views and feelings of the Governor apparently experienced quite a change. His hopes of finding gold seem all to have vanished. He was far away in unknown wilds, having lost half his troops and nearly all his horses. The few horses that remained, were many of them lame, not having been shod for more than a year. He did not hesitate to confess, confidentially to his friends, his regret that he had not joined the ships at Pensacola. He now despairingly decided to abandon these weary and ruinous wanderings, and to return to the Mississippi river. Here he would establish a fortified colony, build a couple of brigantines, send them to Cuba with tidings of safety to his wife, and procure reinforcements and supplies. It seems that his pride would not allow him to return himself a ruined man to his friends.

With the early spring he broke up his cantonment, and commenced a rapid march for the Mississippi. He had heard of a village called Anilco, at the mouth of a large stream emptying into that majestic river. They followed down the south side of the Arkansas river for ten days, when they crossed on rafts to the north or east side. It was probably the intention of De Soto to reach the Mississippi nearly at the point at which they had crossed it before.

[Pg 333]

Continuing his journey through morasses and miry grounds, where the horses often waded up to their girths in water, where there were few inhabitants, and little food to be obtained, he at length reached the village of Anilco, and found it to be on the northern bank of the Arkansas river. Here he learned that, at the distance of some leagues to the south, there was a populous and fertile country such as he thought would be suitable for the establishment of his colony. Again he crossed the Arkansas river to the south side, and moving in a southerly direction reached the Mississippi at a village called Guachoya, about twenty miles below the mouth of the Arkansas river.

[Pg 334]

CHAPTER XIX.

Death of De Soto.

Ascent of the Mississippi.—Revenge of Guachoya.—Sickness of De Soto.—Affecting Leave-taking.—His Death and Burial.—The March for Mexico.—Return to the Mississippi.—Descent of the River.—Dispersion of the Expedition.—Death of Isabella.

The village of Guachoya was situated on a bluff on the western bank of the Mississippi, and was strongly fortified with palisades. De Soto succeeded in establishing friendly relations with the chief, and was hospitably entertained within the town. The Cacique and Governor ate at the same table, and were served by Indian attendants. Still, for some unexplained reason, the Cacique with his warriors retired at sunset in their canoes, to the eastern side of the Mississippi, and did not return till after sunrise the next morning.

De Soto's great anxiety now was to get access to the ocean. But he could not learn that the Cacique had ever heard of such a body of water. He then sent Juan de Añasco with eight horsemen to follow down the banks of the river in search of the sea. They returned in eight days, having explored but [Pg 335] about fifty miles, in consequence of the windings of the stream and the swamps which bordered its banks. Upon this discouraging information, the Governor decided to build two brigantines at Guachoya, and to establish his colony upon some fertile fields which he had passed between Anilco and that place. This rendered it very important for him to secure abiding friendly relations with the chiefs of both of these provinces.

The territory indeed upon which he intended to settle, was within the province of Anilco, and on the north bank of the Arkansas. The chief Guachoya, very kindly offered to supply De Soto with eighty large and many small canoes with which a portion of his force with the baggage could ascend the Mississippi, twenty-one miles to the mouth of the Arkansas, and then ascending that stream about forty miles would reach the point selected for the settlement. The Governor and the chief, with united military force in light marching order, would proceed by land so as to reach the spot about the same time as the canoes.

Four thousand Indian warriors embarked in these canoes, and in three days accomplished the voyage. At the same time, the land forces commenced their march. The Cacique led two thousand warriors, besides the attendants. Mr. Irving writes:

[Pg 336]

"The two expeditions arrived safely at the time opposite the village. The chief of Anilco was absent, but the inhabitants of the place made a stand at the pass of the river. Nuño Tobar fell furiously upon them with a party of horse. Eager for the fight, they charged so heedlessly that each trooper found himself surrounded by a band of Indians. The poor savages, however, were so panic-stricken that they turned their backs upon the village, and fled in wild disorder to the forests, amid the shouts of the pursuers, and the shrieks and cries of the women and children.

"On entering the conquered village, they massacred all they met, being chiefly old men, women and children, inflicting the most horrible barbarities.

"In all this they acted in such fury and haste, that the mischief was effected almost before De Soto was aware of it. He put an end to the carnage as speedily as possible, reprimanded the Cacique severely, forbade any one to set fire to a house, or injure an Indian under pain of death, and hastened to leave the village, taking care that the Indian allies should be the first to pass the river, and none remained behind to do mischief."

From this untoward enterprise De Soto returned to the village of Guachoya, renouncing all idea of establishing his colony in Anilco. He immediately [Pg 337] commenced with all energy building his two brigantines, while he looked anxiously about in search of some region of fertility and abundance, where his army could repose till the envoys should bring back a sufficient fleet to transport those to Cuba who should wish to return there, and could also bring those reinforcements and supplies essential to the establishment of the colony. The river at this point was about a mile and a half in width. The country on both sides was rich in fertility, and thickly inhabited.

Upon the eastern bank there was a province called Quigualtanqui, of which De Soto heard such glowing reports that he sent an exploring party to examine the country. By fastening four canoes together, he succeeded in transporting the horses across the stream. To his disappointment he found the Cacique deadly hostile. He sent word to De Soto that he would wage a war of utter extermination against him and his people, should they attempt to invade his territories.

Care, fatigue and sorrow now began to show their traces upon the Governor. He could not disguise the deep despondency which oppressed him. His step became feeble, his form emaciate, his countenance haggard. A weary, grief-worn pilgrim, he was in a mood to welcome death, as life presented him [Pg 338] nothing more to hope for. A slow fever aggravated by the climate, placed him upon a sick bed. Here, the victim of the most profound melancholy, he was informed that the powerful chief, Quigualtanqui, was forming a league of all the neighboring tribes for the extermination of the Spaniards. De Soto's arm was paralyzed and his heart was broken. He had fought his last battle. His words were few; his despondency oppressed all who approached his bedside. Day after day the malady increased until the fever rose so high, that it was manifest to De Soto, and to all his companions, that his last hour was at hand.

Calmly and with the piety of a devout Catholic, he prepared for death. Luis De Moscoso was appointed his successor in command of the army, and also the successor of whatever authority and titles De Soto might possess, as Governor of Florida. He called together the officers and most prominent soldiers, and with the trembling voice of a dying man administered to them the oath of obedience to Moscoso. He then called to his bedside, in groups of three persons, the cavaliers who had so faithfully followed him through his long and perilous adventures, and took an affectionate leave of them. The common soldiers were then, in groups of about twenty, brought into the death chamber, and tenderly he bade them adieu.

[Pg 339]

These war-worn veterans wept bitterly in taking leave of their beloved chief. It is worthy of record that he urged them to do all in their power to convert the natives to the Christian religion; that he implored the forgiveness of all whom he had in any way offended; and entreated them to live as brothers, loving and helping one another. On the seventh day after he was attacked by the fever, he expired.

"He died," writes the Inca, "like a Catholic Christian, imploring mercy of the most Holy Trinity, relying on the protection of the blood of Jesus Christ our Lord, and the intercession of the Virgin and of all the celestial court, and in the faith of the Roman church. With these words repeated many times, he resigned his soul to God; this magnanimous and never-conquered cavalier, worthy of great dignities and titles, and deserving a better historian than a rude Indian."

Thus perished De Soto, in the forty-second year of his age. His life, almost from the cradle to the grave, had been filled with care, disappointment and sorrow. When we consider the age in which he lived, the influences by which he was surrounded, and the temptations to which he was exposed, it must be admitted that he developed many noble traits of character, and that great allowances should be made for his defects.

[Pg 340]

The Governor had won the confidence and affection of his army to an extraordinary degree. He was ever courteous in his demeanor, and kind in his treatment. He shared all the hardships of his soldiers, placed himself in the front in the hour of peril, and was endowed with that wonderful muscular strength and energy which enabled him by his achievements often to win the admiration of all his troops. His death overwhelmed the army with grief. They feared to have it known by the natives, for his renown as a soldier was such as to hold them in awe.

It was apprehended that should his death be known, the natives would be encouraged to revolt, and to fall with exterminating fury upon the handful of Spaniards now left in the land. They therefore "buried him silently at dead of night." Sentinels were carefully posted to prevent the approach of any of the natives. A few torches lighted the procession to a sandy plain near the encampment, where his body was interred, with no salute fired over his grave or even any dirge chanted by the attendant priests. The ground was carefully smoothed over so as to obliterate as far as possible all traces of the burial.

The better to conceal his death, word was given out the next morning that he was much better, and a joyous festival was arranged in honor of his convalescence. Still the natives were not deceived. [Pg 341] They suspected that he was dead, and even guessed the place of his burial. This was indicated by the fact that they frequently visited the spot, looking around with great interest, and talking together with much volubility.

One mode of revenge adopted by the natives was to disinter the body of an enemy and expose the remains to every species of insult. It was feared that as soon as the Spaniards should have withdrawn from the region, the body of De Soto might be found and exposed to similar outrages. It was therefore decided to take up the remains and sink it in the depths of the river.

In the night, Juan De Añasco, with one or two companions, embarked in a canoe, and, by sounding, found a place in the channel of the river nearly a hundred and twenty feet deep. They cut down an evergreen oak, whose wood is almost as solid and heavy as lead, gouged out a place in it sufficiently large to receive the body, and nailed over the top a massive plank. The body, thus placed in its final coffin, was taken at midnight to the centre of the river, where it immediately sank to its deep burial. The utmost silence was preserved, and every precaution adopted to conceal the movement from all but those engaged in the enterprise.

"The discoverer of the Mississippi," writes the [Pg 342] Inca, "slept beneath its waters. He had crossed a large part of the continent in search of gold, and found nothing so remarkable as his burial-place."

Upon the death of De Soto, a council of war was held to decide what to do in the new attitude of affairs. In their exhausted state, and with their diminished numbers, they could not think of attempting a march back for hundreds of leagues through hostile nations, to Tampa Bay. It would take a long time to build their brigantines and to await an arrival from Cuba. In the meantime there was great danger that they might be attacked and destroyed by the powerful league then forming against them.

A rumor had reached them that a large number of Spaniards were in Mexico, not very far to the westward; that they were powerful in numbers, conquering all before them, and enriching themselves with the spoils of a majestic empire. It was consequently determined to march with all speed in that direction, and join this Spanish army in its career of Mexican conquest.

Early in the month of June they commenced their march in a line due west. Their geographical knowledge was so limited that they were not aware that they were in a latitude far above the renowned city of the Montezumas.

[Pg 343]

Day after day the troops pressed on, through many sufferings and weary marches. On the way, one of their number, Diego De Guzman, a very ambitious young cavalier of high rank and wealthy connections, fell so passionately in love with the beautiful daughter of a Cacique that he deserted from the army to remain with her. She was but eighteen years of age, of very amiable spirit, and of unusual gracefulness of form and loveliness of feature. Moscoso sent an embassy to the Cacique, demanding the return of Guzman as a deserter, and threatening, in case of refusal, to lay waste his territory with fire and sword. The chief sent back the heroic reply—

"I have used no force to detain Diego De Guzman. I shall use no force to compel him to depart. On the contrary I shall treat him as a son-in-law, with all honor and kindness, and shall do the same with any others of the strangers who may choose to remain with me. If for thus doing my duty you think proper to lay waste my lands and slay my people, you can do so. The power is in your hands."

It would seem that this manly reply disarmed Moscoso, for the Spanish army continued its journey, leaving Guzman behind. Onward and still onward the weary men pressed, wading morasses, forcing their way through tangled forests, crossing rivers on rafts; now hungry and now thirsty, again enjoying [Pg 344] abundance; sometimes encountering hostility from the natives, when they took fearful vengeance, applying the torch to their villages; and again enjoying the hospitality of the natives, until having traversed a region of about three hundred miles in breadth, they supposed they had reached the confines of Mexico.

They had no suitable interpreters with them. The most contrary impressions were received from the attempts they made to obtain intelligence from the Indians. Lured by false hopes, they wandered about here and there, ever disappointed in their hopes of finding the white men. Entering a vast uninhabited region, they found their food exhausted, and but for the roots and herbs they dug up, would have perished from hunger.

The Spaniards were in despair. They were lost in savage wilds, surrounded by a barbarous and hostile people, with whom, for want of an interpreter, they could hold no intelligible communication. They had now been wandering in these bewildering mazes for three months. Mountains were rising before them; dense forests were around. They had probably reached the hunting-grounds of the Pawnees and Comanches. It was the month of October; winter would soon be upon them. A council of war was called, and after much agitating debate, it was at [Pg 345] length decided, as the only refuge from perishing in the wilderness, to retrace their steps to the Mississippi.

Forlorn, indeed, were their prospects now. They had made no attempt to conciliate the natives through whose provinces they had passed, and they could expect to encounter only hostility upon every step of their return. The country also, devastated in their advance, could afford but little succor in their retreat. Their worst fears were realized. Though they made forced marches, often with weary feet, late into the night, they were constantly falling into ambuscades, and had an almost incessant battle to fight.

Before they reached the Arkansas river the severe weather of winter set in. They were drenched with rains, pierced with freezing gales, and covered with the mud through which they were always wading. Their European clothing had long since vanished. Their grotesque and uncomfortable dress consisted principally of skins belted around their waists and over their shoulders; they were barelegged. Many of them had neither shoes nor sandals; a few had moccasons made of skins. In addition to all this, and hardest to be borne, their spirits were all broken, and they were sunk in despondency which led them to the very verge of despair.

[Pg 346]

Every day some died. One day, seven dropped by the wayside. The Spaniards could hardly stop to give them burial, for hostile Indians were continually rising before, behind, and on each side of them. At length, early in December, they reached the banks of the Mississippi near the mouth of the Arkansas.

The noble army with which De Soto left Spain but three and a half years before, had dwindled away to about three hundred and fifty men; and many of these gained this refuge only to die. Fifty of these wanderers, exhausted by hunger, toil and sorrow, found repose in the grave. Soon the survivors commenced building seven brigantines to take them back to Cuba. They had one ship-carpenter left, and several other mechanics. Swords, stirrups, chains, cutlasses, and worn out fire-arms, were wrought into spikes. Ropes were made from grass. The Indians proved friendly, furnishing them with food, and aiding them in their labors.

The hostile chief of whom we have before spoken, Quigualtanqui, on the eastern bank of the river, began to renew his efforts to form a hostile league against the Spaniards. He was continually sending spies into the camp. Moscoso was a merciless man. One day thirty Indians came into the town as spies, but under pretence of bringing presents of food, and messages of kindness from their Cacique. Moscoso [Pg 347] thought he had ample evidence of their treachery. Cruelly he ordered the right hand of every one of these chiefs to be chopped off with a hatchet, and thus mutilated, sent them back to the Cacique as a warning to others.

Moscoso, conscious of the peril of his situation, made the utmost haste to complete his fleet. It consisted of seven large barques, open save at the bows and stern. The bulwarks were mainly composed of hides. Each barque had seven oars on a side. This frail squadron was soon afloat, and the Governor and his diminished bands embarked.

It was on the evening of the second of July, just as the sun was setting, when they commenced their descent of the majestic Mississippi, leading they knew not where. They had succeeded in fabricating sails of matting woven from grass. With such sails and oars, they set out to voyage over unexplored seas, without a chart, and without a compass. The current of the river was swift and their descent rapid. They occasionally landed to seize provisions wherever they were to be found, and to take signal vengeance on any who opposed them.

It seems that the Indians, during the winter, had been collecting a fleet, manned with warriors, to cut off the retreat of the Spaniards. This fleet consisted of a large number of canoes, sufficiently capacious [Pg 348] to hold from thirty to seventy warriors, in addition to from thirteen to twenty-four men with paddles. They could move with great rapidity.

Two days after embarking, the Spaniards met this formidable fleet. The natives attacked them with great ferocity, circling around the cumbrous brigantines, discharging upon them showers of arrows, and withdrawing at their pleasure. This assault, which was continued almost without intermission for seven days and nights, was attended by hideous yells and war-songs. Though the Spaniards were protected by their bulwarks and their shields, nearly every one received some wound. All the horses but eight were killed.

On the sixteenth day of the voyage four small boats, containing in all fifty-five men, which had pushed out a little distance from the brigantines, were cut off by the natives, and all but seven perished. The natives now retired from pursuing their foes, and with exultant yells of triumph turned their bows up the river and soon disappeared from sight.

On the twentieth day they reached the Gulf. Here they anchored their fleet to a low marshy island, a mere sand bank, surrounded with a vast mass of floating timber. Again a council was held to decide what course was to be pursued. They had no nautical instruments, and they knew not in what direction [Pg 349] to seek for Cuba. It was at length decided that as their brigantines could not stand any rough usage of a stormy sea, their only safety consisted in creeping cautiously along the shore towards the west in search of their companions in Mexico. They could thus run into creeks and bays in case of storms, and could occasionally land for supplies.

It was three o'clock in the afternoon when they again made sail. There was much division of counsel among them; much diversity of opinion as to the best course to be pursued; and the authority of Moscoso was but little regarded. They had many adventures for fifty-three days, as they coasted slowly along to the westward. Then a violent gale arose, a norther, which blew with unabated fury for twenty-six hours. In this gale the little fleet became separated. The brigantines contained about fifty men each. Five of them succeeded in running into a little bay for shelter. Two were left far behind, and finding it impossible to overtake their companions, as the wind was directly ahead, and as there was danger of their foundering during the night, though with quarrels among themselves, they ran their two vessels upon a sand beach and escaped to the shore.

Moscoso, with the five brigantines, had entered the river Panuco, now called Tampico. Here he found, to his great joy, that his countrymen had [Pg 350] quite a flourishing colony, and that they had reared quite a large town, called Panuco, at a few miles up the stream. They kissed the very ground for joy, and abandoning their storm-shattered brigantines, commenced a tumultuous march towards the town. They were received with great hospitality. The Mayor took Moscoso into his own house, and the rest of the party were comfortably provided for.

It is worthy of note that one of their first acts was to repair to the church to thank God for their signal deliverance from so many perils. They were soon joined by their shipwrecked comrades. They numbered only three hundred, and they resembled wild beasts rather than men, with uncut and uncombed hair and beard, haggard with fatigue, blackened from exposure, and clad only in the skins of bears, deer, buffaloes, and other animals. Here their military organization ended.

For twenty-five days they remained at Panuco; a riotous band of disappointed and reckless men, frequently engaging in sanguinary broils. Gradually they dispersed. Many of the common soldiers found their way to the city of Mexico, where they enlisted in the Mexican and Peruvian armies. Most of the leaders found their way back to Spain, broken in health and spirits.

Many months elapsed ere Isabella heard of the [Pg 351] death of her husband, and of the utter ruin of the magnificent enterprise in which he had engaged. It was to her an overwhelming blow. Her heart was broken; she never smiled again, and soon followed her husband to the grave. Sad, indeed, were the earthly lives of Ferdinand De Soto and Isabella De Bobadilla. We hope their redeemed spirits have met in that better land where the weary are at rest.

THE END.

Early History and Settlement of America. Each in one volume, 12mo., fully illustrated and handsomely bound in black and gold; per vol

1st Daniel Boone and the Early Settlement of Kentucky	†
2d Miles Standish, the Puritan Captain	†
3d De Soto, the Discoverer of the Mississippi	
Other volumes to follow. (*In April.*)	

Abbott, Lyman.

Laicus; or, The Experiences of a Layman in a Country	†
Parish. By Lyman Abbott. 12mo.	1.75

Bunyan.

Grace Abounding to the Chief of Sinners. Being an Account of his own Life. By John Bunyan. 18mo., red edges,	1.00

Clark.

The Valley Kingdoms – Egypt and Assyria. By Rev.	†

E. L. Clark, author of "Daleth." With many beautiful illustrations.
(*In preparation.*)

Cruden.

Cruden's Complete Concordance. A Dictionary and Alphabetical Index to the Bible. (The Unabridged Edition). By Alexander Cruden, A.M.

Price in cloth, reduced from	4.00 to 2.75
" " sheep, " "	5.00 to 3.50
" " half morocco, "	6.50 to 4.50

Cumming.

Is Christianity from God? A Manual of Bible Evidence for the People. By Rev. John Cumming, author of the "Great Tribulation." 18mo., brown cloth extra	90

Charles, Mrs.

Schonberg-Cotta Family.	12mo.	1.50
" " "	Hampstead edition	1.00
The Early Dawn.	12mo.	1.50
" "	Hampstead edition	1.00
Diary of Kitty Trevylyan.		1.50
" " "	Hampstead edition	1.00
Winifred Bertram.		1.50
" "	Hampstead edition	1.00
The Draytons and the Davenants.		1.50
" " "	Hampstead edition	1.00
On Both Sides of the Sea.	12mo.	1.50
" " "	Hampstead edition	1.00
The Victory of the Vanquished.	12mo.	1.50
" " "	Hampstead edition	1.00

Sets of the above in boxes.

The 12*mo. edition, seven vols., including Victory, reduced to*	10.50

The New Uniform Edition.

The Hampstead Edition, 16mo., illustrated, and bound in black and gold. Seven vols.	7.00
Mary, the Handmaid of the Lord. New edition, 18mo., red edges	1.00
Poems. New edition, 18mo., red edges	1.25
Watchwords for the Warfare of Life. Selected from the Writings of Luther. 12mo., bevelled boards	1.75

Song Without Words. Cheaper edition	75

Dana.

Corals and Coral Islands. By James D. Dana, Professor	†
of Geology in Yale College, author of a System of Mineralogy, &c. One vol., large 8vo., with colored frontispiece and three maps, and nearly 100 illustrations, cloth extra	6.00

Döllinger.

Dr. J. J. I. Von Döllinger's Fables Respecting the Popes	†
in the Middle Ages. Translated by Alfred Plummer, together with Dr. Döllinger's Essay on the Prophetic Spirit and the Prophecies of the Christian Era. Translated for the American Edition, with Introduction and Notes to the whole work by Prof. H. B. Smith, D.D. One vol., large 12mo.	2.25

Lectures on the Reunion of the Churches. By J. J. I. Von	†
Döllinger, D.D., D.C.L. Translated by Henry Nutcombe Oxenham, M. A. 12mo.	1.50

Fish.

History and Repository of Pulpit Eloquence, (Deceased Divines.) By Henry C. Fish, D. D. A new edition. Two volumes in one. 8vo., over 1,200 pages, with portraits. Cloth, extra bevelled boards	5.50

Pulpit Eloquence of the XIXth Century. With Seven large steel portraits. 8vo., cloth extra, bevelled boards	4.00

Fenelon.

Spiritual Progress or instructions in the Divine Life of the Soul, including Fenelon's Christian Counsel and Spiritual Letters, and Mme. Guyon's Short and Easy Method of Prayer, 12mo., red edges, bevelled boards	1.50

Christian Counsel and Spiritual Letters. In a Separate volume. 18mo., red edges 1.00

Daily Prayer Book.

Daily Prayer Book, The. For the use of Families, with additional Prayers for special occasions. Edited by John Stoughton, D. D. 12mo., bevelled boards, red edges † 1.50

Gray.

Bible Lore. Chapters on the Rare Manuscripts, Various Translations, and Notable Characteristics of the Bible. By James Comper Gray. One vol., 12mo. † 1.50

Garrett.

Premiums Paid to Experience. Incidents in my Business Life, by Edward Garrett, author of "Occupations of a Retired Life," &c. 12 illustrations, 12mo. † 1.75

The Dead Sin, and other Stories. By Edward Garrett. 12 illustrations, 12mo. † 1.75

The Occupations of a Retired Life. 12 illustrations, 12 mo. 1.75

The Crust and the Cake. 12 illustrations, 12mo. 1.75

Hare.

Wanderings in Spain. By Augustus J. C. Hare, author of "Walks in Rome." Finely illustrated † 3.00

Hall.

Papers for Home Reading. By Rev. John Hall, D. D., of New York. One elegant 12mo., with Portrait 1.75

Questions of the Day. By Rev. John Hall, D.D. One elegant 12mo. 1.75

Howson.

The Character of St. Paul. By J. C. Howson, D. D., †

one of the authors of Connybeare & Howson's St. Paul. 12mo. (*In press.*)

Hood.

Lamps, Pitchers, and Trumpets. Lectures on the Vocation †

of the Preacher. Illustrated by Anecdotes, Biographical, Historical, and Elucidatory, of every order of Pulpit Eloquence from the great Preachers of all Ages. By E. Paxton Hood. A New Edition, two series in one vol., 12mo. 1.75

Jay.

Prayers for the Use of Families. By William Jay, author †

of "Morning and Evening Exercises," &c. A New Edition. 12mo. tinted paper, reduced from 1.50 to 1.00

Jay.

Little Hodge. By the author of Ginx's Baby. One vol. 12mo. 1.25

Luchmee and Dilloo. A Novel. (*In press.*)

Moffat.

A Comparative History of Religions. By Jas. C. Moffat. †

D. D., Professor of Church History in Princeton Theological Seminary. One vol., 12mo., Part 1st, The Ancient Scriptures 1.75

Macdonald.

The Book of Ecclesiastes Explained, Critically and Popularly, by James M. Macdonald, D. D. 12mo. 1.75

Manning, Anne.

Maiden and Married Life of Mary Powell.	1.25
Cherry and Violet. 18mo., red edges	1.00
The Household of Sir Thos. More. 18mo., red edges	1.00
The Faire Gospeller, Anne Askew. 18mo., red edges	1.00
Jacques Bonneval: A Tale of the Huguenots. 16mo.	1.00
The Spanish Barber: A Tale of the Bible in Spain. 16mo.	1.25

Marriage Certificates.

Marriage Certificates. From a beautiful and chaste steel engraving. On plate paper, per dozen	1.00
On bank note paper, per dozen	1.00

Mateer.

The Land of Charity: A Descriptive Account of Travancore and its Devil Worship. By Rev. F. S. Mateer, F. L. S. With over 50 illustrations, 12mo., fancy cloth	2.25

Porter.

The Sciences of Nature versus the Science of Man. By	†
Noah Porter, D.D., President of Yale College. One volume, 12mo.	1.00

Parker.

The Initiatory Catechism; an Introduction to the Shorter Catechism, for Young Children. By Rev. Joel Parker, D.D. Per 100	3.00

Rowland.

The Path of Life. By Rev. H. A. Rowland, D.D. 18mo.	60
Light in a Dark Alley. 18mo.	
The Way of Peace. 12mo.	

Raleigh.	
The Little Sanctuary and other Meditations. By Dr.	†
Alex. Raleigh, of London, author of "Quiet Resting Places." 12mo.	1.75
Rauch.	
Psychology; or, a View of the Human Soul, including Anthropology. By Rev. F. A. Rauch, D.D. 12mo.	1.75
Roe.	
Barriers Burned Away. A Story. By Rev. E. P. Roe.	†
12mo.	1.75
Spencer.	
A Pastor's Sketches. By Rev. I. S. Spencer, D.D. A	†
New Edition, two vols. in one, large 12mo., with portrait, reduced from	3.50 to 2.00
Sermons. Vol. 1.—Practical	2.00
" " 2.—Doctrinal	2.00
" " 3.—Sacramental	2.00
Any volume sold separately.	
Stretton, Hesba.	
Bede's Charity. A New Edition, with twelve	†
illustrations	1.50
Max Kromer: A Story of the Siege of Strasburg. 16mo.	75
Nelly's Dark Days. 16mo.	75
Hester Morley's Promise. 12mo. (In press).	†

Spring's Works, (Rev. Gardiner, D.D.)

Attractions of the Cross. 12mo.	1.00
The Mercy Seat.	1.75
First Things. Two vols.	3.50
Glory of Christ. Two vols.	3.00
Short Sermons for the People.	1.50
Power of the Pulpit.	1.75
The Contrast. Two vols.	3.00
Obligations of the World to the Bible.	1.50

Smith.

The Book that Will Suit You; or, a Word for Every One. By Rev. James Smith. 32mo., cloth extra, bevelled boards, red edges	1.00

Simmons.

Scripture Manual. Alphabetically and Systematically arranged. By Charles Simmons. Designed to facilitate the finding of proof texts. 12mo., cloth	1.75

Tytler.

Margaret: A Story. By C. C. Fraser Tytler, author of "Jasmine Leigh," &c., &c. 12mo., twelve illustrations	1.75

Vinet.

Montaine and other Miscellanies. By Alex. Vinet, D.D. 12mo.	1.75
Gospel Studies. By Alex. Vinet, D. D. 12mo.	1.50

Van Oosterzee.

The Theology of the New Testament; A Hand-Book for Bible Students. By J. J. Van Oosterzee, D. D., one of the authors of Lange's Commentary. Translated by Maurice J. Evans. One vol., 12mo.	1.75

Worboise.

The Lillingstones of Lillingstone. By Emma Jane Worboise. 12mo. Twelve illustrations 1.75

World's Laconics.

World's Laconics, The. On the Best Thoughts of the Best Authors, in Prose and Poetry. By Tryon Edwards, D.D. 12mo., cloth extra 1.75

Weitbrecht.

Miracles of Faith: A Sketch of the Life of Beaté Paulus. By Mary Weitbrecht. With an Introduction by Charles S. Robinson, D.D. 18mo., red edges 75

Footnotes:

[A] Life of Ferdinand De Soto, by Lambert A. Wilmer, p. 272.

[B] Conquest of Florida, by Theodore Irving, p. 81.

[C] Conquest of Florida, p. 89.

[D] Irving's Conquest of Florida, p. 100.

[E] History of Alabama, by Albert James Pickett, p. 17.

[F] Portuguese Narrative, p. 719.